Abstracts of the

Wills and Estate Records

of
GRANVILLE COUNTY
North Carolina

1833-1846

Abstracted by
Zae Hargett Gwynn

Compiled by
Trudie Davis-Long

HERITAGE BOOKS
2010

HERITAGE BOOKS
AN IMPRINT OF HERITAGE BOOKS, INC.

Books, CDs, and more—Worldwide

For our listing of thousands of titles see our website at
www.HeritageBooks.com

Published 2010 by
HERITAGE BOOKS, INC.
Publishing Division
100 Railroad Ave. #104
Westminster, Maryland 21157

Copyright © 2005 Trudie Davis-Long

Abstracted by Zae Hargett Gwynn

Other Heritage Books by the author:
Abstracts of the Wills and Estate Records of Granville County, North Carolina, 1846-1863 by Zae Hargett Gwynn

All rights reserved. No part of this book may be reproduced or transmitted in any form or by any means, electronic or mechanical, including photocopying, recording or by any information storage and retrieval system without written permission from the author, except for the inclusion of brief quotations in a review.

International Standard Book Numbers
Paperbound: 978-0-7884-4083-0
Clothbound: 978-0-7884-8527-5

Table of Contents

Introduction. i

Abstracts of Estates

    Volume 13 1833-1837 1

    Volume 14 1837-1840 36

    Volume 15 1840-1844 73

    Volume 16 1844-1846 108

Index. 135

Information about the Compiler. 168

Estate Records of Granville Co, NC Volume 13-16   i

Introduction

This publication continues the series of estate abstracts originally begun by Zae Hargett Gwynn for Granville Co., NC which were published through Estate Docket Book 12 by Joseph W. Watson.

The proofing process involved scanning and Optical Character Recognition (OCR) processing of the Gwynn manuscripts. The result was compared to the manuscript by this compiler and then reviewed by volunteers from the Richard H Thornton Library in Oxford, NC. Items of questionable interpretation were checked against the courthouse records.
It is important to note there were handwritten notes on the original Gwynn manuscript. This information is included. Obvious spelling errors were corrected and some punctuation was changed, however all names are spelled as listed in the manuscript.
The original pagination from the abstract is included for anyone who wants to check individual pages against Ms. Gwynn's work. However since the annotations include the Liber Folio designation for the items listed, it would probably be more practical to reference the originals at the Granville County Courthouse in Oxford, NC or the NC State Archives in Raleigh.

I wish to thank all the volunteers who have helped with this project. During the proofing process, Fann Montague and Kitty Humphries referred to the original docket books when they had concerns about unusual or illegible entries. During their research, the volunteers discovered that Ms. Gwynn left out details from the original records important to contemporary researchers. Most significantly, Ms. Gwynn left out the given names of the slaves that were listed in the docket books.
This work is a guide only to records that are available. The originals should be consulted for verification and to authenticate information.

Royalties from the sale of this volume are being donated to the Richard H. Thornton Library in Oxford, NC which has graciously allowed me to use the original manuscript for this compilation. The manuscript was placed in the custody of the library at the suggestion of George Stevenson. Mr Stevenson's letter to the Library follows.

Trudie Davis-Long
August 2005

Estate Records of Granville Co, NC Volume 13-16

North Carolina Department of Cultural Resources
June 25, 2002

Dear Ms. Montague,

It was good to hear from you that Zae Hargett Gwynn's notebooks of Granville County record abstracts have been useful to you. I wish the donor of them, Mrs. Mary Jeffreys Rogers, were still alive so that I could pass on to her your remarks about them.

Mrs. Rogers and Mrs. Gwynn had been great friends, and after the death of Mrs. Gwynn, Mr. Gwynn gave to Mrs. Rogers all the notebooks of unpublished abstracts of records of North Carolina counties that Mrs. Gwynn had made during her life. Mrs. Gwynn, herself, as you will remember, published her abstracts of Jones County and Onslow County records--but nothing more.

In the early 1970s Mrs. Rogers lent the notebooks of Gwynn abstracts to Joseph W. Watson of Rocky Mount so that he could publish such of them as he chose. You will recall that he issued, six volumes based on the Granville County abstracts: deeds, 1746-1765; wills and estates in two volumes, 1746-1833; court minutes, 1746-1820; guardian accounts, 1810-1856; and "kinfolks" based on land records, 1765-1826. Mr. Watson's opinion was that little market existed for published data later than about 1820.

Fearing that the notebooks would be put out as trash following the death of Mrs. Rogers, I suggested to her that the Thornton Library would be a good home for the three Granville County notebooks if the Library were willing to give them a home. She accepted the suggestion, and it was at that time that I talked with Joanna McDaniel about them. It is probable that Mrs. McDaniel was no longer officially connected with the library when we talked, but she thought the Library would like to have them, and she was willing to pick them up in Raleigh and take them to Oxford if I would collect them from Mrs. Rogers at Louisburg and bring them to the Archives for her. I brought the notebooks to Raleigh, put with them the name and address of Mrs. Rogers (425 Sledge Road, Louisburg, NC 27549), and held them until they were collected for Thornton Library by Mrs. McDaniel on March 7, 2000. I don't know whether the gift was ever acknowledged to Mrs. Rogers, or not, but she was glad to know that they had gone on to the Library as a permanent gift from her. Mrs. Rogers died on December 5, 2000.

If the Library decides to publish such of the abstracts as were not published by Mr. Watson, I assume that Zae Hargett Gwynn will be given credit on the title page as the abstracter in the same way that Mr. Watson gave her credit.

George Stevenson
Private Manuscripts Archivist
North Carolina State Archives

Estate Records of Granville Co, NC Volume 13-16   1

322
1-thru- 6- Granville Co. in Acct. with Thomas J. **Hicks**, County Trustee for 1832.

7-8- Estate of Benjamin **Moody**, deceased, by Arthur **Moody**, admstr-from Nov. 1830- paid to John H. **Ragsdale** as guardian to Ann, Edward, and Mary **Moody**, paif [sic] William **Moody**, Frances A **Moody**, Pomfret **Loyd**, Joseph A. **Norwood**, Wm. A. **Moody**, admstr. of Ann **Moody**-(this is part of legacy due them), Mar. 1833.

9- thru 12- Acct. current of estate of John **Pittard**, Jr deceased, with Thomas H. **Willie**, admstr- from Nov. 1825- mentions Dolly **Pittards** years allowance and Letty **Pittard**, guardian for children, and cash paid distributees: Dolly **Pittard**, the widow, Wesly **Moores** in right of wife, Howell G. **Pittard**, Nancy and Elizabeth **Pittard**, legatees and Nov. 7, 1833- Howel G. **Pittard**, admstr. of Dolly **Pittard**, dec'd- All legatees of full age of 21 yrs.

13-14-Feb. court 1830- Petition of Elizabeth **Jones** widow of William **Jones**, deceased, who died Aug. 1829, leaving surviving him, the widow, asks years provision;- granted-recorded Nov. court 1833.

14- 15- Aug. 27, 1831- proved Feb. court 1834.
John **Lemay** ---- wills to his son Richard W. **Lemay**, the land whereon he now lives which I bought of Peyton **Wood** and which I gave him by deed of gift; to my son Lewis, the land in Wake county which I bought of John **Green**, for which I have made him a deed of gift; to son Samuel, the land on which I reside, containing 205 acres which I bought of Thomas **Cattrell**; To all the children of my daughter Polly T, wife of John **Hicks**, the 156 acres I bought of Ira E. **Arnold** reserving the right for daughter Polly to reside on land for her life; John **Hichs**, husband of my daughter Polly is not to dispose of or use land for payment of his own debts, and if he try such, the executors are to assure possession to the children of Polly; To my daughter Temperance **Crews**, a negro boy; to daughter Susan, wife of Joel **Ussery**, a negro woman and her two children and their increase, and at their death, that is Polly and Joel, to their children to daughter Kitty B, wife of Ashley **Crews** 2 negroes for her lifetime and if she have child, then to her child or children but if not to be equally divided to all my grandchildren; To son Lewis, the 200 dollars he owes me but to be considered in the final settlement of this estate; All remaining estate equally divided between my children.
Exrs: sons. Richard W. and Samuel **Lemay**.
Wts: John R. **Hicks**, Benjamin **Hicks**.

16-July 30, 1833 - proved Feb. court 1834.
Benjamin **Hope** wills to wife Elizabeth, all I die possessed of for life if she does not re-marry, but in that case she gets nothing. After her death or re-marriage, everything divided between my children, wife sole execrtx.
Wts: Gulielmus C. **Wiggins**, W. H. **Lanier**.

17-Nov. 2, 1833- proved Feb. court 1834.
Charles **Clay**---- wills to wife Permele T. **Clay** for her widowhood or lifetime, all I possess and at her death or re-marriage to my children Namely, Fanny, Archer W., Charles W., Sophan H. **Clay** equally divided between them.
Exrs: wife Permele T. **Clay** and John **Bullock**.
Wts: Josiah **Robertson**.

17, 18- Dec. 2 1833- Thomas P. **Hawkins** of Shelby County, Tennessee and Henry A. **Hawkins** of Granville Co., N. C. appoint Wyatt **Cannaday**, attorney, to sell a tract of land for us in Granville Co., N. C.
Wts: Edwd H. **Carter**.

18- thru 20- Nov. court 1833- Petition-- John **Green** died in 1821, leaving surviving him, his wife Elizabeth, daughter Nancy since

323

married to Nathaniel E. **Cannaday**, a son Joseph **Green** now of lawful age, and minor children Isaac, Mary A., William, John B., and George W. **Green** whose guardian is Clement **Wilkins**- The petitioners Elizabeth **Green**, Joseph **Green**, N. E. **Cannaday**, and Clement **Wilkins** as guardian of the minor children ask that personal estate of John **Green**, deceased, be divided between the heirs. On Dec. 31, 1833, the commissioner divided the negroes to the following heirs: Lot 1- to John B. **Green**-- Lot 2, to Mary A. **Green**--Lot 3 to Nathaniel E. **Cannaday**-- Lot 4 to Joseph **Green** Lot 5- to William **Green**--Lot 6- to George W. **Green**- Lot 7-to Isaac **Green**.

20-Jan. 1, 1834- Charles Glover received of Alexander F. **Marrow**, $334.43 and releases him from obligation as executor of Joseph P. **Glover**, deceased.
Wts: Thos. L. **Williams**, Jas. W. **Hegee**.

21-Nov. court 1833- Commissioner laid off to Charles P. **Glover**, son of Daniel Glover, deceased, his part of his father's estate. He was allotted 150 acres of land and 6 negroes, as near equal to that given Absalom **Glover** by his father, as possible Dec. 11, 1833.
Also allotted to Charles P. **Glover**, his share.

22-Feb. 3, 1834- James **Wyche**, guardian of George, Elizabeth, David, Thomas and William **Evans**, children of David L. **Evans**, deceased, asks permission to sell certain negroes that are property of wards, to pay debts due on estate and also to complete the education of the two not yet out of school- They were sold.

23-24- Madison **Slaughter** of Sullivan County, Tennessee, one of the heirs of Jacob **Slaughter**, deceased, late of Granville Co., N. C. whose will dated Aug. 29, 1821, willing to me, then unknown to my grandfather Jacob **Slaughter**, only as one of the youngest children of Jacob **Slaughter** Jr. (see will on record in Granville Co., N. C.)-and I appoint Daniel 2**Branstetter** Esq. of Sullivan Co., Tennessee, my

Estate Records of Granville Co, NC Volume 13-16   3

attorney, to receive for me, my inheritance, from the executor, Abraham **Slaughter**, of estate and will of Jacob **Slaughter** Sr. deceased, my grandfather. Oct. 28, 1833- wts: Joseph **Everitt** J. P., George W. **Netherland**, clerk, Thomas **Rockhold** presiding Justice of Sullivan Co., Tenn.

25-thru-29- Rendered to Feb. court 1834- by John L. **Eaton**, trustee, sold estate of E. J. **Fruar**, deceased-

29- Feb. 1, 1834- Sale of estate of Robert H. **Burchett**, deceased, by Bart **Kimball**, admstr-

30- thru 32- Feb. court 1834- Nancy J. **Read**, execrx. of estate of Dr. Thomas H. **Read**, deceased, - Inventory of estate includes 1220 acres of land in one tract and 380 in another tract, 37 negroes, much household furniture, plantation tools and a very large collection of books (the largest any inv. in this county has had yet. zae) mostly medical and Religious- also lists debts due estate-

33-34- Inv. and sale of estate of Lewis **Bledsoe**, deceased, by Richard **Bullock**, admstr- rendered to Feb. court 1834- Among buyers were Francis Jechoniah, Caroline, Elizabeth **Bledsoe** and Clark **Landers** and others.

34- thru 36- Inv. and sale of Elizabeth **Ellis**, deceased, by Benjamin **Bullock** executor- Oct. 15, 1823 and sale on Oct. 15, 1831.

36- thru 44- Rendered to Feb court 1834- Inv and sale. of estate of James **Smith**, deceased, by Porteus **Moore**, excr. and Harriot W. **Smith** excrx lists 865 acres of land, 19 negroes -- also sale Nov. 22, 1833.

44 thru 54- Sale of estate of William **Hunt** estate, deceased, by Memucan **Hunt**- excr. rendered to Feb Court 1834- Among buyers were Spottswood and John A. **Burwell**, Gan. Joseph **Bryan**, Edward **Bryant** bought a piano forte and books, Maj. Thomas T. **Hunt**, Edmund **Towns** bought many things, Memucan **Hunt** bought among much else, an English Stud Book, William **Reavis** bought a small Buffalo Steer and a gun.

54-55- Estate of Elizabeth **Ellis**, deceased, in acct. with Benjamin **Bullock**, excr, from July 1828- gives acct of estate left children: Rheany, Stephen, Leaven, Squire, William **Ellis**; and to a slave $10.00 rendered Feb. Court 1834.

324
56- thru 62- Sale of estate of James **Satterwhite**, deceased, by Howel, Solomon and James **Satterwhite** rendered to Feb. court 1834.

62 thru 65- Oct. 4, 1833- Division of land of Charles **Yancey**, deceased, By petition Aug, court 1833- by Kesiah **Yancey**, Ann **Yancey**, Nathaniel **Robards** state that Charles **Yancey** died intestate leaving the following children: Absalom, Charles,

Ann, Kesiah, Jane who married Lewis **Tapp**, Martha who married Nathaniel **Robertson**, Mary who married Lewis **Cosby** -Nathaniel **Robards** has purchased the rights of Absalom (who had bought the right of Nathl **Robertson** and wife) **Yancey**. Now Charles **Yancey** says he owns the right of N. **Robertson** and wife, so we wish the proper and rightful owner decided upon. Charles **Yancey** surrendered his right and land divided into lots for each of heirs, each of about 33 ½ acres.

    65- thru 69- Feb. court 1834- Estate of Henry L. **Graves**, deceased, by Elijah **Graves**, excr.- will probated Mar. 5, 1829-paid James **Nunn** for coffin Dec. 9, 1829- mentions clothes for children: Ralph H.[enry] **Graves**, Betsy C. **Graves**, Selina F. **Graves**, Jesse D. **Graves**, Elizabeth C. **Graves**, Elijah C. **Graves**, Ralph Henry **Graves** was in college Jan. 1833.

    69- thru 71-. On Nov. 12, 1833- Sylvanis **Puryear** conveyed to the heirs of John **Puryear** Sr., deceased, certain valuable property which now is the common property of all the heirs of John **Puryear**, namely: William **Amis** who married Elizabeth **Puryear**, William C. **Tucker** who married Martha **Puryear**, John **Puryear** Jr., Peggy **Neal** (who is dead) leaving as her representatives Harriet who married George W. **Tucker**, Martha who married David C. **Wilkerson** and William H. **Neal** and Alexander G. **Neal**(minors) and Sarah **Boyd** (now dead) leaving Amy who married John **Junel**, George W. **Boyd**, John **Boyd**, Martha who married Thomas **Amis**, Sylvania who married Aplin **Puryear**(now dead) leaving children but names and number unknown (all minors)- the property was bought by William **Amis** with understanding that each of the heirs or representatives could buy back by paying their 1/5th part.
Wts: Fabian A. **Royster**, Archibald **Clark**.

    71- Power of Attorney, Dec. 12, 1833- from Sylvania **Puryear**, widow of John **Puryear** deceased, relinquished all interest in **Puryear** estate and appoints William **Amis**, attorney, to transact business of selling said estate.
Wts: Fabian **Royster**, Archibald **Clark**.

    73, 74- The children, legatees and others interested in the estate of Francis **Royster**, deceased, namely: Elizabeth, widow of said deceased, Banester **Royster**, Willie **Royster**, Thomas Lorton **Williams**, claiming the interest of Robert **Royster**, Marcus D. **Royster**, William **Royster**, Joseph A **Norwood** and wife Letty, Thomas J. **Farrarr** and wife Martha, their agent Baren **Oliver**, Berrin **Oliver** and wife Mary and Emily **Royster** ask a division of the property remaining of the late Francis **Royster** which has not been divided and is in hands of executor Banester **Royster** and exrx. Widow Elizabeth **Royster**, reserving to Mrs. E. **Royster** certain portion for her personal use forever, and the remainder sold by said Banester **Royster**. Sept. 19, 1833-

    74, 75- Feb. 26, 1834- Power of Attorney from William D. **Jones** to Thomas L. **King** to collect all due him.
Wts: John L. **Eaton**.

75-76- Mar. 8, 1834- proved May court 1834.
Martha **Anderson** to son Thomas P., 2 negroes and a feather bed and it's (sic) necessary furniture; To daughter Mary W., 3 negroes, and my silver divided between my two children here mentioned; My daughter Mary to have her share of what is left when or if she married before she is 21 otherwise the guardian to keep the estate of both children until they are of age and be sure they are divided equally in this. Clement **Wilkins** to be executor and guardian.
Wts: Thomas J. **Hicks**, Sarah **Norman**.

325
76- A quit claim from W. S. **Hart** to his guardian John G. **Hart** Apr. 20, 1833.

77- Henry County, Tennessee- William C., John and Lewis M. **Hutcherson** appoint Elijah **Hester** of Granville Co., N. C., attorney, to recover for them all lands belonging to them.- Jan. 3, 1834.
Wts: Eli **Kendall** and William G. **Hogan** J. P., Thomas K. **Porter**, clerk, William **Porter** chairman and presiding magistrate of Henry Co., Tenn.

78- May 8, 1834- Green **Stanton** and his wife Mary **Stanton** have decided to live separate and apart and hereby agree that under penalty of bond of $1000.00, he will leave her free and not enter her dwelling house without her permission or attempt to take possession of or expect any services from her, and he deeds to her ½ of the dower she has from her former husband, the late Southern **Higgs**, which land he now lives upon. and has right to in right of his wife, Mary- and Mary in turn releases Green **Stanton** from all responsibility of her support and any right she may have now or ever in any property he may acquire and since they can not agree to property settlement now, three persons are to make the division and Green **Stanton** under penalty of $1,000.00 must abide thereby.
Wts: H. W. **Peace**, Saml **Fuller**.

79 Wardens of the Poor of Granville Co., N. C., in acct. with Anderson **Paschall**, acting Warden for 1833.

81- Apr. 25, 1834- Property sold belonging to estate of Lewis **Bledsoe** deceased, by Richard **Bullock**, Admstr.

82- Feb. 1834 Personal estate of Sarah **Jeffrets**, deceased, by Wm. C. **Patton**.

82- Inv. of estate of John **Lemay**, deceased, mentions Susa, Richard, Samuel, John C. and Robert M. **Lemay**.

83- Sale of property by Mrs. Elizabeth **Norman** of estate of George **Norman**, deceased. Nov. 24 1834.

84- Sale of estate and hire of negroes of estate of Jos. **Barnett** Sr. deceased, by Jos. Jr, and Thos. B. **Barnett**, excrs.

85- Sale of estate of Sarah **Jeffreys**, deceased, Feb. 25, 1834 by Wm. C. **Patton**, admstr. among buyers was Elizabeth **Jeffreys**.

86- thru 88- Inv. and sale of estate of Southan **Higgs** deceased, Mar. 28, 1834 by Anderson **Paschall**, special Admstr. -sold Apr. 21, 1834- among buyers were Allen and Mrs. Rebecca **Higgs** and Southan J. **Higgs**.

89- thru 100- Inv. of and sale of the estate of Leonard **Henderson**, deceased, by John L. **Henderson**, executor.
Dec. 16, 1833- among buyers were A. **Henderson**, Robert and Hardy **Patterson**, Dr. **Sturdivant**, John L. and A. E. **Henderson**. Dr. **Hare**, A. E. **Henderson** bought most of household goods, dishes, silver etc., Dr. Wm. V. **Taylor** bought books, (this is a law library and a beautiful one, zae) (the top price on these beautiful books per volume was 900) (they is also here, names. of some of his students of law, namely Hiram W. **Husted**, Wm. A. **Graham**, Hutchuns B. **Mitchell** deceased), Edward **Chatam**, B. **Butler**, C. **Cordle**, Jas. **Jordan**, Jas. **Knott**, Edward **Owen**--Inv. and sale by John L. **Henderson**, excr.

101- thru 105- Inv. and sale of estate of Anne C. **Vaughn**, deceased, Feb. 25, 1833- devised much to Mariah **Howerton**, Ann C. **Howerton**; Eugenia **Saunders**--by Thomas **Howerton**, excr.

105- thru 106- Feb. 6, 1834- Division of Estate of Jonathan **Davis**, deceased, 1/7th to Mary **Davis**, the daughter.

106- Inv. of estate of Benjamin **Hope**, deceased, Feb. 10, 1834, by Eliza Elizabeth **Hope**, excrx.

107- Acct of estate of Vines **Short** by Horace T. **Royster**, admstr. Feb. 1834.

109- Estate of James **Forsythe**, deceased, by Joseph **Hester**, excr. Apr. 19, 1834.

110 thru 116- Acct. of estate and separation and division of estate of James **Smith**, deceased, by John P. **Smith** proved by John **Webb**. May 1834.

110-Estate of Jeremiah **Bailey**, deceased, by John **Bailey**, excr. Nov. 1834 mentions Martha **Bailey** and children, also Wm., Israel, Anderson **Bailey**.

111 - thru 116- Acct. of sales of estate of James **Smith** Sr., deceased, by order of will for purpose of division of estate. Legatees were J. H. **Smith**, Martha P. **Webb**, (Exrs were Amy **Smith** and began 1824- To Martha P. **Smith Webb**, youngest child of James **Smith** Oct. 13, 1824, her legacy– Samuel Henry **Smith**, 1823, legacy-- William H. **Smith** in 1824 James and Ann H. **Webb** legacy– Stephen

and Sarah D. B. **Dance**-- Martha P. and Thomas **Webb**, Jr.– Stephen **McDaniel**, Sarah **Dance**, Thomas **Webb** Jr., David **Mitchell**, William F. **Smith**, James **Webb**, James **Smith** Jr., John P. **Smith** Jr., all were legatees.

117- William A **Taylor** appoints George **Terry** of Mecklenburg County, VA. attorney, to collect all money due him.
Wts: John A. **Burwell**, H. **Woodwirth**.

118– Estate of Henry **Graves** in acct. with Elijah **Graves**, excr. from 1829- paid for preaching funeral $5.00, probate of will 80¢, James **Nunn** $8.00 for coffin, mentions money paid Salina, Mrs. Betsy, Jessee D. **Graves** paid board for Ralph **Graves**, E. C. **Graves**, Selina and Betsy **Graves**; Board for Jesse and Elijah **Graves**.

120- Orange county, N. C.- Hillsborough, N. C.- Apr. 24, 1834----
Elijah **Graves** exr. of James L. **Graves** deceased, in his office, came James **Marrow** who married Selina **Graves** --

121- Oct. 8, 1829--proved Aug court 1834.
Margaret **Carnal**----wills to the lawful heirs of son James **Carnal** all my right in the property willed James by his father Moses **Carnal** and which I deeded in trust to Wm. and Stephen **Terry** for a debt owing them of $41.10 with interest from Feb. 6, 1828 and James must pay this debt; All other estate divided between my six children: Moses and James **Carnal**, Jane **Brinkley**, Sarah and Elizabeth **Dean**, Catharine **Watson**.
Exrs: James **Carnal**, William **Terry**.
Wts: Howel **Brigs**(?), Sterling W. **Duncan**.

122- Inv. of estate of Jeremiah **Moore** July 30, 1834 at Mrs E. **Blackwells** residence the place he resided, by Nathl **Daniel**, Admstr.

122- June 9, 1834- Additional acct of sale of Reuben **Jones**, deceased by D. J. **Young**, excr.

123- Aug. court 1834- Inv. of personal estate of Martha **Anderson**, deceased, by Clement **Wilkins**; excr.-

124-Sale of property of William E. **Dortch**, deceased, Dec. 16, 1834 by John **Bullock**- Admstr.

125-126- Dec. 9, 1828- proved Aug. court 1834.
Isham **Eppes**— wills to wife Mary **Eppes**, 5 negroes, a horse, 2 feather beds and furniture, ½ the live stock, all household and kitchen furniture and I lend to her 6 other negroes, 248 acre of land, 3 horses and the other half of live stock, and furniture for her lifetime and after her death I will to my son-in-law Joseph **Hester**, negroes and the land; To Elizabeth Ann, daughter of Elijah and Mary W. **Hester**, a negro; to Isham E., son of William and Nancy **Veazey**; all stock and two beds and

furniture sold and money divided between my nephews and nieces: William son of William and Elizabeth **Murphey**, Elizabeth **Smith**, Rebecca **Wartman**, John H. **Wartman** all children of John H. and Tabitha **Wartman**.
Exrs: son-in-law Joseph **Hester** and friend Elijah **Hester**.
Wts: David F. **Coaly**, Thomas **Rogers** Jr.

126-May 27, 1834- negroes of John **Lemay**, deceased, divided to heirs; Samuel **Lemay**, Gideon **Crews** and wife Temperance, Joel **Ussery** and wife Susan.---Wts: Benj. **Kittrell**, clk.

127- thru 130- Hire of negroes and sale of property of Southan **Higgs** deceased, by Anderson **Paschall**, admstr.- Stephen **Cook** bought furniture returned Aug. court 1834.

131-Estate of John **Diment**, deceased, in acct. with Howard **Dement**, Exr. from 1828 mentions Willis **Diment**- recorded Aug. court 1834.

327
131- July 12, 1834- proved Aug. court 1834.
Feabay **Seegroves**--- wills all she has which is 3 cows and yearlings and household and kitchen furniture to Elizabeth, daughter of Charles **Heflin** and she executrix.
Wts: Zachariah Allen, Charles **Heflin**.

132-133- Estate of Dick H. **Dolby**, deceased, in account with William **Fleming**, admstr. July 11, 1834-mentions acct. paid Micajah B. **Dolbey** Cost of suit in Tennessee to Richard **Bullock**, widows support, hire of negroes for year 1832, 33, 34.

134, 135- May 15, 1834- Thomas **White** and wife Cassandra of Sumner Co., Tennessee appoint Henry A **Brinkley**, attorney, (**Brinkley** of G Co., N. C.) to collect all legacies due us in North Carolina.
Wts: A. H. **Douglas**, clerk of Sumner Co. court, Stephen H and Seaton H. **Turner**, took examination of Cassandra as to her willingness herein M. **McFarland** deputy clerk of Sumner Co., Tenn.

136- June 3, 1834- John **Gordon** appoints William L. **Owen**, attorney to collect money due him.
Wts: James **Royster**, Robert **Beasley**.

137- Aug. 8, 1834- Edward T. **Bryant** appoints Rhodes W. **Herndon**, attorney, to transact any and all business he might have left undone or unfinished since he is removing from the State.
Wts: Benja **Kittrell**, Wm. N. **Sneed**.

137- Feb. 3, 1834- Benjamin **Merritt**, admstr. of estate of Temperance **Leamon**, deceased.

138- Acct. of estate of Ransoms **Hubble**, deceased, with Robert G. **Gilliam**, admstr. from Nov. 1828 mentioning sale of May court 1828-- mentions not on Richard **Wynn**, judgement, mentions Levi **Hubble**.

141- Acct. of estate of Jeremiah **Bailey**, deceased, Aug. 2, 1834- by John **Bailey**, excr, mentions Martha, Anderson, William and Isreal **Bailey** being paid.

142- Nov. 26, 1832- proved Aug. court 1834-
Hugh **Bragg**----wills that excrs. sell that which they think best to pay debts; To sons Stephen and Joel **Bragg**, 5 shillings each; To daughters Patsey **Henley**, Cisbey **Callet**, Betsey **Weartress**, each 5 shillings; All I own to be the property of my wife for her life or widowhood, then to be sold and divided, among my last eight children: Peggy **Bragg Weatherman**, Fanny **Bragg**, Thomas **Bragg**, Beckey **Bragg**, David **Bragg**, Robert **Bragg**, Suaney, James **Bragg**.
Exrx: wife Massey **Bragg** and John **Harris** excr.
Wts: C. H. **Cook**, John **Henley**, George **Winston**.

143- Notice of a sale at house of Southan **Higgs**, Esq. deceased, May 30, 1834--and slaves hired the same day. Any persons owing to the estate requested to pay immediately and those with claims against estate to come forth. signed A. **Paschall**, admstr.

144- Estate of John **Tippett** Sr., deceased, in acct. with John **Tippett** Jr. admstr. from 1830- to Aug. 5, 1834.

145- William **Harris**; orphan of Charles **Harris**, deceased; in acct. with his guardian Lewis **Parham**, from May 1833- Aug. Court, 1834.

147, 148- Aug. 14, 1834- Kenelin (Kenchen?) F. **White** and wife Elizabeth of Sumner Co., Tennessee appoint Henry A. **Brinkley** of Granville Co., N. C. attorney, to collect from Anderson **Paschall**, admstr. of Southan (Southern) **Higgs**, deceased, all due us in right of wife Elizabeth.
Wts: Jno. L. **Bugg**, Alfred H. **Douglas**, clerk of court of Sumner Co., Tenn.

148- Oct. 4, 1832- proved- Nov. court 1834.
David **Parker**---- wills to wife Chloe, the 150 acres whereon I live called 'The Old Tract' and 4 negroes for her lifetime, and I lend her as much of crop and as many cattle as excr. thinks she needs for her lifetime and at her death to go to Eady **Addcock** and 2 of the negroes for as long as she is single, but if she marry then to take it away

328
from her and give to my grandchildren, ½ to the children of Nancy **Jones** and the other half to the children of Saly **Jones**; to my daughter Sally **Jones**, the land I devised to my wife and Eady **Adcock**, at their deaths; to granddaughter Polly **Jones** daughter of Nicholas and Nancy **Jones**, a negro girl; to granddaughter Martha **Jones**,

daughter of Nicholas and Nancy **Jones**, a negro; to granddaughter Rebecca **Jones** daughter of Nicholas and Nancy **Jones**, a negro; At death of wife and Eady, the property sold and divided to the children, yearly, of Sally **Jones**.
Exr: William **Clement** who relinquished and John **Shearman** appointed Admstr.
Wts: C. H. **Carrington**, Samuel **Clement**.

150 Jan. 13, 1834 proved Nov. court 1834.
James **Oakley**----wills to daughter Francis, a feather bed and furniture, a cow and calf; to daughter Prudence **Cash**, a featherbed and furniture a cow and calf; to son Haywood **Oakley**, a horse and a feather bed and furniture; to daughter Martha, a featherbed and furniture and cow and calf; to daughter Nancy **Cash**, a feather bed and furniture, a cow and calf; To daughter Lucrecia a featherbed and furniture, a cow and calf; to daughter Hannah, a featherbed and furniture, a cow and calf; to son James W.-a horse, a featherbed and furniture; To son Elijah a horse, a featherbed and furniture; To son Elsbey, a horse, a feather bed and furniture; To son William Y. a horse, a featherbed and furniture (the last six children are minors); The land I own in Person Co. sold and a half the money given my wife Rebecca and the other half to my brother John **Oakley**; I lend my wife the land on which I live, all furniture and stock for her lifetime of widowhood, then sold and money divided among all my children, if they are of age or married, otherwise to remain on the land with all other property given my wife until each is of age or married.
Exrs: son Haywood **Oakley** and wife Rebecca **Oakley**.
Wts: Joseph **Hester**, Willie **Mangum**.

152, 153- Oct. 14, 1830-proved Nov. court 1834.
James **Haskins**-----wills to daughters Mary and Pirsely, a feather bed and furniture, a negro, a cow, each and if either die the survivor to get the negroes; to daughter, Ann **Haskin**, Rachel **Gran**, a featherbed, and furniture a negro a cow and calf, a piece, and if either die then to the survivor; To grandchildren Nancy **Bullock**, a featherbed and furniture, a cow and a calf, Mary **Green**, the same things; to sons Aaron, and George, a negro each, a horse and colt, featherbed and furniture; To son Isaac, a negro a featherbed and furniture, horse, saddle and bridle, 100 acres of land adjoining Richard **Bullock**, being the upper part of my land; to son Thomas $25.00 cash; to son-in-law John **Jinkins** and my daughter Elizabeth **Jinkins** $75.00; to son James, $50.00, son John $25.00; All estate to remain with and belong to my wife as long as she is a widow or living, but she to give the beds and cattle to the children when they are of age or marry.
Exrs: son George and Aaron **Haskins**.
Wts: Hester **Moore**, Thomas R. **Moore**.

153, 154, 155-- June-12- 1830- proved Nov. court 1834.
Lucretia **Bailey** ---wills to son Samuel **Bailey** a negro;- to sons Israel, and Ephriam and daughters Mary **Eastes** formerly Mary **Bailey** to each 5 shls. To daughter Lucretia **Moore**, formerly Lucretia **Bailey** $5.00 and a cow and calf; to son Jeremiah, a negro girl; to son William, several negroes, a mare and colt, and he is to give my grandson William **Bailey** son of my daughter Nancy **Bailey**, a good,

Estate Records of Granville Co, NC Volume 13-16

horse when he arrives of age and if it please providence to take my grson out of town, and to the city before he is 16 yrs. old then to sell the horse and colt and divided the money to his two sisters Lucretia and Glaphry; to daughter Cairy **Dillard**, formerly Cairy **Bailey** all my wearing apparel except my straw bonnet, negroes and $5.00; to granddaughter Glaphrey **Bailey** daughter of my daughter Nancy a bed and furniture, and a side saddle, my straw bonnet; all else I own

329
including the crop to be sold and money divided to my three grandchildren.
Exrs: son William **Bailey**.
Wts: Thomas **Due**, J. W. **Harris**.

156- Inv. of property of Margret **Carnal**, deceased, July 9, 1834 by William **Terry**, excr.

156- Note to Clerk of court authorizing him to release Mr. Joseph A. **Norwood** from deed of trust on land purchased of heirs of John **Taylor** signed by John **Taylor** Dec. 26, 1832--wts: Jno. **Lewis** Jr.

157- Oct. 30, 1834- Inv. of estate of William **Floyde**, deceased, by Wm. **Floyd** Jr., excr. and acct. of sale of property mentions William **Floyd**, Charles, Elizabeth **Floyd**, William **Floyd** (son George), George **Floyd** Jr., Sally **Floyd**.

160, 161, 162- Oct. 7, 1834- Nov. court 1834- Inv. and sale of property of Isham **Epps**, deceased, not included in his will, by Joseph **Hester** excr.

162 Sept. 16, 1834- Acct. of sale of estate of Robert H. **Harris** deceased, mentions William **Harris**, Mrs. **Harris**, as buyers, also John **Harris**. Sold by Thomas H. **Harris**, admstr. Nov. court 1834.

164-Estate of Thomas **Lile** deceased, with Parker **Rand**, admstr. with will annexed. Nov. 4, 1834.

165- Estate of Sarah **Glendening**, deceased, in acct. with Parker **Rand** admstr. and among list is Allen **Simms**, also money collected for sale of estate of Wm. **Glandening**, deceased Jan. 8, 1830, as his will directs and sale of house in Raleigh, N. C. also bank stock sold- return made Nov. 4, 1834 by **Rand**, admstr.

167- Estate of Rowland **Harris**, deceased, by Saml J. **Reaves** mentions amount due Artethy **Daniels** heirs, Elizabeth **Harris** and Cephos **Daniel**.

168- Estate of David **Wilkerson** Jr., deceased, with John **Buckhannon** admstr. from Sept. 1832-returner Nov. court 1834.

169- Estate of Francis **Royster**, deceased, by Banester **Royster** excr. from August 1828- mentions amount paid William and Emily E. **Royster**, Marcus D.

Royster Nov. 3, 1834.

170, 171- William V. **Taylor** and Leonard **Henderson** indebted to George **Thomason** Dec. 3, 1829 for $1000.00 being a bond- George **Thomason** sold, as directed by the will of Thomas **Thomason**, that tract of land which was to be sold at death of both his daughters Mally and Lydia -and money divided among the children of Thomas **Thomason**, and William V. **Taylor** bought land which is the interest of John, James, Nathaniel and, four other shares, Nelson, Elizabeth, Anne and Thomas **Thomason's** shares. This is to assure clear title from children of Thomas **Thomason** now deceased. recorded Nov. court 1834.
Wts: John L. **Henderson**.

172-Granville County in acct with Thomas J. **Hicks**, county Trustee Nov. 4, 1834.

174- thru 177- Jurors were paid 20¢ a day.
May term 1830- Petition of Elizabeth **Jones**, widow of William **Jones**, deceased, asks her dower in property stating that her husband died in 1829 leaving the widow and children Portheus A. and Indianna **Jones**, both minors with William M. **Sneed** as guardian and executor with Thomas D **Norman** and will probated Nov. court 1829. That William **Jones** had several tracts of land, the Bevil Tract whereon the mansion house stand(s) and 2 other tracts described as that bought of Thomas W. **Norman**. That Indianna **Jones** has since married Horace T. **Royster**. She was allotted her third of estate Aug. court 1831 -recorded Nov. court 1834.

178- John **Shurman** and George W. **Shurman** of Maury county, Tennessee. Parsons **Shurman**, Mary F. **Shurman** of Maury Co., Tennessee, James B. **Davis**, and wife Martha **Davis** of Rutherford Co., Tenn. William **Prewitt** and wife Nancy of Rutherford Co., Tenn., heirs of Squire **Shurman**, deceased appoint John **Shurman** of Granville Co., N. C., attorney to sell the land

330
one tract called The Hedgrith Tract, one whereon James **Logan** formerly lived in Orange Co., N. C. containing 47 acres adjoining Chargls **Glenn** and others, a tract of 23 acres adjoining and one of 84 acres whereon William **Russell** formerly lived, a mill seat adjoining Nathaniel Harris **Upstead**, a tract whereon Timothy **Russell** formerly lived, which lands were devised to us by Squire **Shurman**, deceased- May 15, 1834.
Wts: Peter **Campbell**, Thos. L. **Watkins**, G. W. **Smith**, Robt. **Espy**, Maury Co., Tenn. Judge of Circuit Court was Lonsford M. **Bramblett**, James Coffield **Mitchell**, Judge- William **Carroll**, Governor. Recorded Feb. court 1835.

180- May 26, 1834- Parsons M. **Shurman** of Little Rock, Arkansas appoints John **Shurman** of Granville Co., N. C., attorney, to sell all land he owns in North Carolina.
Wts: William **Badgett**, county Clerk of Pulaski Co., Ark., William S. **Fuller**

Estate Records of Granville Co, NC Volume 13-16

Secretary of Arkansas Territory.

181, 182- Aug. 28, 1834- James B. **Davis** and wife, Martha and William **Prewitt** and wife Nancy of Rutherford Co., Tennessee, appoint John **Shurman** of Granville Co, N. C., attorney, to sell all land that descended to us from Squire **Shurman** deceased, which land is in Granville and Orange Counties, N. C.
Wts: Richard **Ledbetter**, clerk of Rutherford Co. court, James Coffield **Mitchell**, Judge of circuit court of Rutherford Co., Tennessee.

183-Nov. 27, 1834- proved Feb. court 1835.
Ann **Hunt** -----wills to brother, Samuel **Hunt** a negro slave; to half sister Parthena **Hester** and half brother Hiram T. **Hester** negro slaves. To step-father Hamilton **Hester** for the great love I have for him, $550.00 which is money I got from M. V. **Taylor** for my negro Alfred; After debts paid if anything left in hands of my guardian to give it to my brother Samuel **Hunt**.
Exrs: Hamilton **Hester**.
Wts: James **King**.

184- Aug. 13, 1834- proved Feb. court 1838(5).
Joseph **Priddy** ---- wills to wife Mary my negroes, stock and furniture for her life then to daughter Betsey Ann **Jones**, a negro; to daughter Harriot Amanda, a negro; to daughter Virginia Kivon, a negro slave; All else at death of wife to the three daughters.
Exrs : my wife Mary.
Wts: John P. **Lemay**, Benjamin **Clopton**.

185- Feb. 5, 1835- Estate of Daniel **Fuller**, deceased, with John P. **Lemay** and Ozborn **Fuller** excrs.- mentions William **Hendley** as paid a bill, Legatees were Lucy **Estes**, Mary **Nowlin**, Crofford **Fuller**, children of Daniel **Fuller**, Temperance May, Ozborn **Fuller**.

186, 187 Jan. 1, 1835 Estate of Southern **Higgs**, deceased, by Anderson **Paschall**, admstr. hire of slaves and sale of estate.

188 Estate of Martha **Roberson**, deceased, by Henry **Woodworth**, admsr Nov. 1834 sold Jan. 19, 1835 sold for $2.59.

189 Dec. 1834 Amy **Smith**'s legacy, receipt given and witnessed by John P. **Webb**, Stephen **Beasley**.

190 Feb. court 1835 Estate of William T. **Lawrence**, deceased, by John P. **Lawrence** from 1832.

191- Estate of John **Puryear** Jr. deceased,- Nov. 27, 1834 by Sarah T. **Puryear**, admstr.

192, Jan, 28, 1835 Estate of James **Oakley**, deceased,-by Elijah **Hester** one of excrs.

193- Inv. of estate of Lucretia **Bailey** by William **Bailey**, excr. Dec. 10, 1834 and acct. of sale Nov. 25, 1834- buyers include William T., John, Ephraim, William Y., Israel **Bailey**, Samuel **Bailey**.

194 thru 197- Sale of property of David **Parker**, deceased, -Dec. 5, 1834 by John **Shearman**, admstr.

331

197 thru 200- Feb. court 1835- Estate of William **Royster** Sr. deceased, with William **Royster**, Jr., admstr.-from Aug. 1832.

200 thru 206- Feb. court 1835- Estate of Ann P. **Dortch**, deceased, by Jesse **Cobb** Nov. 27, 1834- and sale thereof.

206 thru 208- Nov. term 1834, David L. **Evans** died leaving estate to be equally divided between wife and children, one child George W. **Evans** is of full age, the other two Elizabeth J. and David L. **Evans**- Ask that estate be divided to them that the younger children may have use of it for education which is now in hands of James **Wyche** -their guardian, and other children Thomas J. W. and William Henry **Evans**.

208- thru 212- May court 1834- Petition of Obeda **Blockley**, widow of Halyard **Blockley**, deceased, states that her husband died possessed of land on Middle Creek adjoining the lands of Thomans Y. **Cooke**, Wm. **Blacknall**, Stephen **Johnson** and Wm. **Champion** containing 110 acres. Asks for her dower in land. There was 82 acres instead of 110 as stated of which she was given 27 1/3rd acres.

210-Nov. court 1834- Obeda **Btockley** widow of Halyard **Btockley** and Sally **Btockley** one of children of James **Btockley**, deceased, as that land of James **Btockley** which he willed to his wife for her lifetime then to his three children, namely Halyard, Sally, James **Btockley**, James **Stockley** sold his share to Halyard **Btockley**, now deceased, leaving Obeda, the widow and children Joseph and Mary **Stockley**. The lands to be divided 1/3rd to Sally and 2/3rds to Halyard **Btockleys** children The land adjoins that of Thomas Y. **Cooke**, Mrs. Elizabeth **Blacknall**, John **Nuttall**, deceased. Jan. 15, 1835- land divided (the name is **Blockley**).

212- 213, 214- Robert H., Alfred M, and Horace A. **Burton** state that their mother Agatha **Burton**, deceased, willed her land and mansion house called Montpelier to Robert H, Alfred M, James M. and Augustus **Burton** and Augustus died prior to his mother so Agatha **Burton** then willed his share of and to Horace A. **Burton**. She also devised to her daughter Fanny H. who has since married Samuel **Deekins** and Elizabeth who married James **Anderson**. James M. **Burton** conveyed his share of land to Horace A. They ask the property be divided to them, Eliza and

Fanny--were given land jointly. The land adjoins that of John **Bullock** and L. **Henderson** and contains 494 acres.

214 thru 216- Petition of James **Marrow** and wife Selina, Ralph H. **Graves**, Jesse Deekins **Graves**, Elizabeth **Graves**, Elijah Calvin **Graves** by their guardian James **Marrow** state that Henry L. **Graves** died in 1829 willing all he had to the above named and that it was to be divided when one of his daughters married, and now Selina is married to James **Marrow** so they ask a division of land and property. He owned land adjoining that of Dr. Thomas **Read**, John **Norman**, Ralph **Graves** and a tract at John **Hunts**, Wm. **Bullocks**, William **Hesters**, Wm. **Read** and Dr. C. **Read**. Also negroes to be divided. Ralph **Graves**, the grandfather of the above named children gave one negro- to his grandson Ralph Henry **Graves**; Dec. 24, 1834- division made. The negroes that belonged to their father Henry L. and their mother Elizabeth **Graves** now dead, Legatees were Elizabeth **Graves**, Elijah C. **Graves**, Ralph H. **Graves**, Jesse D., James and Selina **Marrow**, Betsey B. **Graves**.

218 thru 219- May term 1833- Southern **Higgs**, Allen H. **Higgs**, Susan A. **Higgs** and Calvin **Higgs**, heirs and devisees of Kinchn **Higgs**, deceased petition against Thomas H. **Willie** guardian of Woodson **Higgs**, Kenchen **Higgs** and Sibert J. **Higgs** (minors) and also heirs and devisees of Kinchn **Higgs** who left a will with his widow Susan **Higgs** and Allen **Higgs**, admstrs, The he owned 1260 acres called the Harrisburg Tract out of which the widow was given her dower and a tract of 263 acres. The heirs ask a division of this land -It was divided among them.

220- Apr. 29, 1835- John C. **Maclin** of Greenville Co. Virginia appoints Edward **Terry** of Granville Co., N. C., attorney to sell land in Granville Co., N. C., which he owns cojointly with his brother William M. **Maclin**.
Wts: William A **Wardlaw**, clerk of court of Greenville Co., VA, John **Roberson** presiding justices and Thomas Dillahay.

332
222- Mar. 18, 1835- John **Boyd** of Halifax county, Virginia appoints George W. **Boyd** of same place, attorney, to receive that to which I am entitled from the estates of John **Puryear** Sr., and John **Puryear** Jr., deceased, of Granville Co., N.C. Wts: Peyton **Puryear**, Simon **Puryear**.

222-Nov. 11, 1834- Bailee **Peyton** and wife Ann C, of Sumner Co., Tennessee appoint Samuel W. **Smith** of Granville Co., N. C. to sell lands in Virginia and North Carolina which came to us thru right of wife Ann C. **Peyton**.

223-224- Feb. 21, 1835- Cassander **White**, widow and relict of Thomas **White**, deceased, of Sumner Co., Tennessee appoints Henry A **Brinkley**, attorney, to receive for her from estate of Southern **Higgs**, deceased, of Granville Co, who died last Spring, intestate and whose admstr. is **Anderson Paschall**.

225- Apr. 7, 1835- Thomas B. **Littlejohn**, admstr. of estate of Dr. William **Vaughn** and Sarah Matilda **Vaughn** places notice to all claimants against estate or owed to estate.

226- May 8, 1835- Estate of Osborn **Ball**, deceased, by Samuel **Duty**, admstr. settle estate.

227- Inv. and sale of the property of Elijah and Jesse **Veazey**, deceased sold Feb. 25, 1835 by Jacob **Hester**, admstr. mentions Mary **Veazey**, John C. and John R. **Veazey**, Joseph H. **Veazey**, Anderson **Veazey**.

229- thru 231--Apr. 29, 1835- Inv. of property of James **Haskins**, deceased by George **Haskins**, excrs. and Aron **Haskins** sold Feb. 27, 1835.

232--Inv. of estate of Mrs. E. **Norman** by Dudly **Mingay** May court 1835 sold by **Mingay** Feb. 1835-estate of Mrs. Elizabeth **Norman**.

233 thru 236- Inv. of property of Alexander **Hamilton**, deceased, by Patrick **Hamilton**, admstr. Apr. 27, 1835.

237- Apr. 28, 1835- Estate of Morris **Carnal**, deceased, by Wm. **Terry**, admsr.

237- Feb. 1835- Inv. of estate of Ann M. **Hunt** by Hamilton **Hester** excr.

238- Acct.-of estate of Elizabeth **Hillyard**, deceased, by Donaldson **Paschall**, admstr.

239, 240- Inv. of estate of Samuel R. **Parkam (Parham)**, deceased, by Lewis **Parham**, admstr. May 1, 1835.

240 thru 242- Estate of John **Harris** Sr., deceased, by William **Yarbrough** admstr. from Sept. 1828- mentions legatees but not named.

242 thru 250- Mar. 19, 1835- Estate of James **Philpott**, deceased, by Simeon **Philpott**, Inv. and sale of estate- mentioned in sale was Elizabeth **Hubbard**, Emily, Solomon, Lindon, James **Philpott**, William, Samuel, Mary Ann **Philpott**..

250, 251, 252- Wardens of the Poor of Granville Co., N. C. by A. **Paschal** one of acting wardens. for May court 1835.

253--Estate of Robert A. **Burchitt**, deceased, by Bart **Kimball**, admstr.

254- Mar. 26, 1834- William **Webb** appointed James **Hart** Sr., attorney to collect that owing him in North Carolina and Virginia.
Wts. A. L. **Webb**.

255--Accts of estate of Joshua **Hutcherson**, deceased, by James **Blackley**, admstr. Aug. 4, 1835 mentions John, Asa, Willis, James M. **Hutcherson**.

Estate Records of Granville Co, NC Volume 13-16   17

255- Inv. of estate of Isreal **Hargrove**, deceased, Aug. 1, 1835 by Charles M. **Hargrove**, admstr. mentions William **Hargroves** legacy and Charles M. **Hargrove**.

257, 258- Inv. of estate of Gabriel **Jones** Sr., by John Y. **Sandford**, admstr. Aug, court 1835.

259, 260- Estate of Joseph **Barnett** Sr., deceased, in acct. with Thos. B. **Barnett** excr. from Jan. 1831- lists board-for Elizabeth Ann, Martha, Robert S., Joseph W., Mary **Barnett**, James **Barnett**.

260, 261- Jesse H. **Cobb** administrator of estate of Ann P. **Dortch**, deceased Aug. 7, 1835.

333

262- July 18, 1835 Inv. of personal estate of Lemuel **Peace**, deceased, by Josiah **Peace**, admstr. and sale of same July 29, 1835-

263 - Aug. 6, 1831- proved Aug. court 1835.
John **Puryear**---- wills to John **Pomfrett**, Henry **Smith**, son of John P. **Smith** negro children; To wife Sarah T. **Puryear**, all else I own including my part of my father's estate John **Puryear** Sr, and all I will receive from my mother.
Exrs.; my wife Sarah T. **Puryear**.
Wts: Maurice **Smith**, James **Smith**.
William C. **Tucker**, George W. **Tucker**, William and Thomas **Amis** and David S. **Wilkerson** state that this is not the will of John **Puryear** and a publication made as to George and John **Boyd**, John Junior, and wife Amey Aplin **Puryear** as guardian of his children to appear. Feb. term 1835 and continued to May 1835-- proved by jury and recorded.

264- May 5 1835- proved Nov. court 1835.
Fleming **Lumpkins**---- wills to wife Polly, my land and negroes for her widowhood or lifetime and at her death to my children or the representatives of them that are dead; My property kept together, and my youngest child Meredith remain with my wife and she executrix.
Wts: John C. **Taylor**, E. W. **Norwood**.

265-Apr. 29, 1831- proved Aug, court 1835.
Allen **Howard**---- wills to son **Anderson**, a negro slave; to daughter Elizabeth **Lunsford**, 2 negroes; to son Thomas, a negro; to son William 2 negroes; to son Joseph, 4 negroes and land I bought of Benjamin E. **Person**, except about 20 acres; to daughter Phebe **Voss** 4 negroes, a bed and furniture, a mare, saddle; to son Solomon the remainder of my land, 3 negroes, a silver ladle, a saddle; all rest of silver to two-daughters. All else of my property sold and money divided to the children.
Exrs: son Joseph Howard and James **Gooch**.
Wts: James **Gooch**, Daniel **Gooch**, John **Webb**.

266--Jan. 1, 1835- Estate of Joseph **Barnett** Sr., deceased, by Thos. B. **Barnett**, excr.

267- Inv. of property of John **Jinkins**, deceased, by Joel **Swinney**, admstr.

268- Estate of James M. **Moody** with Wm. A. **Moody**, admst.

269 Aug. 1, 1835- Estate of Phillip **Pool**, deceased, who died Mar. 25, 1834, by Clarborn **Pool**, admstr.

270- Sale of estate of John **Smith** deceased, which he willed to his wife Nancy **Smith** during her lifetime and now she deceased- sold by John **Smith**, excr. June 6, 1835- Henry, Guy, James, Jno. **Smith** bought at sale. Also Thomas J. **Smith**, Lucy **Smith**; Alexander **Smith**, Sudy **Smith**.

273, 274- Sale of property of Benjamin **Hope**, deceased, by Elizabeth **Hope**, admstr.- July 25, 1835. among buyers were Mariah, Mary, Nancy **Hope**.

275- Estate of Charles D. **Tucker** by H. **Hare** (Dr. Len. H. **Hare**).

275, 276- Mar. 8, 1835- Benjamin **Bullock** became owner of the interest David **Mitchell** acquired when he married Elizabeth **Smith**, daughter of James **Smith** deceased, in her legacy from her father which property was devised to his wife Amey **Smith** for life and rest to children, they accounting for that given them in the lifetime of parents- **Bullock** assigns to Amey **Bullock** for $200.00 by trust to pay certain debts.

277- Oct. 7, 1835 John **Webb**, of Breckenridge Co., KY. appointed Isaac **Webb**, of Person Co., N. C., attorney to receive from Thomas **Webb**, of Granville, Co., N. C. as the excr. of the will of John **Webb**, deceased, to collect from Thomas **Webb** that due me.
Wts: William H. **Webb** Jr., John W. **Owen**.

278, 279- Nov. 16, 1829-- Breckenridge Co., Kentucky- James **Barclay**; John W. **Stotts**, Cornelius **Hough**; Robert **Stephens**, Henry N. **King**--before whom James **Owen** came and asked administration on estate of Thomas **Owen**, Esq. deceased, with Thomas G. and John W. **Owen** and Lewis **Moreman**, securities and James **Owen** appoints his brother John W. **Owen**, attny. or admstr. of

334
Thomas **Owen** Esq., deceased, to go to North Carolina and call upon Thomas **Webb** of Granville Co., excr. of John **Webb** Jr, deceased, and collect from him all money due me as admstr. of Thomas **Owen** deceased, who married Elizabeth **Webb**, now deceased, who was a daughter and heir of John **Webb** Jr., deceased, and also appoint Isaac **Webb** of Person Co., N. C., attorney to recover for me all due from. estate of John **Webb**, deceased. 10/8/1835.

Estate Records of Granville Co, NC Volume 13-16   19

Wts: Jo **Allen**, clerk of Breckenridge Co., KY., court; Nathan D. **Anderson** Acting Justice.

279- William M. **Sneed** gives receipt to Protheus E. A. **Jones** Oct. 30, 1835 for his half of money due as executor of his fathers estate and Dr. H. T. **Royster** and wife paid other half--about $462.00.

280- John **Puryear**, William C. **Tucker**, David W. **Wilkerson**, George W. **Tucker**, George M. **Boyd**, Thomas **Amis**, John **Junel**, John **Boyd** appoints William **Amis**, attorney, to sell all property belonging to us which was possessed by the late Sylvania **Puryear**, deceased, as her heirs at law and also as heirs of John **Puryear** deceased.
Wts: Simon **Puryear**, Harmon **Puryear**.

281-Oct. 15, 1835- proved Nov. court 1835.
James **Stuart**---- wills to wife all of which he dies possessed to use for the support of herself and children; to son Thomas A **Stuart**, land on which I reside, a horse, a cow and calf, bed and furniture, sow and pigs, corn, pork, to receive this after death of my wife; All else to be divided among the other children at death of my wife.
Exrs: my wife and John S. **Eaton**.
Wts: John **O'Brien** Jr., Thomas **Wilson**, Samuel **Edwards**.

282- Acct. of Thomas J. **Hicks**, county Trustee for the year-1835.

284- Estate of Benjamin **Hope** deceased, by Elizabeth **Hope**, excr. from Jan. 7, 1834 at which date paid for coffin $4.00.

285- Estate of William E. **Dortch**, deceased, by John **Bullock**, admstr. Oct. 5, 1835.

288 thru 303- Estate of Maurice **Smith** deceased, by Richard J. **Smith**, admstr. Nov. court 1835-Mentions gifts to Samuel W. **Smith**, John B. **Smith**, Allen R. **Smith**- He had a very large library and many negroes.

303- Oct. 14, 1835- Stephen K. **Sneed** appoints Thomas H. **Willie**, attorney to sell his land in Granville County and his town property in Oxford, N. C. since he is moving to the west and also to collect all that is owing him.
Wts: S. S. **Downey**, Wm. M. **Sneed**.
He also wishes his 1/3rd of land that formerly belonged to William M. **Sneed**, sold with approbation of Richard **Sneed** and Thomas D. **Ridley**.
Oct. 20, 1835- Wts: B. **Bullock**, L **Gilliam**.

305- Sale or hire of negroes of estate of George **Norman**, deceased by Dudley **Mingay**, excr.

305, 306--Inv. of estate of Fleming **Lumpkin**, deceased, Sept. 1, 1835 by Thos.

H. **Willie**, admstr. mentions widows support.

306 thru 309- Estate of Israel **Hargrove** by Charles W. **Hargrove**, admstr. Sept. 30, 1835- and among buyers at sale were Hartwell W., Israel W., Mary **Hargrove**.

310 thru 312- Inv. of estate of Southern **Higgs**, deceased, bonds, judgements etc. May court 1835- by Anderson **Paschall**.

312- Oct. 29, 1835- Inv. of property of estate of William **Norwood** by Philip H. **Norwood**, admstr.

313- Estate of Gran **Ellington**, deceased, by Willis **Harris**, admstr. Nov. 4, 1835.

314- Sale of estate of Samuel R. **Parham** deceased, Oct. 28, 1835 by Lewis **Parham**, admstr. and among buyers were Elizabeth, Lewis, Asa, Willie J. **Parham**, Williamson, Lewis R. **Parham**.

317- Sale of estate of Phillip P. **Pool**, deceased Oct. 27, 1835 by Clabourn P **Pool**, admstr. and among buyers were Anna, Margaret, Phillip P. **Pool**, Joshua **Nunn**, Charles W. P. **Pool**.

335
319- Inv. of estate of Allen **Howard**, deceased, which was willed away and not sold and some that was sold Aug, 28, 1835- by Joseph **Howard**, excr.

325 thru 327 Aug. term 1835- petition of Mary **Hargrove**, William R. **Hargrove**, Isreal **Hargrove**, Charles W. **Hargrove** and Hartwell W. **Hargrove** state that Isreal **Hargrove** Sr. departed this life May 3, 1835, leaving his widow Mary, and his children Wm. R., Isreal W, Charles W and Hartwell W. **Hargrove** and administration on estate given to Charles W **Hargrove**. They ask division of estate for there is more than enough to pay the indebtedness. 27 negroes divided between them.

328 thru 335- Nov. court 1835- Petition of Leonard **Higgs**, Ella **Higgs**, Willis **Johnson** and wife Mary, Kenchen H. **White** and wife Elizabeth, Alfred, and William **Higgs**, George P. **Thomason** and wife Nancy, Willis **Johnson**, Willis H. **Higgs**, minor who sues by guardian Allen H. **Higgs**, Warner **Parham** and wife Mary W., Thomas **White** and wife Cassy, Daniel **Johnson** and wife Eliza, Green **Stanton** and wife Mary, Southey J. **Higgs**, Allen H., Susan A, Calvin **Higgs**, Woodson, Kinchen H., Sebert J. **Higgs**, minors, with and by guardian Thomas H. **Willie**- against minor and heir at law of John **Higgs** deceased, son of John **Higgs** Sr. deceased whose name is unknown.
State that Southern **Higgs** died Mar. 1834 without leaving issue, and he owned land in Granville Co., N. C., containing 972 acres and left surviving him the petitioners

Estate Records of Granville Co, NC Volume 13-16   21

and the defendant whose relationship is as follows: Leonard **Higgs** a brother, Ella **Higgs**, Mary who married Willis **Johnson**, Elizabeth who married Kinchen H. **White**, Alfred **Higgs**, William **Higgs**, Nancy who married George P. **Thomason** who are children and heirs at law of John **Higgs** deceased, who was a brother of said intestate, Willis. Willis **Higgs** married a **Johnson** and had son Willis **Johnson** and was a sister (she now deceased) of Southern **Higgs**, deceased, Willis H. **Higgs**, a minor who sues by his next friend Allen H. **Higgs**, Mary W., who married Warner **Parham**, Willis H. and Mary W. children of Mary **Johnson**, daughter and heir of aforesaid Willey **Johnson** who married John **Higgs**, who is now dead, Cassey **Higgs** married Thomas **White**, she a sister of Southern **Higgs**, deceased, Eliza **Higgs** married Daniel **Johnson**, sister of Southern **Higgs**, deceased, Southern J., Allen H., Susan A., Calvin, Woodson, Kinchen H., Sebert J. **Higgs** children of Kinchen **Higgs** Sr, deceased, who was brother of Southern **Higgs** deceased and these children minors and sue by guardian Thomas H. **Willie** and defendant who is a minor child and heir of John **Higgs** Jr., deceased who was one of children of John **Higgs** Sr. deceased who was a brother of Southern **Higgs** deceased. The land should be divided into 7 lots and one part was given Leonard **Higgs**, one part to the children of John **Higgs** Sr., deceased, one part to children of Nelly **Johnson**, deceased, one part to Casey **White**, one part to Eliza **Johnson**, one to Mary **Stanton**, one to children of Kinchen **Higgs**, deceased, subject to dower of Rebecca **Higgs**, widow of Southern **Higgs** deceased Land was divided to them.

332- thru 335- Nov. court 1835- Division of negro property of Southern **Higgs**, deceased, who died without issue.
Rebecca **Higgs**, widow of Southern **Higgs**, deceased, Leonard **Higgs**, brother of deceased, and sisters Kesiah who married Thomas **White**, Polly married Green **Stanton**, Nelly who married William **Johnson**, now deceased, leaving children, who are entitled to 1/7th of 2/3rds of the negroes, to wit: Elly, John, Alfred, William, Betsy, **White**(petitioner), Polly who married Willis **Johnson**, Nancy **Thomason**, all living outside the State, except John who is dead and whether he left issue is not known. Southern **Higgs** had the following brothers who preceded him in death, namely, John and Kinchen **Higgs**. Kinchen left a widow Susan and the following children: Southern, Allen, Calvin, Woodson, Kinchen H., Jackson and Susan **Higgs** who are entitled to 1/7th of 2/3rds of the negroes. Calvin sold his share to Dennis T. **Paschall**. Nelly **Johnson** left the following children: Willis **Johnson**, Polly who married John **Higgs** and

336
said Polly left children (she preceding testator in death) Willia **Higgs** and Polly who married Warner **Parham**) who are entitled to a share and they reside in Tennessee. Anderson **Paschall** was admstr. of estate of Southern **Higgs** deceased, and asks widows thirds be set off first and 2/3rds to other heirs, Granted and division made.
336-Apr. 18, 1835-- proved Feb. court 1836.
William **Mallory**---- wills to son Charles, John, William, $1.00 in addition of all given them; to son James, a bed and furniture, a horse; To son Pleasant, $1.00 in addition to that already given him; to daughters Lucy **Miner** and Nancy **Hopkins**

and daughter Agathy M. **Parrish**, each $1.00 in addition to that already given them; To wife Mary, land whereon I live, a negro and the rest of my property for her lifetime and at her death to my daughters that are now single and if either marries then the single one have the negro slave.
Exrs: sons John and James **Mallory**, Robert **Longmire**.
Wts: Augustin **Harris**, Meredith **Pool**.

337- Nov. 5, 1835--proved Feb. court 1836.
Elizabeth **Green**---wills to daughter Mary A., 2 featherbeds equal to beds given my daughter Nancy, and a chest; to 2 daughters Nancy and Mary, all silver and bed curtains; to sons Isaac, William, John B., George W., a feather bed, sheets, counterpains with remainder of my bed clothes, table cloths, etc. to be divided among my seven children: namely Nancy, Mary, Joseph, Isaac, William, John B., and George W. **Green**.
Exr.- none named.
Wts: James **Beasley**, Thomas **Hicks**.

338- Mar. 5, 1831- proved Feb. court 1836.
Frederick **Wiggins**--- wills to have debts paid and that left to his wife Nancy for life and at her death to be equally divided between my children namely: Nancy **Bowdon**, Gulielmus, John, Hundley, Harold **Wiggins** and Elizabeth **Reavis**, each 1/8th part; To children of Thomas **Wiggins**, dec'd 1/8th part; To children of Jaqueline **Wiggins**, 1/8th part.
Exrs: wife Nancy and son John **Wiggins**.
Wts: Joseph W. **Hawkins**, Franklin **Moss**, Hardy **Harris**.

339, 340, 341- Jan. 23, 1833- proved Feb. court 1836.
Robert **Lanier**---- wills to daughter Sally **Jiles**(?) and John **Jiles**, for their lifetime, a slave, and at their death to my granddaughter Polly **Hester** to be divided among her heirs; to John **Jiles** $1.00; to daughter Elizabeth **Landis** and John **Landis**, a negro slave; to daughter Polly **Lanier**, 2 negroes, a horse, 2 cows and calves, sow and pigs, 4 sheep, half the geese, 2 beds and furniture, and all the furniture marked with the first letters of her name, a loom, a spinning wheel, 6 chairs, a pot and an oven, one spider, 6 knives and forks and her choice of 6 earthen plates and a side saddle and bridle; To daughter Nancy **Jenkins**, to be paid annually the interest on $250.00 and as soon as. her youngest child is of age the principle to be divided among her children; To grandsons Zachariah and John **Lyon**, all property I bought at sale of Zachariah **Lyon**, deceased, now in hands of Walter and Nancy **Jenkins**; to daughter Wilmouth **Adams**, 3 negroes ; to grson John Pinkney **Adams**, a still; to wife for her lifetime, negroes, 2 featherbeds and furniture, live stock and household goods, side saddle and at her death to be divided between my children and grandchildren: 1/5th part to Wilmouth **Adams**, Elizabeth **Landis**, to children of Benjamin **Lanier**, my son, deceased; to Jennett and Barsheba **Cash**(?) 1/5th together, to Nancy **Jenkins**'s children 1/5th, when they are 21 yrs. old; to son-in-law William **Cash** $1.00, to granddaughters. Jennet C. **Cash** and Barsheba **Cash** a negro girl sold and money divided between them; to Elizabeth and John **Landis** a negro

slave. Land divided as follows: To Wilmouth and Isaac **Adams** 1/3rd part whereon they now live; to wife 1/3rd with the dwelling house; to Polly **Lanier** 1/3rd part, all else sold and divided between my children and grchildren 1/5th to each of the following: Wilmouth **Adams**, Elizabeth **Landis**, to

337

children of Benja A. **Lanier**, my son, deceased; 1/5th to Jennett and Barsheba **Cash** jointly; 1/5th part to children of Nancy **Jenkins** when 21 yrs. old.
Exrs: son-in-law Isaac **Adams** and if he needs counsel to pay from estate for same.
Wts: James A. J. **Burchett**, Allen **Wilkins**.
Elizabeth, widow of Robert **Lanier** contested will but withdrew and will was proved (since James A. **Burchett** and Allen **Wilkins** were dead) on oath of Clement **Wilkins** and Dr. James **Young**.

341, 342- Aug, 12, 1835- Daniel **Johnson**, admstr. of Elizabeth **Johnson** deceased of **Roberson** county, Tennessee, appoints William **Johnson** of said county, attorney, to call on admstr. of estate of Southern **Higgs** of Granville County, N. C., to receive her share in estate as she was a sister of Southern **Higgs** and sell the part for her, Elizabeth **Johnson**, dec'd. Wts: W. **Seal**, clerk of court and John **Hutchinson** magistrate of county of **Roberson**, Tennessee.

343- Nov. 10, 1835- William **Howard** of Madison County, Tennessee, appoints James W. **Cozart** of same county, attorney, to receive all money due me in Granville Co., N. C.
Wts: Roderick **McIver**, clerk of Madison Co., Tenn and Jacob **Perkins** Chairman of court.

344- thru -350- Inv. and acct of sales of property of Mark **Veazey**, deceased, by William **Veazey**, excr. Feb. court 1836. Mentions Joseph, John C., James L., Abner, John C. **Veazey** buy at sale, and Andrew J. and William, Ezekiel **Veazey**.

351- thru page 358- Inv. and sale of estate of Coleman R. **White**, deceased, Nov. 10, 1835- by James **Wyche**, admstr.--mentions Frances Shelia (or Celia) and Eaton J. **White** in cash, and cash spent by G. W. **White** before he was appointed admstr. also mentions as buyers at sale: John, Wm. G. V., Phillip **White**, Thomas O. **White**, Eaton J. **White**, Francis **White**, Celia **White**, Guilford D. Sims. negro slaves willed to John **White**, Elizabeth **Allison**, Mary **Vincent**, Susan **McGehee** and children of Rutha **Crook**, also 3 negroes bed and furniture to Wm. G. V. **White** (if will is established), To Thomas P. **White** bed and furniture, to Francis L. L. **White**, negroes and Celia C. **White**.

358- thru 363- Sale of estate of Robert **Lanier**, deceased, by Elijah **Hester**, admstr. Dec. 1, 1835.

363- Sale of estate of Joseph **Barnett** Sr., deceased, by Thomas B. **Barnett**, excr, Dec. 28, 1835.

364- Estate of Isham **Epps** by Elijah **Hester**, excr. Feb. court 1836.

365- Estate of Elijah and Jesse **Veazey** by Joseph **Hester**, admstr. Feb. court 1836.

366- Estate of John C. **Whitfield** by John W. **Whitfield**, excr. mentions money paid Mary J. **Hester** as specified in the will, to heirs of Sarah **Young**, to Samuel **Young**, to James **Hester**, to Mary **Hester**, heirs of Eliza and D. Proddy, to Wm. **Whitfield**, to Joseph Booth, to John W. **Whitfield**.

367- Estate of Joseph **Barnett**, deceased by T. B. **Barnett**, excr. Feb. 6 1836.--mentions Mrs. Mary **Barnett**, James and William **Barnett**.

368- Jan. 28, 1836- Inv. of Lucy **Lemay**'s property by John P. **Lemay**, admstr.

368- Acct. of sales of Wesley W. **Paschall**, deceased, by John P. **Lemay**, admstr. Feb. court 1836.

369, 370- Estate of Robert **Lanier**, deceased, Inv. Nov. 5, 1835 by Elijah **Hester**, admstr.

370 thru 372- Estate of Samuel **Bryan**, deceased, by Washington H. **Thomas**, admstr. Dec. 7, 1835. Among buyers at sale were Mrs. Mary **Bryan**, Thomas **Bryan**.

372- thru 374- Acct. of estate of Leonard **Henderson** deceased, by John L. **Henderson**, excr. from Aug, 1833-

375- John **Gilliam**, sheriff, accounts of Granville Co., N. C. 1836.

338

376, 377- Sale of estate of Gabriel **Jones**, deceased June 6, 1835, by John Y. **Sandford**, admstr.

378- Negro girl of estate of Allen **Howard**, deceased, as per will to Joseph **Howard**, Nov. court 1835.

379- thru 381- Acct. of estate sold of Allen **Howard**, deceased, Nov. 17, 1835- by Joseph **Howard**, excr. and among buyers were Thomas, Joseph, Solomon, **Anderson Howard** Feb. court 1836.

381, 382- Inv. of estate of Samuel **Bryan** deceased, Dec. 7, 1835, by Wash. **Thomas**, admstr.

382- thru 384- Inv. of estate of and sale of Margaret **Carnal**, Dec. 3, by Wm. **Terry**, excr. mentions land in Orange Co., N. C.

384 thru 386- Acct. of sales of Fleming **Lumpkin**, deceased, Sept, 28, 1835 by Thomas H. **Willie**, admstr. mentions Mrs. **Lumpkin** and John **Lumpkin** as buyers at sale among many others.

387- Feb. court 1836- Commissioners to sell negroes of estate of Southern **Higgs**, deceased, allotted to heirs of Kinchen **Higgs**, deceased.

387- Inv. of estate of Elizabeth **Johnson**, deceased, Feb. 5, 1836 by William **Johnson**, admstr. there is money due from Southern **Higgs** estate.

388- Additional Inv. of property of L. **Henderson** deceased, by John L. **Henderson**, excr.

389- thru 397- Acct. of sale of estate of Col. Maurice **Smith**, deceased, Apr. 10, 1835 being 2nd sale- by Richd. J. **Smith**, admstr.- among buyers were Mrs. Amy **Smith**, William **Smith**, Saml Henry **Smith**, Francis S. **Smith**, Amy W. **Smith**, the widow.

397-- thru 400- Inv. and acct of sales of estate of Mrs. Elizabeth **Green**, deceased, by Clement **Wilkins**, admstr. Jan, 25, 1837 among buyers at sale were William, Joseph and Mary A. **Green**.

401- thru 407- Acct. of sales of estate of Hubbard **Cozart**, deceased, Feb. 1836 by William **Clement**, admstr, gives allotment to Mrs. Mary **Cozart**, wife of deceased. James C. **Cozart** among those buying at sale, also Robert and Allen **Cozart**, William **Cozart**, Simeon **Cozart** also.

407- thru 412- Inv. and of account of sales of James A. **Buchannon** deceased, Feb. 25, 1836, by James **Wyche**- Hillyard **Buchannon** bought at sale, Mary, Priscilla **Buchannon** also bought at sale, Rosa **Buchanon** also.

412-413, 414- Inv. and sales of estate of Fred **Wiggins**, deceased, Feb. 18, 1836, by L. H. **Hare**, admstr.- mentions buyers at sale being Nancy and Howel **Wiggins**, John **Wiggins**, and others.

414-415- Hire of negroes of estate of Moses **Carnal**, deceased, by from 1834 and Feb. 1835 by William **Terry**, admstr.

415- Estate of Robert **Lanear**, deceased, sale Mar. 1, 1836 by Isaac **Adams**.

417- thru 419- Sale of estate of William **Madison**, deceased, by Samuel P. **Forsythe**- May court 1836-sold Feb. 26, 1836 and among, buyers were Mary Ann, Levin, James, Peyton **Madison**.

419- 420- Apr. 13, 1834- proved May court 1836.
Claborn **Parrish**---- wills to Capt. Alfred **Jones** 10 acres, at the Orange Co. line

adjoining William **Parrish** to Mark **Roberts** corner, in trust for my daughter Patsy **Moore** and her husband to have no control over it and at her death to the heirs of her body; All else to my wife, Polly, and my. granddaughter, Rheaney **Parrish**, to live with her and have a home with her for the lifetime of my wife, also to wife a horse, live stock, and furniture and anything else necessary; to grdaughter Rheaney **Parrish** a bed and furniture, a chest, weaving loom; all else sold and my exrs. divide to my children: Christian **Forsythe**; Sibon **Parrish**, Nancy **Worsham**, Polly **Mangum**, William **Parrish**, Ready **Olmstead**, Eady **Jones**, Reamy **Parrish** and Patsy **Moore** and grdau Rheany, a saddle and bridle, and cow.
Exrs: Capt. Alfred **Jones** and son William **Parrish**.
Wts.: B. **Bullock**, Wm. **McFarlin**.

339
421- Aug, 29, 1835- proved May court 1836.
George **Thomason**--- wills to wife Martha, after debts paid all my estate for her lifetime and after her death, to daughter Martha $100.00 for her services heretofore; to son James, bed cow and calf, hogs; to Elizabeth **Montague**, a bed; to son George, a bed, cow and calf; To daughter Martha a bed and live stock; To Martha a horse and saddle; All else sold and equally divided between son James and daughter Elizabeth **Montague**, son George, daughter Martha **Thomason**, son Garland **Thomason**.
Exrs: sons James and George **Thomason** To son William $1.00.
Wts: John **Barnett**, Young **Montague**.

421, 422- May 22, 1832--proved May court 1836.
Mary **Jinkins**--- wills to cousin Richard **Bullock**, a negro man, a negro woman, live stock, household and kitchen furniture, tools and all else and he executor.
Wts: Samuel **Lemay**.

422- 423- Inv. of estate of David **Jones**, deceased, by Jonathan **Jones**, admstr.-May court 1836.

423- Additional Inv. of estate of Ann M. **Hunt**, deceased, by Hamilton **Hester**, excr. May court 1836.-

423, 424- Inv of estate of Thomas **Dickerson**, deceased, by Dennis T. **Paschall**, admstr. May term 1836-- money due this estate from estate of John **Stone** deceased.

424- Inv. of estate of Penelope **Dew**, deceased, May 2, 1836, by Thomas **Dew**, admstr. whole estate $31.2 ½ cents.

424- Feb. term 1836- Jury allotted to J Robert **Maben** and wife their proportion of estate of Jonathan **Davis**, deceased. Feb. 4, 1836.

425- 426- Acct. of estate of Martha **Anderson**, deceased, by Clement **Wilkins**, excr. May court 1836.

Estate Records of Granville Co, NC Volume 13-16

426, 427- Estate of Israel **Hargrove**; deceased, with Charles M. **Hargrove**, admstr, from May 1835-to May term 1836.

427 thru 429- Nov. 14, 1835- William **Higgs** and Nancy **Thomason** of Weakley Co. Tennessee, appointed Alfred **Higgs** their attorney Sept. 29, 1835 to receive for them any land or other estate that descended to them from Southern **Higgs**, deceased, late of Granville Co., N. C. and also to collect from **Anderson Paschall** that due from, estate of **Higgs**, deceased, and all negroes belonging to them and Alfred **Higgs** appointed Col. Lewis **Parham**, in his stead, of Granville, Co, N.C. Wts: Benjamin **Kittrell** (who was dead May 1836 and Thomas H. **Willie** proves his handwriting).

429- Nov. 14, 1835- Alfred **Higgs** of Weakley Co., Tennessee appoints Col. Lewis **Parham**, of Granville Co., N. C., attorney, to collect from **Anderson Paschall**, admstr. of Southern **Higgs**, all due me.
Wts: Benjm **Kittrell**.

430- 431- Apr. 4, 1830- proved Aug court 1836.
Barbary **Washington**---- wills to daughter Elizabeth **Avey**, Matildy **Askew** the land whereon I live, live stock, bed and furniture and a chest; To sons William and Woodson **Washington** and daughter Elizabeth **Avey**, Matilda **Askew** all else I own; to William **Terry**, land whereon I now live, stock etc to hold in trust for my daughter Elizabeth for her support and her children's support or he to take property and support her from same.
Exrs: William **Terry**.
Wts: Stephen **Terry**, Daniel **Dear**.

431- Dec. 19, 1833- proved Aug. court 1836.
Sarah **Jeffrys**---wills to son Littleton Washington **Jeffrys**, a negro named Mack who was willed to me by my father William **Jeffrys** to be mine at death of my mother, ½ of my household goods and he live on my land till 21 yrs. old; to grandson Sidney Turner **Pettiford (Peddyford)** land left me by my father William **Jeffrys**, live stock and ½ household goods.
She died Dec. 19, 1833- and will written by Jeremiah **Rust** Aug. court 1836 William C. **Patton**, admstr.

340

432-Estate of James **Satterwhite** May court 1836, in acct with Howel **Satterwhite** and Solomon **James**, excrs.

433- Estate of William **Floyd**, the elder, deceased, in acct with William **Floyd**, Jr., excr. Aug. court 1836.

434- Estate of Ann M. **Hunt** in acct with Hamilton **Hester**, excr. Aug. court 1836.

435- Estate of Halyard **Blockley** deceased, with Howel **Cooke**, admstr. May court 1836.

436- Inv. of estate of Nathaniel **Robertson**, deceased, by Henry **Woodsworth**, admstr.-Aug. court 1836.

437- Further Inv. of estate of Robin Hood **Harris**, deceased, by Thomas **Harris**, admstr. Aug. court 1836.

437- Sale of negroes of estate of Alexander **Hamilton**, deceased, in Williamsborough, N. C. by P. **Hamilton** admstr. July 1, 1836.

437, 438- Sale of negroes of estate of Hubbard **Cozart** deceased, by William **Clement** admstr. May 31, 1836-

439- Acct of sale of property of Lydia **Lyon**, deceased, Mar. 4, 1836 by C. B. and Elkanah **Lyon**, admstrs.

440- Inv. of estate of George **Thomason** Sr. deceased, May 10, 1836 by James **Thomason** excr.

441, 442- Estate of Claborn **Parrish**, June 3, 1836- sale by Alfred **Jones**, excr.

443 thru 445- Acct. of sale of estate of John **Lyon** by C. B. and Elkanah **Lyon**, excrs. Mar. 4, 1836. Among buyers were John W., James **Lyon**, Elk. **Lyon** and others.

446- Nov. term 1835- petition of Alfred, William **Higgs**, Willia[m] **Johnson** and wife Mary, Ann **Thomason** against Ella **Higgs**, Francis M. **Higgs**, infant son of John **Higgs** and Kinchen **White** and wife Elizabeth- state they are the representatives of John **Higgs**, deceased, and that their father, John **Higgs**, was one of brothers of Southen **Higgs** who died in Mar. 1834 and they are entitled to a share in estate. We received 2 negroes at division of negroes and ask permission to sell them to make equal division between ourselves of the money- granted and sold.

447-448- Feb. court 1836- petition of Francis A **Hodge** against Lucy L., Margaret B., James B., and William H. **Hodge**, minors, states that she is widow of William H. **Hodge**, deceased, and at his death he had a large estate consisting of 100 or more negroes; that he left the petitioner and minor children as heirs, and next of kin. Archibald **Henderson** is guardian of defendants. Asks division of negroes. Widow Frances A. received 27 negroes, May 3, 1836 by her agent Richard **Bullock** of Warren county, N C.- the children given 70 negroes.

449, 450- Feb. court 1836- Petition of Salley, Mariah, Stephen and Susan **Floyd** by their guardian Daniel A. **Paschall** and James **Floyd** minor. State that Henry **Floyd** died and left will appointed Robert **Harrison**, excr. and we ask settlement of estate and distribution of slaves, and Salley **Floyd**, widow of Henry **Floyd**, deceased, and one of the petitioners entered dissent and asked for division of estate- She was allotted her part of negro estate and children Ann Mariah **Floyd** and Susan George **Floyd** their share, and sons Stephen and James **Floyd**-

451- Aug. term 1835- John D. **Maclin** is a tenant in common with the heirs of William W. **Maclin** to a tract of land and since he is entitled to one moiety or ½ of land, asks division,- but he is ignorant of names and ages of other children so petition can be granted without aid. Was allotted his half the land and other half set off to heirs of Wm. W. **Maclin** (there is a plat of this land and division here).

453 thru 455- Petition of Mrs. Amy W. **Smith**, widow of Maurice **Smith**, deceased, states her husband died in 1835 intestate, and admstr. is Richard J. **Smith**. She asks division of lands. Home tract of 1000 acres, **Hennings** 1,072 acres, **Stiths** 600 acres, **Jonathan Creek** 300 acres, **Fosters** 300 acres, **Olivers** 126 acres, **Stanly** 415 acres, **Peach Grove** 185 acres. **Gooch** tract 100 acres, **Beasleys** 35 acres-- buildings in Oxford and lots.

341
She was allotted the 1000 acre home tract and part of the **Henning** tract adjoining including the dwelling house.
There were children: Mary A. G., married to Richard I. **Smith**, Francis S. **Smith**, William **Smith**, John B. **Smith**, Ann R. **Smith**, Men R. **Smith**, James W. and Thomas M. **Smith** surviving their father.

455- Sally **Robertson** of Henderson Co., Kentucky, Oct. 28, 1822, on motion of Sarah **Robertson**, widow of Leonard **Robertson**, deceased, was given letters of administration on estate of her late husband and was secured by George **Robertson** and George **Lyne**.
Wts: Wm. D. **Allison** clerk of county court of **Henderson** Co., KY, and Thos. Toles was presiding justice.

456, 457- Power of attorney from Sally **Robertson** to Larkin **White** Nathaniel **Robertson** of Mecklenburg Co., VA. devised by his last will to Martha **Robertson**, a negro woman and at her death to his two grsons Charles and Leonard **Robertson** sons of said Martha, and, now Martha is dead, and Leonard **Robertson** removed to Henderson Co, KY, and there died intestate and Sally **Robertson** his widow, and admstrx appoints Larkin **White** of Henderson Co., KY attorney to sell my interest in negro slaves.
Wts: James **Alves** J. P., Joseph **Cowan** J. P., Wm. D. **Allison** clerk of court of Henderson Co., KY.

458, 459- Dec. 4, 1824.- proved Nov. court 1836.
John **Woods**---- wills to wife Molley, for life or widowhood, all my property, but if she re-marry then divided between her and children or at her death the division to children namely: Joannah **Oakley**, Molley **Boles**, Anthony **Wood**, Sally **Carnal**,

Patsey **Oakley**, Caty **Oakley**, Nancy Wood, Lucy **Carnal**.
Exrs: son Anthony **Wood**, sons-in-law Thomas and Yancey **Oakley**.
Wts: William **Oakley**. Howel L. **Ridley**, Ezekiel **Wood**.

459- Sept. 17, 1836- proved Nov. court 1836.
George A. **Nuttall**--- wills to wife Salley, all property for her widow-hood but if she marry to go to my son John, all estate. If she remain widow till son 21 yrs. old, she is to deal out to him a half of my estate and at her death all estate to son John **Nuttall**. If he die to her.
Exrs: wife Sally.
Wts: James H. **Bryant** George **Kittrell**.

460- 461- Sept. 14, 1831- proved Nov. court 1836.
Lucy **Parker** ----wills to daughter Priscilla **Weathers**, a negro slave for her lifetime then to her children, also $5.00; to daughter Ann **Lemay**, negroes and furniture, stock and all money I have on hand; to my granddaughter Lucy **Freeman**, a negro girl for life then to her children; to granddaughter Lucy A. **Lemay** a negro slave.
Exrs: son-in-law John T. **Lemay**.
Wts: Saml **Young**, Stephen **Bragg**, Thomas **Cole**.

461- Estate of Martha **Wilkerson**, sold Oct. 29, 1836 by Howell G. **Pittard**, admstr.

462-463- Inv. of estate of Mansfield D. **Jenkins**, taken by James **Wyche**, admstr. Jan. 20, 1836- there was firm **Jenkins** and **Morris** retailers of liquors.

463- Inv. of estate of Charles **Glover**, deceased, by Mary **Glover**, admstr. Nov. 2, 1836.

463- Inv. of estate of Lucy **Parker**, deceased, by John P. **Lemay**, excr. Nov. court 1836.

464- thru 470- Inv. and sale of estate of William **Cozart**, deceased, Aug. 25, 1836 by James C. **Cozart**.

470- thru 475- Inv. and sale of estate of Benjamin **Kittrell**, deceased, by James **Howze**, admstr. Nov. 4, 1836.

476, 477- Acct. of estate of George **Thomason**, deceased, by James **Thomason**, excr. June 8, 1836.-

477 thru 480- Sale of estate of John **Webb**, deceased Nov. 19, 1836 by Thomas **Webb**, excr.

480, 481- Acct. of negro hire of estate of Southern **Higgs**, deceased, Jan. 1,

1836 by **Anderson Paschall**, admstr.

481 thru 483- Sale of estate of Barbary **Washington**, deceased, June 27, 1836- by William **Washington**, admstr.

483, 484- Estate of David **Jones**, by Jonathan **Jones**, admstr. Nov. court 1836.

484- 485- Nov. 9, 1836- Estate of Lucretia **Bailey** with William **Bailey**, excr.- paid Benjamin **Rogers**, agent for Jubilee **Rogers**, excr. of Peleg **Rogers**, deceased.$198.00 ½.

485- Estate of Robbin H. **Harris** with Thomas **Harris**, admstr. Nov. 5, 1836 speaks of balance due widow and legatees but not named.

486- Estate of John **Smith**, deceased, with John **Smith** Jr., excr. from May court 1833- to Nov. court 1836 -and gives that paid legatees: Executors part as legatee; James **Smiths** part; Elizabeth **Smiths** part; Guy **Sthiths** part; Alexander **Smiths** part; Leroy **Smiths** part; John **Bradfords** part in right of his wife Nancy.

487- 488-Estate of John **Lemay**, deceased, by Samuel and Richard W. **Lemay**, excrs. from 1833- to Nov. court 1836- a legacy due Gideon **Crews** and Lewis **Lemay** mentioned herein.

488- thru 491- Estate of Col. William **Hunt**, deceased, with Memucan **Hunt**, excr. from Mar. 1834 to Nov term 1836.

492- 493- May term 1836- Petition by Mary **Buchanon** widow of James A. **Buchanon**, deceased, who died possessed of certain lands and leaving survivors: the widow Mary, children: Hinton, & Patsey **Buchanon**, Prudence **White** who reside without the jurisdiction of this court, Hilliard **Buchanon**, Willis **Hutcherson** and wife Agnes, Lewis **Montague** and wife Hixey, Peter **Hayes** and wife, and Priscilla **Buchanon** who live in this county and are all of full age, and Rosa and Ruffin **Buchanon** (minors) The widow asks her dower in land. Was given 83 ½ acres Aug. 18, 1836.

493-494- Aug. term 1836- Petition of Elizabeth **Parham**, widow of Saml R. **Parham**, deceased, who died Jan. 1835 possessed of 650 acres of land, and asks her dower in said land, The deceased Samuel R. **Parham** left surviving him the widow Elizabeth, and children: Mary, wife of Joseph **Howard**, Lewis R. **Parham**, Robert B. **Parham** (last two minors). She was given 225 acres and the dwelling house Oct. 8, 1836.

495-496- June 6, 1836- proved Feb. court 1837-
John **Eastwood**---- wills to wife Mary, all the land on east side of Persimmon Branch on both sides of Hampton Mill creek, being part of land whereon I live, for her lifetime or widowhood; To wife a bed and furniture. 3 negroes, 2 horses, cows and calves and sheep, tools, a flax wheel, a linen wheel, 2 potts and an oven etc for

her life or during widowhood; To wife Mary, a years support out of my crop on hand to be allotted by my excr.; To Dicey **Jones**, wife of Abner **Jones**, 3 three negroes; to Elizabeth, daughter of Charles **Eastwood**, 2 negroes. To Elijah H. **Eastwood**, a negro man; to Lucy daughter of Charles **Eastwood** a negro at death of my wife; to Wiley son of Charles **Eastwood**, a negro at death of my wife; to Robert, son of Charles **Eastwood**, a negro ; To Nancy daughter of Charles **Eastwood**, a negro; to my brother Abraham **Eastwood**, the land whereon I live containing 561 acres excepting, to my wife that part given her for life or widowhood and a negro slave; To Isabella daughter of Charles **Eastwood** $250.00; My executor to sell all that remains and also all I gave my wife (at her death or re-marriage) and divide the money between the children of Charles **Eastwood** herein named and Abner **Jones** to be executor.
Wts: Edward **Kimball**, Wm. **Clement**.
The widow entered her dissent and Abner **Jones** renounced executorship.- Thomas **Gooch** was appointed Administrator May court 1837.

343
497- Aug. 29, 1836- proved Feb. court 1837.
Ann **Haskins**--- willed to her four daughters Polley, Prissey, Anney **Haskins**, Rachel **Green** household and kitchen furniture, live stock; To son Aron **Haskins**, a pine chest and pair of steelyards; to sons John, James, Thomas, George, Isaack and daughter Elizabeth, one shilling each;
Exrs: son Aron **Haskins**.
Wts: William **Fleming**, John **Husketh**.

498- Dec. 31, 1836- Inv. and sale of estate of Isaac **Green**, deceased, by Clement **Wilkins**, admstr.- also admstr. of Elizabeth **Green**, deceased- Clement **Wilkins** is a distributee of estate.

499- Estates of Moses and Margaret **Carnal** deceased with Wm. **Terry**, admst.

499- Nov. 18, 1836- Inv. of William **Satterwhite** by David **Satterwhite**, admstr., mentions only the money received from excrs of James **Satterwhite** deceased which was $409.12 ½.

499- Additional Inv. of goods of James **Philpott**, deceased, mentions that received of estate of Wm. **Philpott** by excr. Thomas **Philpott** and of Ambrose **Davie** which was willed to Jas. **Philpott** by Kendal **Davie**. Simon **Philpott** is admstr. of James **Philpott** estate- report Feb. Ct. 1837.

500- Nov. 12, 1836- Inv. of estate of John **Wood**, deceased, by A.S. **Webb**, admstr.

500- Additional Inv. of estate of Hubbard **Cozart**, deceased, is a judgement against James **Cozart** as admstr. of William **Cozart**, deceased, with Wm. **Clement**, admstr. Feb. court 1837.

501-Amount of assets in hands of guardian James **Ridley**, of estate of his ward Thomas **Neal**, deceased- and transferred to Jos. Jas. **Ridley**, admstr. from Feb. 1836--gives his hire of 2 negroes, 1/4 of land rent on Person land, board paid Mrs. **Neal**, medical services for Sept. 8, 1836.

502- thru 507- Feb. court 1837- Winifred P. **Kimball**, admstrsx of estate of Bartholomew **Kimball**, deceased, returns inventory and acct. of sales made Dec. 16, 1836- Jacob **Davis** bought most of household goods.

507- Oct. 1836- Willis **Johnson** of Weakley Co, Tennessee appoints Lewis **Parham** of Granville Co., N. C., attorney, to collect all due him.
Wts: John W. **Cooke**, Judge of 9th Judicial District of Tenn., Newton **Cannon**, Governor.

508-509- Ordered to divide[d] estate of Absalom **Glover**, deceased- and negroes divided into 6 lots thus: Elisabeth **Norwood** lot 1, David **Glover** lot 2, William B. **Glover** lot 3, William and Weldon **Griffin**, heirs of Phebe **Griffin**, lot 4, To Alexander F. **Marrow** and wife Polly, lot 5, to David **Glover** lot 6- Dec. 24, 1836.

510- Acct of estate of Joseph **Barnett**, deceased, by Thomas B. **Barnett**, excr paid legacy as per will, to Elijah and Robert S. **Barnett** Feb. court- 1837.

510-Feb. 7, 1837- Sterling **Hobgood** appoints John P. **Webb** of Person Co. N. C. attorney to receive his legacy from estate of John Wood, deceased.

511-Feb. 7, 1837- Drury S. **Marrow** releases negroes to John W. **Stovall** and J. R. **Patterson**, that had been left in trust with him by Daniel **Marrow**, Sr. deceased for use of Hester **Stovall** and at her death to go to her 2 children John W, and Elizabeth **Stovall**. (Elizabeth md James R. **Patterson**).

512- Feb. court 1837- Estate of Capt. William **Jones**, deceased, by William M. **Sneed**, excr. from 1835- Aug. 29, 1835 divided between widow and the two children unnamed here.

513- 514- Jan. 12, 1837- Estates of Moses and Margaret **Carnal**, deceased by William **Terry**, Esq., excr. mentions again that due legatees, not named.

515- Nov. court 1836- Ordered that accounts of Dudley **Mingay**, excr. of estates of George **Norman** deceased and of Elizabeth **Norman** deceased be settled - coffin paid for May 1835 on Elizabeths acct. and 1834 of George **Norman**s acct.

517- Acct. of sales of perishable property of James A, **Buchanon**, deceased, Nov. 5, 1836 by James **Wyche**, admstr. Feb. 6, 1837.

518-Nov. term 1836- Fleming **Beasley** and William O. **Gregory** petition to build grist mill on Grassy creek-

344
519- thru 522- Apr. 29 1827- proved May court 1837.
John **Taylor**, Sr. ---- wills to son John C. **Taylor** in addition to that already given him, the tract of land bought of Timothy **Driscoll** and also all my lands of northwest side of **Taylor**s Ferry road except a part of the original tract lying northwest of road adjoining land of the late Stephen **Sneed** and south of Bartholomew **Strum**s, I give to my son James H. **Taylor** and also all land on east side of **Taylor**s ferry road, and all other land except that given John C. **Taylor**; To daughter Agness B. **Taylor**, $1500.00, and 18 negroes; To sons John C. and James H. **Taylor** and sons-in-law Henry **Young** and Thomas **Allen** or the survivors of them, 13 negroes and increase thereof from Apr. 1822 in trust for my grandson John Taylor **Walton** and if he should die before 21 yrs. old then to fall back to residuary of my estate; To my two sons all the negroes and property of every other kind, that the negroes may not get separated from each other, except those herein already given; To the other children they must pay $4000.00 to be paid $1000.00 yearly with the child of the deceased one to receive the share of the parent.
Exrs: sons John C, and James H. **Taylor**.
Wts: Richard **Bullock**, H. L. **Plummer**, Wm. **Hunt**.
Codicil places the part of estate given daughter Nancy **Young** to stay in trust with her brothers for her benefit and not with her husband, Henry **Young**, dated Aug. 6, 1832.
Codicil takes back the $1500.00 given daughter Agness and gives to sons since Agness had now married James **Somerville** dated Jan. 3, 1837. (William **Hunt** was dead when will probated and Thomas D. **Ridley** dead.)

522- Mar. 22, 1835- proved May court 1837.
Thomas D. **Ridley**----wills to wife Mary R., the land whereon he lives and also the mill and land with it, many negroes, the carriage and horses, also all other live stock, furniture, tools, utensils and also all money due me including that which is to come to me in right of my former wife Elizabeth **Taylor** or in right of my present wife and all my right in lots in Williamsborough, Louisburg and Chatham courthouse. codicil added giving a negro boy to his brother Dr. James **Ridley** Exrs: wife Mary R. **Ridley**.
Wts: Sally **Middleton**, Jno. C. **Taylor**, Thomas **Tippett**.

523- Feb. 21, 1837- proved May court 1837.
Jonathan **Stone**---- wills to have all estate consisting of 2 negroes household furniture and stock, sold and money given to: daughter Polly **Jones** $100.00 but Wiley **Jones** not to control the same; to granddaughter Averilah G. **Rust** $100.00; and after excr. paid 6% for trouble the others to receive 1/8th part of my estate: daughter Judith **Lemon**, dau. Peggy **Bobbitt**, dau. Delphia **Washington**, son Claiborn **Stone**, daughter Susan **Rust**, son Jonathan M. **Stone**, daughter Sarah **Welch**, to children of Nancy **Thomason**-
Exrs: son Jonathan M. **Stone**.

Wts: Thomas T. **Cooke**, William **Whitfield**.

524- May 6, 1837- May court 1837.
William **Pruett**, son of Parker **Pruett** and his wife Elizabeth, died on Sunday Apr. 30, 1837. On the 27th he spoke of distribution of his estate in the presence of his parents who state that he said he wished all to go to his brothers and sisters and his brother Robert to manage it, Robert **Pruett** qualified as executor May court 1837.

524- Nov. 12, 1836- Power of Attorney from John **Hobgood** Jr, to John P, **Webb** of Person Co., N. C., to collect his legacy in estate of John Wood of Granville Co., N. C., deceased.
Wts: Portius **Moore**, **Barnett Hobgood**.

525- Apr. 14, 1837- Arrenia **Ellington** of Wilson County, Tennessee appoints Joseph J. **Ridley** of Granville Co., N. C., attorney to collect for her her share as legatee of John **Pittard**, deceased, which is in

345
hands of Robert B. **Gilliam**.
Wts: Robert M. **Burton**.

526- thru 531- Apr. 28 1837- Sheriff's accounts examined by James **Wyche**, for Leslie **Gilliam**, sheriff.

531 thru 533- Granville County in account with The Wardens of the Poor of the county for 1836--

533- thru 538- Feb. 27, 1837- Inv. of property belonging to estate of James **Cheatham** Sr., deceased, sold by Isham **Cheathem**, admstr. **Cheatham** names mentioned among buyers were: James, Isaack, Sally.
End Book "13".

346

1-2-May 1, 1837- Power of Attorney from Alfred **Higgs**, Nancy **Higgs** who married John B. **Dent**, and more lately Nancy **Thomason**, Willis **Johnson** who married Mary **(Higgs) Johnson**, all of Weakley County, Tennessee, to William **Higgs** of same place, to demand of Lewis **Parham**, our present agent to settle with **Anderson Paschall**, admstr. of estate of Southern **Higgs**, deceased, late of Granville Co., N. C.
Wts: Jno. A. **Gardner**, David **Winston**.
Wm. H. **Johnson** clerk of county court of Weakley Co., Tenn., Caleb **Brasfield**, chairman of court.

3- May court 1837-Current acct of estate of John **Webb**, deceased, by Thomas **Webb**. executor-

3, 4, 5, 6- May court 1837-:Acct. of sale of estate of Mansfield D. **Jinkins**, deceased, by James **Wyche** admstr.

6 thru 8- Sale of property of C. **Parrish**, deceased, Oct. 1, 1836- Apr. 22, 1837 by A. **Jones** excr. May court 1837.

8-Sale of negroes of William **Cozart**, deceased- Mar. 30, 1837- by James C. **Cozart**, admstr.

9--Sale of property of Erasmus **Knott**, deceased, by Caleb **Knott**, admstr. and names buying were, among others, Risdon, George, John, Elizabeth and Milly **Knott**- May court 1837.

10- thru 12- Estate of Henry **Floyd**, deceased, by Robert **Harris**on excr. May 5, 1837-

12- Inv. and acct. of sales of property of Jesse **Dean**, deceased, by John **Shearman** admstr. and Sarah **Dean**, widow of Jesse **Dean**.- Cash received of William **Terry** as legacy to Sarah **Dean** from estate of Moses **Carnal**, deceased.--Estate sold Mar. 3, 1837.

14 Dec. 1, 1836-, Sale of estate of Sarah **Johnson**, deceased by Stephen **Johnson**, admstr.

15- Sale of estate of Stephen **Johnson** deceased, by Stephen **Johnson** Jr., admstr. Dec. 1, 1836.

16- thru 18- Aug. 27, 1831- proved Aug. court 1837.
Coleman R. **White**---- wills to son John **White** and daughters Elizabeth **Allison**, Mary **Vincent**, Susan **Magehee** and to children of daughter Ruthy **Crook** (they dividing their mothers share) 3 negroes; To daughter Ruthy **Crook** for her lifetime, 3 negroes and their increase, a mare and colt which she has in her possession, and

at her death to her children or the survivors of them; To daughter Haskey Ann Nelson **Jinkins**, 3 negroes and their increase, - 1/4 of my land on Tarr river and a saddle; to son, William George Vaughn **White**, counterpaines, quilts, bed and furniture, a corner cupboard, a table, 3 slaves and part of tract of land called **Calebs**, horse, saddle, bridle; to son Thomas Person **White** a horse, saddle, bridle, bed and furniture, 3 quilts, 2 counterpains, a walnut desk, 3 negroes, 1/4 of land on Tar river; to daughter Frances Lany Jane **White**, Hester Coleman **White** ½ of land on Tar river and 6 negroes to be equally divided between them when they marry or come of age 21; To daughter Frances Lany Jane **White**, a horse, saddle and bridle, bed and furniture, 3 quilts, counterpains; to: daughter Ceily Coleman **White** a horse, saddle, bridle, bed and furniture, quilts and counterpains; to son John **White** all in his possession; to daughter Mary **Vincent**, Susan **McGehee**, Elizabeth **Allison**, Haskey Ann Nelson **Jenkins**, Polly **Crook** all now in their possession; All debts paid by selling that which is left of my estate and anything left divided to all my children; Exrs: son John **White**, nephew William R. **White**.
Wts: Anderson H. **Walker**, Abraham **Lawrence**.
Exrs. renounced executorship and James **Wyche** became admstr.

18, 19, 20- July 25, 1835- proved Aug. court 1837.
Thomas **Blacknall**---- wills to son William **Blacknall**, the land whereon

347

he lives known as "**Robertson** Tract"; to sons John, Charles and Jonathan **Blacknall**, the land whereon I live on both sides of Tabbs creek divided between them; to daughters Nancy **Hayes** and Lucy **Hicks** no part of my estate having already received their share; The rest of estate divided between all my children except those named in foregoing clause and any child that may be dead is to be represented by their child or children for their share excluding completely Lucy **Hicks** and Nancy **Hayes**. My grandson Thomas, son of my son George **Blacknall**, deceased, is to pay my estate $500.00 for that he has had either to himself or thru his father; No part of my estate, shall be subject to the debts or control of either Harry **Cook** or Charles **Nuttall**, but the share that would go to my daughter Elizabeth **Cooke** is to be held by my executors and used for her support for her life time then to her children at her death; The part that would go to my daughter Frances **Nuttall** is to be used as that above and strictly for her support only and then to her children or child of her child.
Exrs: brother-in-law William **Kittrell** and son William **Blacknall**.
Wts: Thos. L. **King**, John K. **Jones**.
John K. **Jones** is now resident of Tennessee so signature proved by Robert **Jones**.-
Exrs. renounced executorship.
and James **Wyche** appointed Admstr. with bond of $50,000 and bondsmen Wm., John, Jonothan **Blacknall**, Gideon H. **Macon** and Tryon **Yancey**.

20, 21- Jan. 2, 1835- proved Aug. court 1837.
Nathan **Bass**---- wills to wife Martha, a desk, bed and furniture, a spinning wheel, flax wheel, a cow and calf, sow and pigs, horse, saddle a pot and oven, set of knives

and forks, 6 pewter plates, 2 decanters, 10 acres of land to include the dwelling house, reserving an acre for the family grave yard, and a still; At wife's death the s[t]ill and 10 acres to Warner **Tanner**, better known as Warner **Bass**; To Warner Tiner the land south of Big Path running from William **Bradfords** to Mrs. Ann S. **Taylors** to the line of Lewis **Petifords** land, a horse, a cart, 6 pewter plates; To Lewis **Petiford** who married my daughter Diza (Iliza) 50 acres being land they now live on at Joshua **Hutchinsons** line dec'd and others, and a pot; to daughter Honon **Jones** the rest of land on Pathway at William **Diments** line; To son Jesse **Bass**, grandson Lemuel **Valentine**, daughter Sally **Pettiford** to each 5 shillings; all remaining to be sold and debts paid and if any left divided between wife Martha and Warner **Tiner**.
Exr: William **Bradford**.
Wts: D. A. **Paschall**, Benja **Kittrell**, A. H. Walker.
Benjamin **Kittrell** is now dead- handwriting proved by others.

22- Aug. 7, 1837- Acct. of estate of Lemuel **Peace**, deceased, by William C. **Patton**.

23- May term 1837- Estate of James **Philpott** by Simeon **Philpott**, admstr. settled Aug. 3, 1837.

23-24-25- Estate of Ann **Vaughn** by Thomas **Howerton**, excr. Aug. 2, 1837

25-26- July 3, 1837- Willis L **Higgs** of Weakley Co., Tennessee appoints Col. Lewis **Parham** of Granville Co., N. C. attorney, to transact all my business with the admstr. of estate of Southern **Higgs**, deceased, late of Granville Co., N. C., as I am one of legatees since I am the son of Mary **Higgs** deceased, wife of John **Higgs**, now resident of Granville Co., N. C. and grandson of Ellen er [sic] **Johnson**, deceased, who was sister of Sothorn **Higgs**, deceased.
Wts: Wm. H. **Johnson**, clerk of Weakley Co., Tenn court, Caleb **Brasfield** chairman of court.

26-27- Estate of Isham **Epps**, Inv. and sale taken Nov. 12, 1836 by Elijah **Hester** excr.

28- Inv. of estate of Mary **Eppes**, deceased, Nov. 12, 1836 by George **Rogers**, admstr. Aug. court 1837.

348
33- thru 41- Aug. court 1837- Sale of estate of Edward W. **Norwood**, deceased, by Robert **Jinkins**, admstr. mentions among buyers, Nathaniel M. **Norwood**, Rebecca **Norwood**, John **Norwood**, Thomas **Norwood**, George **Norwood**. (He must have owned a store.)

41- thru 43- Aug. court 1837- Sale of estate of Long **King** by Saml P. **Forsythe** admstr.

43, thru 46- Aug. court 1837- Sale of estate of John **Eastwood**, deceased, by Thomas **Gooch** admstr. mentions wife Mary **Eastwood**, Charles **Eastwood**, among buyers.

47-48, 49- July 8, 1837- proved Nov. court 1838.
William **Floyd** Sr--- wills to wife Martha, instead of her thirds, my dwelling house and other outhouses with orchard and gardens, 3 negroes and as much land as she needs to cultivate, household and kitchen furniture, horses, other livestock, and enough provision for her use and for support of Rebecca **Loyd**, Martha and Abagail **Mann** whom I wish to live with my wife as long as they are single; To niece Rebecca **Loyd**, after death of my wife, bed and furniture and she may work my farm while single with negro Allen, free of rent and after her death to grdaughter Martha and Abagail **Mann**, a featherbed, a chest, to each $15.00 when married and if either die before married then all to the other: To son George, $2.00, to daughter Delilah, $2.00; To son Stephen all timber and ½ of my shop tools, my half of our saw mill, all blacksmiths tools and he to keep his mothers plantation tools in repair while she live; All else divided into 9 equal parts and to go to sons Pleasant, Joshua, Samuel, William, Stephen, Presley, Charles and a half of 2/9ths to son George and his wife Obedience and the other half to daughter Delila at death of her husband Thos. **Mann** and at her death to her children; All else divided to all children.
Exrs: Samuel **Duty**, son Pleasant **Floyd**.
Wts: James **Murray**, W. **Ellington**, Jno. S. **Eaton**.

49, 50, 51- Sept. 23, 1837- proved Nov. court 1837.
Daniel **Gooch**---- wills to daughters Hannah and Nancy **Goock** [sic], a tract of land and a yoke of oxen and cart, but if they marry or die to go to my children: Samuel, Joseph, James, Thomas, William **Gooch**, daughter Jane **Clement**, Hannah **Gooch**, Amos, Dudley S., Daniel T. **Gooch**, Nancy **Gooch**. To daughter Rachel, wife of Thomas **Howard**, her share of estate and at her death to her children or in case any be dead and leave issue then to the issue that part that would have gone to the child, and if no issue living to all my children; all else divided into 12 parts and each to receive ½th [should be 1/12th].
Exrs. sons Joseph, James, William, Amos, Dudley S. and Daniel T. **Gooch**.
Wts: Jas. A. **Russell**, Samuel **Rogers**, Joseph **House**.

51-52- Lucetta R. **Thomason** of Lauderdale county, Alabama appoints Horace **Somerhill** attorney to recover for me 5 negroes of estate of Richard **Thomason** and from Thomas **King**, my agent in Granville Co., N. C. Oct. 3, 1837-
Wts: George W. **Sneed** J. P., William W. **Garrard**, clerk of court of Lauderdale Co., Alabama, John T. **Haraway**, Judge of court James **Powell** and Southern **Thomason** swore to signature of L. R. **Thomason**.

53- 54-May 1, 1837- proved Nov. court 1837.
Lucy **Parham**---- wills to son Williamson **Parham**, a negro; to grdaughter Arseneth, daughter of son Williamson **Parham** a set of china and a negro; to grdaughter Nancy, daughter of son Williamson, a negro; to grdaughter Emily, 2 blue checked

counterpains, a sealskin trunk; to son Lewis a negro; to grdaughter Judah Woodson, wife of William **Paschall**, one blue check counterpane; to grchildren: Lewis R. **Parham**, Mary **Howard** wife of Joseph **Howard**, Robert E. **Parham**, children of my deceased son Samuel **Parham** the money from sale of negro girl and her increase; to John F. **Bryant** and Nancy **Fuller** children of my deceased daughter, Nancy **Bryant** the money from sale of negroes; To grdaughter Nancy **Fuller**, featherbed, sheets, counterpane, bed curtains; to son Asa, 3 negroes

349
and a horse; to Martha **Green**, daughter of my son Asa **Parham** a figured counterpane; All else sold and divided to sons Williamson, Lewis and Asa **Parham** and the children of my son Samuel **Parham**, deceased.
Exrs: my brother Samuel T. **Reavis**, executor.
Wts: John C. **Taylor** (Exr. refused so Williamson **Parham** became admstr.)

54- thru 57- Daniel **Johnson**, husband of Elizabeth, formerly Elizabeth **Higgs** (now deceased), Zachariah and **Anderson Johnson**, Aveyrilla Shannon widow of Samuel Shannon, deceased, formerly Aveyrilla **Johnson**, Eleanor **Johnson**, William K. **Smith** and wife Kasandra, formerly Kasandra **Johnson** all of Robertson County, Tennessee and Southern H. **Johnson** of Graves Co., Kentucky, all children and heirs at law of Daniel **Johnson** and wife Elizabeth (**Higgs**) **Johnson** (she now dead) and all of us over 21 yrs. old appoint William **Johnson** of Sumner Co., Tennessee but now in Granville Co. N. C. attorney to recover for us all that is due us thru our mother Elizabeth from the estate of her brother Sothorn **Higgs**, deceased, of N. C. which is 1/7th of the estate of said Sothern **Higgs** late of Granville Co. Feb. 10, 1836 at Springfield, Tennessee.
Wts: John **Hutcherson**, magistrate of Roberson Co., Tenn., Wm. **Seal**, clerk.

58-Nov. 6, 1837- John F. **Bryant** appoints Col. Lewis **Parham** and Daniel A. **Paschall**, attorneys, to collect all due him.
Wts: Thomas **Wilson**.

58, 59- Nov. 10, 1837- Lucy **Parham** widow of Lewis **Parham**. Sr., deceased recently died, leaving a will which has caused dissension among her children and grandchildren and to alleviate any further dissension or costs in caveat, we wish to have the estate that was left in hands of widow by her late husband Lewis **Parham** Sr., sold to highest bidder and distributed by legal order and Asa **Parham** who has lived with and taken care of all business, working farm and paying all debts accrued since the death of their father, no accounting is to be made but he is to share equally with accts past settled. And each to receive 1/5th part of estate after sold, that is the money from sale to Williamson, Lewis Jr., Asa, Lewis R. **Parham** and 1/5th to Joseph **Howard** and wife Mary and Robert E. **Parham** and 1/5th to Samuel **Fuller** and wife Nancy and John F. **Bryant** Jr.

60- thru 86- Nov. court-1837- Inv. and acct of sales of estate of Henry **Woodworth**, deceased; sold by John **Read** special admstr. on Oct. 11, 12, 13, 1837-

Estate Records of Granville Co, NC Volume 13-16   41

This was stock of a store, dry goods etc. also sale of live stock.

86-87- Apr. 16, 1834- proved Nov. court 1837.
Jesse **Barnett**---- wills to have executor dispose of as much of estate as necessary for paying debts and educating two young sons, Benjamin and Samuel **Barnett** and when they are of age they are to be given that estate which is left equally between them.
Exr: John **Barnett**, my son, and he guardian to two youngest sons. I have given to the older children all I think I can afford. Wts: Elisha B. **Hart**, Thos. **Williams**, Thomas G. **Barnett**.

88- thru 94- Inv. and acct. of sales of estate of Thomas **Jones**, deceased, by Lunsford A. **Paschall**, admstr. Sept. 22, 23 1837 - and among buyers were Jane, Abner, Edward Jr., Alfred **Jones**.

95- thru 99- Inv. and acct. of sales of estate of Leonard **Bullock**, deceased, by William **Fleming** admstr. Nov. 1, 1837. Among buyers were Pamela, Phillip P., Edward, the widow, Agnes, Sarah, Benjamin F., Leonard H. **Bullock**, Richard H., Benjamin T. **Bullock**, John D. **Bullock**.

100- thru 106- Estate of Zachariah **Hester**, deceased, by Hamilton **Hester** admstr. and sale Aug. 30, 1837.

106- thru 113- Inventory and acct, of sales of estate of Thomas **Blacknall**, deceased, by James **Wyche**, admstr. July 25, 1838 and among buyers were Thomas B. **Cooke**, Jas. **Bullock**.

113-114- Inv. and sale of property of Jonathan **Stone**, deceased, by Jonathan M. **Stone**, excr.

350
115-Estate of Dr. William **Vaughn** of Mississippi, in account with Thomas B. **Littlejohn**, admstr.-- Money paid to Eldred G. **Roberts** in full of the hire of negroes received from excr, of Col. James **Vaughn**, he being legally entitled to receive the same -$254.18- Money received from hire of the negroes bequeathed to Dr. William **Vaughn** by Col. James **Vaugn** since death of Mrs. Ann **Vaughn**- The negroes from estate of Col. James willed to Dr. Wm. **Vaughn** were received and turned over to Eldred G. **Robert** of Parrish of Avovyelles, Louisiana who is entitled in right of his wife Dorcas (formerly Dorcas **Stafford**) and by assignment from Elouisa A. **Stafford** to receive sd legacy of Dr. Wm. **Vaughn**, they Dorcas and Elouisa being half sisters of Sarah Matilda **Vaughn**, dec'd, the only child of Dr. William **Vaughn** deceased.

116- thru 121- Inv. and account of estate and settlement of estate of Coleman R. **White** by James **Wyche**- Aug. 15, 1837- The slaves devised to the children of Rutha **Crook** were not in possession of testator when he died and I do not have them in my possession; the property devised to William G. V. **White** is in his possession; As Frances and Celia **White** have no guardian I have made advancements to their estate which was a negro woman and increase and from date of will when says and increase of negro woman, and date of death in Sept. 1835, there were 2 children born and so under terms of will they would be directed sold. There is a suit in which many of the slaves are involved and since the suit is not yet decided they cannot be divided.

122- Power of Attorney Nov. 10, 1837- from James **Howze** of Franklin Co., N. C. Admstr. of Benjamin **Kittrell**, deceased, to George **Kittrell** of Granville Co., N.C., to act as administrator and agent for me in the settling this estate. Wts: Thomas H. **Willie**, D. T. **Paschall**.

122-Feb. court 1836- Current Acct. of estate of Mark **Veazey** by William **Veazey**, excr.--

124-Acct. of estate of Philip P. **Pool**, deceased, by Claborn P. **Pool** admstr. Nov. court 1837.

125 Acct. of estate of Henry **Woodworth** deceased, by John **Read**, special admstr.

125, 126- Additional Inv. of E. W. **Norwood** deceased by Robert **Jinkins** admstr. Nov. term 1837.

129-127 [sic]- Acct. of estate of William **Satterwhite** deceased, by David **Satterwhite**, admstr. mentions receipt for money from estate of James **Satterwhite**.

127- Nov. court 1837- Estate of Lewis **Bledsoe** by Richard **Bullock**, admstr. mentions Meekins **Bledsoe** and Mrs. Frances **Bledsoe**, widow.

128- Estate of Moses **Carnal**, deceased, by Wm. **Terry**. Nov. court 1837 with will annexed.

128- Dec. 5, 1834- Acct. of sale of estate of Philip P. **Pool** deceased by Claborn P. **Pool** admstr.

129- Accts. of estate of Isaac **Green** by Clement **Wilkins** admstr. mentions amt, due from his mother's estate (but name not given).

130-131- Proved Aug. court 1837.
Thomas **Jones**---- wills to wife Jinsey, 300 acres of land on Green Creek being tract of 100 acres my father gave me and the land I had granted to me, and at her death to my two sons: Lotan and Thomas **Jones**, also to her 1/5th of my slaves being 25, and at her death the negroes and all their increase to be divided to all my children living or dead. Also to wife 1/5th of all personal property and at her death to all my

children and she to have $500.00 for improving the place I have given her; All my children those by my first wife that is: Amos P., Ruffin and Duffy **Jones** and by 2nd wife: Loton and Thomas **Jones**, they to be equally divided for when are of age; Amos **Gooch** deceased, willed to the three children of my first wife the tract of land whereon I live which is valuable; To my mother $50.00, and all else among children.

351
Exrs: Abner **Jones**, Millington **Blalock**, Dr. James A. **Russell**.
Wts: **Willie Mangum**, Benj **Hester**, Henry W. **Jones**.
Executors renounced and Lunsford A **Paschall**, appointed admstr.

132, 133- Power of Attorney Feb. 9, 1838 from Robert **Taylor** and wife Mildred (formerly Mildred **Kennon**), Thomas B. **Lewis** and wife Elizabeth (formerly Elizabeth **Cobb**), Lewis K. **Willie**, Thomas H. **Willie** in right of Lewis **Kennon** appoint John **Cobb** of Fayette County, Tennessee, to receive their legacy from estate of the late Willis **Lewis**, deceased, of Tennessee.
Wts: L. **Gilliam**, Jas. **Nuttall**.

134- Aug. 22, 1837- proved Feb. court 1838.
Vincent **Vaughn**---- wills to wife Martha the land whereon I now live and at her death to my son Vincent **Vaughn** and he to live on land and care for his mother, and to wife 3 negroes, 3 bedsteads and furniture, live stock, some furniture and at her death all given her to be sold and money divided between the children.
Exrs: my wife Martha, son-in-law John **Bowdon**.
Wts: William B. **Mann**, Pumphrey **Edwards**.

135- Dec. 12, 1836- proved Feb. court 1838.
Jacob **Fane**---- wills to wife Sally all estate. He states here that he has lived with her as his wife for many years and many years ago set her free, going into the courts of Oxford and not only setting her free but also my brother James **Fane**, I had set free. If any doubt arises that Sally **Fane** was liberated by the laws of North Carolina, I then place this estate in the hands of Howel L. **Read** Esq. in trust for the benefit of my said wife and to secure the freedom of my brother James **Fane** whom I have also liberated. If necessary that they leave the State then I authorize Howel L. **Read** Esq. to attend to this matter, and upon their settlement wherever they can live then to give up all my estate to said Sally **Fane**.
Exrs: Howel L. **Read**.
Wts: Abraham W. **Venable**, Charles L. **Read**, Henry **Yancey**.
Howel L. **Read** renounces executorship and the emancipation of Sally **Fane** was then proved by William V. **Voss** a witness to same, and John **Bullock** was appointed admstr. with bond of $6000.00 with securities Thomas L. **Williams**, Abraham W. **Venable**.

136- Inv. and acct. of sales of estate of Henry **Woodworth** by Benjamin **Norwood**, admstr. Dec. 5, 1837. covers pages 136 thru-145--mentions years support for widow and cash from John **Read** special admstr. recorded 1838.

145- thru 155- Acct of sales of estate of Daniel **Gooch**, deceased, by Amos and James **Gooch**, excrs. Dec. 6, 1837 mentions as buyers at sale Hannah, Joseph, Daniel T., Dudley S. **Gooch**, William **Gooch** and others.

156 thru - Sale of estate of Millington **Blalock**, deceased, by Thomas **Blalock** admstr. Dec. 1, 2, 1837 -gives list, of property given Rebecca **Blalock** for years support and John P. **Blalock** bought at sale and also Lucetta **Blalock** -recorded Feb. court 1838.

166 thru 168--Sale of estate of Thomas **Jones**, deceased, by Lunsford A. **Paschall**, admstr. Nov. 13, 1837. Among buyers were Jane **Jones**, Henry W. **Jones**, Henry **Jones** Jr., Thomas W. **Jones**, William **Jones**.

169- Sale of estate of Zachariah **Hester**, deceased, by Hamilton **Hester**. Admstr. sale Nov. 27, 28, 1837--buyers included: Drucilla, Hiram G. **Hester**, Francis G. **Hester**- and mentions provision for widow.

174-175- Sale of estate of Nathan **Bass**, deceased, by **Anderson** H. Walker admstr. Dec. 22, 1837- and among buyers were Warnes, William, Patsy **Bass**, Hudson **Hendley**, and also mentions wife Martha **Bass**.

176-177- Sale of estate of Willie **Grisham**, deceased, by Anderson H. **Walker**, Dec. 7, 1837- among buyers were H. J., Hilliard J., E. **Grissom**, Salley **Grisham**, Shem **Cooke**, John **Blacknall**, Nancy **Grisham**- years support for the widow.

352

177- thru 181- Sale of estate of Jesse **Barnett**, deceased, by John **Barnett**, excr. Nov. 14, 1837- mentions among buyers Thos. G., Jesse. F., William, James **Barnett**- mentions two youngest Samuel and Benjm. **Barnett**.

181 thru 183- Inv. and sale of estate of John C. **Ridley**, deceased, by William D. **Sims**, admstr- Was in business (Confectionary concern) with Charles **Sims** in Oxford, N. C.

183 thru 187-Inv. and sale of estate of William **Floyd**, deceased, by Samuel **Duty**, excr. Nov. 25, 1837- mentions Stephen, George, Charles **Floyd** among buyers at sale, also Pleasant **Floyd**.

187-188- Inv. and sale of estate of Archibald **Cawthorn** deceased, by Stephen **Morris**, admstr. Aug. 29, 1837- mentions James H. **Cawthon** as buyer.

189, 190- Hire of negroes of estate of John **Eastwood**, deceased, by Thomas **Gooch**, admstr. Aug. 16, 1837- mentions Mary, Elizabeth, Charles **Eastwood**, Henderson **Eastwood**, Abraham **Eastwood**; also mentions and sell negroes devised to Mary, the widow of John **Eastwood**, to have for her lifetime or widowhood.

191- thru 193- Inv. and sale of estate of Lucy **Parham**, deceased, by

Williamson **Parham**, excr. Nov. 13, 1837.

193- thru 194- Estate of Frederick **Wiggins**, deceased, sold by Len. H. **Hare**, admstr.

195-196- Estate of Nathaniel **Williams**, Sr., deceased, by Nathaniel **Williams** Jr., excr. Feb. court 1838- paid for coffin in 1831 --

197-198- Sale of estate of James **Satterwhite** deceased, which was left to his wife for her lifetime, by Howel, James and Solomon **Satterwhite**. Wife's name was Frankey **Satterwhite**.

198, 198- Acct. of estate of Robert **Lanier**, deceased, by E. **Hester**, admstr. mentions wife and mentions daughter Mary.

199, 200- Ordered that years support be set off to Jane **Jones**, widow of Thomas **Jones**, deceased, as directed by his will, Feb. court 1838.

200- Sale of estate of John **Champion**, deceased, by Wm. **Huskey**, admstr. Nov. 4, 1837.

201, 202, 203- Account of Thomas V. **White** child and devisee of Coleman R. **White**, deceased, with James **Wyche**, admstr. Nov. 16, 1837- states amount to William **Ashley** and others which they recovered in U.S. court in Raleigh against me for hire of negroes devised to you from testator.

203- Inv. of estate of James P. **Butler**, deceased, by Lewis **Reavis** Dec. 24, 1837-

204- Inv. of estate of Woodson **Wilkerson**, deceased, by William G. **Ellixson** admstr. Feb. 5, 1838.

204- Inv. of estate of Elizabeth **Johnson** deceased, by William **Johnson** admstr- states that Nov. 1737 received $735.53 from Southern **Higgs**, estate. she was a legatee.

204-205- Inv. of property of Benjamin **Kittrell** deceased, by James **Howze** admstr. Feb. court 1838.

205- thru 209- Acct. of estate of Mansfield D. **Jinkins** by James **Wyche** admstr. Feb. court 1838.

209- Feb. term 7837- Petition of Mrs. Amy W. **Smith** and James A., and Thomas M. **Smith** who sue by their next friend Amy W. **Smith**, stating that her late husband Maurice **Smith** died in 1835 and Richard J. **Smith** was appointed admstr. of estate. He was possessed of many slaves and we ask division of said slaves;

Maurice **Smith** left surviving him the widow Amy **Smith** and two infant children James A and Thomas M. **Smith** and other children by a former marriage, namely: Mary G. **Smith** who had married Richard J. **Smith** prior to her fathers death, Francis S., Saml W., Ann Rebecca, John B., Mann R. **Smith**, the last five being minors who with the petitioners are legal heirs to the negroes. James L. **Wortham** appointed guardian of the 5 minors named above.

353
    211- thru 213- Nov. term 1836- Petition of Mary **Glover**, admstr. of Charles **Glover**, deceased, in her own right, of William B. **Glover**, Alexander F. **Marrow** and, wife Polly, Thomas F. **Marrow**, assignee of Daniel **Glover**, Elizabeth **Norwood**, David K. **Glover** (minor) by Alexander F. **Marror**-- against William **Griffin**, Weldon **Griffin** and said Daniel **Glover**--
stating that Charles **Glover** died intestate and Mary **Glover** became admstr. of estate. Charles **Glover** was never married and his next of kin are: his mother Mary **Glover**, his brothers William B. and Daniel **Glover**, sisters Polly **Marrow**, Elizabeth **Norwood** and the defendants William and Weldon **Griffin** who claim in right of their mother Phebe **Griffin**, another sister of Charles **Glover** deceased. Joseph Sims is guardian of William and Weldon **Griffin** of Warren County, N. C.- Thomas F. **Marrow** bought the interest of Daniel **Glover** one of the brothers of Charles **Glover**, deceased. They ask division of negroes of estate or to sell, them and divide money according to law. Allotted Feb. 16, 1837. Lot 1 to David K. **Glover**-- Lot 2 to Elizabeth **Norwood**, Lot 3 to Thomas F. **Marrow**, lot 4 to Alexander and Polly **Marrow**, lot 5- to William B. **Glover**, lot 6 to William and Weldon **Griffin**.

    213- thru 216-Nov. term 1836- Petition of Joseph **Howard** and wife Mary, Lewis R. **Parham** and Robert E. **Parham** (minor) by guardian Williamson **Parham**- stating that Samuel R. **Parham** died intestate possessed of land on Tabbs creek containing exclusive of dower already laid off to widow 450 acres and that they are only heirs of said land. The children Mary who married Joseph **Howard**, Lewis R. and Robert E. **Parham** ask land divided between them. Nov. 26, 1836 the land divided between them.

    214- Nov. term 1836- Petition of Elizabeth, widow of Samuel **Parham** deceased, who died in 1835, leaving widow and three children (named above; with Lewis **Parham** admstr. of estate. The petitioner asks division of negroes of estate of Samuel **Parham**, deceased allotted to them.

    216- thru 218- Feb. term 1837- Petitioners are Raleigh and Gaston Railroad stating that in locating and making the road (see Act of General Assembly of 1835 Chapter 25, entitling Railroad to Incorporate) the company have found it necessary to occupy a portion of the lands of Josiah **Crudup** in Granville Co., N. C. and said Railroad cannot agree with **Crudup** for purchase of land, and we therefore ask court for relief and that land may be condemned for use of railroad for a fair price. Ask commissioners to put a fair price on land. on Apr. 5, the commissioners met and decided the land was worth $1500.00.

218, 220- The Raleigh and Gaston Railroad vrs. George **Kittrell**.- same as above---valued at $256.00.

220- thru 222- Railroad vrs Charity **Powell**-- land valued at $67.00 same petition as above.

222- thru 224- Railroad vrs. Thomas L. **King**--- valued at $169.00 same petition as first.

224, 225, 226- May term 1837- William **Dean**, Jesse C. **Dean**, Moses C. **Carnal** and wife Margaret vrs Elizabeth J. and Joseph R. **Dean**--State that Jesse **Dean** died intestate possessing 460 acres of land, which descended to your petitioners and the defendants. Sarah **Dean** is entitled to dower in land and asks for her dower be laid off and the part to the defendants which is legally theirs. The defendants are minors with guardian. The land was divided into five parts and allotted them.

226, 227- May term 1837- Sarah **Dean**, widow of Jesse **Dean**, deceased, who died intestate leaving the widow and children named above-- asks her dower be laid off to her in the land. Allotted to her.

228 thru 231- Petition of Elizabeth **Peace**, widow of Joseph **Peace**, deceased, Elizabeth, Willie, Anderson and Francis **Peace** children of Celia **Peace** deceased-vrs-- John and Elizabeth **Cothron** children of John **Cothron** deceased, Lemuel **Cothron**, Charlotte **Diment** and James **Cothron**, children of William **Cothron**, deceased--- Stating that Archibald **Cothron**, late of Alabama, died in 1832 or 1833.

354
Intestate, leaving land in Granville County, N. C. on which William **Cothron** deceased, the father of said Archibald lived and died, containing 12 to 1500 acres and Archibald **Cothron** was never married and land came to petitioners and defendants as next of kin, being brothers and sisters and issue of such. Elizabeth **Peace** widow of Joseph **Peace** was a sister and Elizabeth, Anderson and Francis **Peace** children of Celia **Peace** who was a sister of Archibald **Cothron**, and all of full age; The defendants John and Elizabeth **Cothron** children of John **Cothron**, a brother of said Archibald, deceased, who live in Tennessee, and the children of William **Cothron**, deceased, who was a brother of Archibald **Cothron** are not known by names but they are of full age and live in Tennessee, also Lemuel **Cothron**, is a brother and lives in Tennessee, Charlotte **Diment**, widow of Mathew **Diment**, is a sister and resident of Tennessee, and James **Cothron** of Granville Co., N. C. is a brother. They are advised that the land is subject to division into seven equal parts and ask this done. The land was divided and allotted them Aug. 2, 1837.

231- thru 234- Acct of estate of James A. **Buchannon** by James **Wyche** admstr. beginning July 1836- recorded. Gives names of those advanced money from estate of **Buchannon** were the widow Mary **Buchannon**, John R., Priscilla, Rosa, Hillyard and Hinton **Buchanon**, Patsy **Mitchell**, Lewis **Montague** and wife, Joshua A. **White** and wife, Peter **Hayes** and wife, Willis **Hutcherson** and wife--

234, 235- Feb. term 1837 -Petition of Frances **Elliott** widow of Alexander **Elliott**, deceased, states that he died in 1829, intestate leaving widow and following children: Stephen, Samuel, Polly Ann, Robert, Elizabeth, Nancy and Alexander **Elliott** all infants under 21 yrs. old and without guardian. The deceased owned 117 acres of land and since he was indebted to several persons, the land was sold and bought by William L. **Owen** by judgement against it. She asks that her dower in land be laid off to her. She was given 39 acres Oct. 25, 1837-
Wts: John **Shearman**.

236- thru 237-May term 1837- Petition of Susan **King**, widow of Long **King**, deceased, who died early this year, leaving the widow and children: Mary Ann **Madison**, Sally and John **King**-who are minors. The widow asks her 1/3rd or dower in a tract of 217 acres. She was given 57 acres, not quite a third but she consents. Nov. 1, 1837.

237, 238- Feb. term 1837- Petition of Cephas **Daniel** and wife and heirs of Lethe **Daniel**, wife of John **Daniel**. who are the only heirs at law of Rowland **Harris** deceased, ask that the land be divided to them. The widow of Rowland **Harris** has had her dower laid off in the land, and Cephas **Daniel** who married Arena the daughter of Rowland **Harris** asks his part. John **Daniel** married the other daughter of Rowland **Harris**, namely Lethe **Harris** by whom he had children, (she is now deceased). They moved to South Carolina and later to the Western country and names of children unknown. They are represented by their guardian Archibald **Henderson**. The land was divided to them, Aug. 5, 1837.

239- Aug. term 1837- The Raleigh and Gaston Railroad petition to have a fair price put upon land of Mrs. Martha **Rufuf** and Leonidas **Butler**, that the Railroad may purchase it at fair price. The price was $105.00.

241- thru- Acct. of estate of Southern **Higgs**, deceased, with Anderson **Paschall**, admstr. from 1834- and the distribution of estate-To Archibald **Davis** and wife (1/3rd); to Leonard **Higgs**, Cassandra **White** (1/7th of 2/3rds); To Green **Stanton** (½ of 1/7th of the remaining 2/3rds); To Mary **Stanton**, the same amount; and to each of the following 1/7th part, namely Nelly **Johnson**, John **Higgs**, Kenelin **Higgs**, Elizabeth **Johnson**.

355
245- Anna **Pool** appoints her son William **Pool**, agent and attorney to attend to her business affairs and to receive all due her from estate of Gabriel **Jones**, deceased. Apr. 13, 1838.
Wts: William P. **Ligon**, Gabriel **Jones**.

245, 246- Jane **Winfrey** appoints William P. **Ligon**, agent and attorney to

receive all due her from estate of Gabriel **Jones**, deceased May 1, 1833.
Wts: William P. **Pool**, Willis **Royster**.

246, 247- Lucy **Jones** appoints John Y. **Wilkerson**, agent and attorney to receive all due her from estate of Gabriel **Jones**, deceased. 5/8/1838.
Wts: William P. **Logan**, Willie **Brooks**.

247, 248- May 8, 1838- James G. **Rainey** of Caswell Co., N. C. appoints Howell G. **Pittard** of county and State aforesaid, agent and attorney to receive the deed of trust or transfer made to me by William B. **Williams** in trust for Caleb H. **Richmond**--a certain bond to secure payment to **Richmond** for certain debt of **Williams** to him.
Wts: Lewis **Heflin**, R. G. **Maddox**.

248- Jan, 29, 1838- proved May court 1838.
Mary **Buchanon (Buckhanan)**---- wills all she has to her son John Ruffin **Buchanon**, but if he die under age or without heirs then to nephew and niece William D. **Allen** and Hickly **Bradford** with Wm. D. **Allen** executor.
Wts: Frederick S. **Carter**, Edwd H. **Carter**.

249-Jan. 28, 1838- proved May court 1838.
Simon J. **Clement**---- wills to wife Nancy, the land whereon I live and the tract adjoining **Cozart**s on Nap of Reeds creek, for her lifetime; All other land to my children divided between them or sold and money divided between them; Also to wife Nancy all negroes, money, bonds etc as long as is a widow or for lifetime; if she re-marry all divided to her and children; When each child comes of age or marries to give each a negro and anything else she can spare of my estate.
Exrs: wife Nancy.
Wts: Abner U. **Gay**, Wilborn L. **Hampton**.

250- 251- Apr. 3, 1832- proved May court 1838.
Benjamin **Hester**--- wills to granddaughters Julia **Wiggins** and Edney **Wiggins**, the beds and furniture in the front room; to grandson Benjamin **Wiggins**, a horse; to grandson Thomas Hundley **Wiggins**, a horse and a negro boy;. to grandson Isaac **Hester**, a negro boy and $50.00 to buy a horse but to remain in hands of William M. **Sneed** to be delivered when he think best; And also 50.00 for his education; To daughter Rebecca **Wilson**, a negro; to daughter Francis **Veazey**, a negro; to granddaughter Nancy **Hester** daughter of Thomas T. **Hester**; a negro; to grandson Benjamin **Williams**, the land I bought of David S. **Goodloe**; To daughter Milley **Barnes** $20.00; to Wm. M. **Sneed**, the guardianship of Isaac **Hester** my grandson. If any child die under age or without issue the part to go to the sisters and brothers; All else of my estate to son Thomas T. **Hester** and he executor with William M. **Sneed**.
Wts: Lot G. **Watson**, L. **Gilliam**, Augst **Landis**, Wm. **Jones**.

251- Inv. of estate of Benjamin **Hester** March 1, 1838 by Thos. T. **Hester**.

252- Inv. of estate of Jacob **Fane**, deceased, Feb. 19, 1838 by John B. **Bullock**, admstr. included 2 negroes (see will) and all else left in possession of the widow Sally **Fane**.

253- Aug. 5, 1837- proved May court 1838.
Nelly **Daniel**--- wills to granddaughter Nelly **Daniel** the bed 1 lie on; to grandson John Sondser **Daniel**, my big horse and next best bed; to granddaughter Almire **Farrow**, a bed; to daughter Lucy **Farrow**, a chest and filly colt; to Molly **Ascue**, a bed quilt and counterpane and sheet; to daughter Eliza **Daniel**, all my crop and my mare and all other property. My negro girl Ritty is to have my little bed; My daughter-in-law Arrena **Daniel** receive from Capt. Wm. H. **Gilliam**, the money from last years crop and pay him what I owe him, also to pay Archibald **Henderson** and Madison **Hawkins** what I owe them and all else to her with an iron pot and all I have in hands of Thos. **Daniel** to be for benefit of his wife

356
Eliza and her children.
No. executors named---
Wts: John **Daniel**, Wm. H. **Lewis** - Leonard **Hare** appointed admstr.

254- Inv. of property of William **Hester**, deceased, by Lewis **Parham**, Sr. admstr. May 8, 1838- states that the interest William **Hester** has in estate of Benjamin **Hester**, deceased, had been deeded in trust to Rodes N. **Herndon** and Robert G. Gilloom (**Gilliam**?) trustees- Suit in court now.

254, 255- Jan. 14, 1837- proved--an attempt to probate was contested in Feb. term of court, but withdrawn and probated May term 1838.
Simeon **Cozart**--- wills all he owns to his mother Mary **Cozart** for her life then to his sister Gemima **Lyon**, a negro boy; to sister Mary Ann **Rogers** a negro slave; To brother Allen **Cozart** 6 negroes all live stock and other property I possess after death of my mother.
Wts: Pinckney **Cozart**, James C. **Cozart**, James **Philpott**.
Will objected by Alexander **Lunsford** and others but withdrawn- Allen **Cozart** made admstr. with $10,000 bond secured by James C. **Cozart** and Simeon **Philpott**.

255, 256- June 16, 1835- proved May court 1838.
Mary **Perkinson**---- wills to have all her property of every description sold and debts paid and that left thus: To son Thomas **Wilson**. $30.00; to children of son Richard **Wilson** all else as they come of age; My negroe woman choose with whom she wishes to live and also her children and that person to pay a fair price for them.
Exrs: Richard **Sneed** and Archibald E. **Henderson**.
Wts: Robt. **Wilson**.
A caveat entered by Thomas **Wilson** Aug. term 1837.

256- Acct of sale of estate of Thomas **Blacknall**, Sr, deceased by George **Kittrell**, admstr. among buyers were Caroline **Blacknall** who bought almost

everything. May court 1838.
256, 257- Inv. and Acct of sales of estate of Nelly **Daniel** by Leonard H. **Hare**, admstr. Oct. 9, 1837-

258- Inv. of estate of and sale of property of Vincent **Vaughn**, deceased Mar. 8, 1838 by John **Bowdon**, excr.- covers four pages with sale-- mentions Vincent, John, Martha **Vaughn** as buyers.

261- Inv. of property of Mrs. Martha **Vaughn** given her by will of Vincent **Vaughn**, deceased, for her lifetime. May 5, 1838.

263- Inv. and sale of estate of Solomon **Bailey**, deceased by John **Davis**, admstr. Mar. 29, 1838 mentions among buyers, Israel, Allen, John W. **Bailey**, Israel **Bailey** Sr., William P. **Bailey**, Jones **Bailey**, Henderson **Bailey** and Claborn H. **Cooke**.

266- Inv. of Simeon **Cozart**, deceased, by Allen **Cozart**, admstr. May 5, 1838.

269- Negroes of estate of Simeon **Cozart**- hired Mar.ee, 1837 and acct of sales Mar. 12, 1838.

269, 270 Acct with Wardens of the Poor- May court 1838.

270 thru 277- Vouchers etc of the Sheriff, Leslie **Gilliam**, to County for 1837-1838-

277- Mar. 10, 1826- proved Aug. court 1838.
Mary **Somerville**---- wills to all her children and grandchildren all given them and what is left of estate.
Wts: Hardy **Patterson**, James **Somerville**, George C. **Eaton**. William A. **Somerville**, admstr. with bond of $30,000.00.

278- Apr. 8, 1838- proved Aug. court 1838.
Gideon E. **Gill**---- wills to wife Polly and children that which excrs. think sufficient for their support for as long as she live or is a widow and all else sold and divided between them; if wife re-marry to sell all property and divided between wife and children then living.
Exrs: brother William A. **Gill** and William R. **White**.
Wts: Henry H. **House**.
Executors refused to act- Wyatt **Cannaday**, admstr-

357
279-Apr. 28, 1837- proved Aug. term 1838.
David **Chandler**--- wills to have all estate sold and money to children: Daniel, Littleberry, William, John, Thomas **Chandler**, Nancy **Overby**, Mary Ann **Overby** and Phoebe **Chandler**, to each 1/8th part of money: To daughter Rebecca **Downey**

$1.00 and 1/9th part of my estate left in trust for her with Littleberry and Thomas **Chandler**, and at her death that remaining to her children: Margaret **Downey**, Mary Ann **Royster**, and Izabella **Downey**, John and Susan Ann **Downey**; Two of my negroes may choose their master but if not wanted there then to be sold and money divided as before stated.
Exrs: Littleberry and Thomas **Chandler**, my sons.
Wts: Marcus D. **Royster**, William **Royster** Jr.

280- Mar. 14, 1838- proved Aug. court 1838.
John R. **Sneed**-- wills to wife Elizabeth, for life or widowhood, four negroes and increase, household furniture, stock and provisions and if she re-marry then to have a childs part; to son Lemuel, a gun, money from sale of a negro and smiths tools; to Lemuel all that is left my wife at her death and if she be alive when he is of lawful age she to give him what she can; All debts be paid by that left wife.
Exrs: John C. **Veazey**, E. **Hester**.
Wts. Wm. **Parrish**, Fielding **Veazey**.

281- Aug. court 1838- Inv. and sale of estate of John **Wiggins**, deceased, by John **Jordon** admstr., bought mostly by Thos. **Stovall** and James M. **Hawkins**.

282- Estate of William **Madison** by Samuel P. **Forsythe**, admstr. from Feb. 26, 1837 mentions widows support for a year.

283- List of sale of property of Solomon **Bailey**, deceased, May 28, 1838, by John **Davis**.

284- June 2, 1838- Sale of property of Moses **Bass**, deceased, and buyers included Mason **Bass**, Wouton **Bass**, Chesley **Bass**-sold by Thos. T. **Hester** admstr.

285, 286- Estate of Allen **Howard** deceased, by Joseph **Howard** excr. from 1835 to Aug. 8, 1838.

287, 288- Negro hire of estate of John **Eastwood**, deceased, by Thomas **Gooch** admstr.

288- Negroes sold to Carolina **Blacknall**, widow of Thomas **Blacknall**, deceased, July 3, 1838.

289- Aug. 1, 1838- Alexander **Marrow** paid over to David K. **Glover** all that is due him from estate of Joseph P. **Glover**, deceased, for which he is executor.
Wts: Thos. and W. D. **Williams**.

289- Estate of William **Cozard**, deceased, by James C. **Cozart** admstr. Aug. court 1838.

290- Estate of Thomas **Neal**, deceased, by Jos. James **Ridley**, admstr. June 4,

1838.

290-291- Estate of Barbery **Washington** by William **Washington**, admstr. Aug. 7, 1838.

291, thru 293- Petition of Raleigh and Gaston Railroad against Margaret, Mary, Betsy, John **Freear** minor children of Elizabeth **Freear** deceased, asking fair price be put on land Railroad needs from them price set was $143.00 Apr. 3, 1837.

294-295- Nov. term 1837- Petition of Richard J. **Smith** and wife Mary G. **Smith** and Francis S. **Smith** against Samuel N., Ann Rebecca, John B., and Man B. **Smith** minor children of Maurice **Smith**, deceased-In 1837, Amey **Smith** the widow with two children James A. and Thomas M., asked division of estate of Maurice **Smith** deceased, and their shares were allotted them. James L. **Wortham** appointed guardian of minor children, and represented them in division- Francis J. and Richard J. **Smith** allotted their share of negroes Dec. 26, 1837.

358

296- thru 298- Jan, 22, 1838- James **Wilkerson** departed this life leaving survivors, his widow Sarah **Wilkerson** and the following children: John **Wilkerson**, Anne wife of John **West**, Katey wife of Burgess **Adcock**, George **Wilkerson**, James **Wilkerson**, Sarah, wife of William Ellixson, and Alexander **Wilkerson** (minor) and Woodson **Wilkerson** who died in 1834 without issue. The will of James **Wilkerson** was administered by Howell L. **Ridley** until he died and then admstrs. became John **West** and John **Wilkerson**. And the estate of Woodson **Wilkerson** (a child of James) is administered by William **Ellixon**- Ask division of negroes of estate of James **Wilkerson** deceased, to the heirs above, granted.

298-299-Aug. term 1837-Petition of Pamela **Bullock**, widow and relict of Leonard **Bullock** deceased, who died possessed of 600 acres and mansion house thereon adjoining lands of Edward **Bullock**, Dick H. **Dolby**, Obediah **Winston**, Susan **Bullock** and heirs of Dick H. **Dolby**, deceased, leaving a widow, Pamela **Bullock** and children: Susan wife of Willis B. **Hutcherson**, Pamela, wife of Obediah **Winston**, Agnes **Bullock**, Phillip P. **Bullock** who are of full age and minor children: Sally, Weldon E., Christian, Mildred and Mary L. **Bullock**- The widow Pamela **Bullock** asks dower in land. She received 192 acres with dwelling house etc. Jan. 16, 1838.

300-301- Nov. term 1837- Rebecca **Blalock** widow of Millington **Blalock** deceased, who died Oct. 1837, possessed of several tracts of land, one of 100 acres bought of Sarah, Solomon and John **Mangum** and a tract of 201 acres on Tar river bought of Solomon **Philpott**, 117 acres bought of Lemuel **Goodwin** on Shelton Creek, 220 acres bought of William and Martha **Johnson** and 250 acres bought of Rowlin **Gooch**, 202 acres, and a tract whereon he lived of which he deeded part to his son Thomas **Blalock**. The widow asks dower in the lands. She was allotted 455 ½ acres Dec. 2, 1837.

302- thru 305- Aug. term 1837- Betsy **Hillyard**, Mary **Hillyard**, John A. **Thomas** and Wm. **Bodenhammer**, Loton L. **Watson** and wife Martha, Thomas B. **Littlejohn**-- state that Benjamin **Hillyard** deceased, died possessed of 936 acres which descended to the following heirs at law: Martha **Watson**, Sally **Paschall** wife of Dennis T. **Paschall**, Harriet wife of Edwin **Paschall**, Joseph W. **Hillyard**, Benja F. **Hillyard**, Elizabeth **Hillyard** and Mary **Hillyard** subject to the dower of Betsy the widow of Banjamin **Hillyard**. They also state that Elizabeth **Hillyard** has departed this life, and by her will left Thomas B. **Lewis**, Jas. **Cooper** and John R. **Hicks** as exrs. of her will, and directed her part of land sold and the exrs named refusing to qualify. Donaldson S. **Paschall** was made admstr. but land could not be sold for was left to Betsy **Hillyard** for life then to Mary **Hillyard** for life by will---The **Bodenhammers** have bought the interest of Dennis T. **Paschall** and his wife Sally as they deeded it in trust to Stephen K. **Sneed** who deeded to the **Bodenhammers**. Also Thomas B. **Littlejohn** has bought the interest of Edwin **Paschall** and his wife Harriet and also right of Benjamin F. **Hillyard**. Mary **Hillyard** has one share in her own right and bought the share belonging to her brother J. W. **Hillyard**. The widow has had her dower set off and agrees to take no more land. Therefore the division of land is asked to be made to set off to each his proper land. The land was divided and laid off to proper owners Dec. 4, 1837.

306- Nov. term 1837- Petition of Druciller (Drucilla) **Hester**, Nancy **Currin**, John, Jeremiah **Hester**, Patrick **O'Brient** and wife Faith, Isaac **Duncan** and wife Aphia, Hiram G. **Hester** (minor) by his guardian John **Bates** and William, John, Susan, Ann Eliza, and Candis **Bates** (minors) by John **Bates** their guardian - against Hamilton **Hester** admstr. of Zachariah **Hester**, deceased, Thomas **O'Brient** and wife Elizabeth, Calvin **Gorden**, Sarah, Lawson N., James, William, Samuel and Mary Jane **Gorden**. Zachariah **Hesters** children were: Nancy, John, Jeremiah, Faith, Alphia and Hamilton **Hester**. A son Benjamin **Hester** died, in lifetime of his father Zachariah leaving issue Hiram G. **Hester** and Elizabeth **Bates** a daughter of Zachariah died leaving issue William, John, Susan, Ann Eliza **Bates** children of John **Bates** and also child Candis **Bates** of Elizabeth and John **Bates**. And another

359
daughter of Zachariah **Hester**, deceased, was Mary, wife of John **Gorden** who also died prior to her father death, leaving children: Elizabeth who married Thomas **OBrient**, Calvin, Sarah, Lawson N., James, William, Samuel and Mary Jane **Gordon** all living in Tennessee, the last six being minors. Petitioners ask division of negroes- granted Mar. 1838.

309 thru 313- Division of land to above mentioned heirs of Zachariah **Hester**, deceased--- May 1838-

313- thru 318- Nov. term 1837- Petition of John S. **Blalock**, Joseph D. **Hobgood** and wife Nancy, Lucretta **Blalock** (minor) sues by guardian Samuel **Philpott** and Milley **Phillpot** by her guardian Saml **Philpott** against Thomas **Blalock**, Woodson **Washington** and wife Sally, Edward **Boswell** and wife Milley,

Estate Records of Granville Co, NC Volume 13-16   55

Robert **Blalock**, William, Millington and Etna **Blalock** infant children of William **Blalock**, deceased. Milly **Philpott** is daughter of Martha **Philpott**, daughter of Millington **Blalock** Sr., deceased, and she, Martha, also deceased leaving the one child. William **Blalock** was also son of Millington **Blalock** deceased, and he too is dead leaving the children named above, who live in Tennessee. Their respective shares were allotted them. Aug. court 1838-plat here.

318 thru 321- Feb. term 1838- Petition of John D. **Bullock** and wife Sophia, and of John A. **Dolby**, Anna **Dolby**, James **Dolby**, Edward **Dolby**, and Penelope **Dolby** minors by their guardian John D. **Bullock**---- state that Dick H. **Dolby** died Aug. 1832 possessing about 750 acres of land of which the widow Prudence **Dolby** has been allotted her dower right. Petitioners ask division of remainder of land to them the heirs of Dick H. **Dolby**, deceased, being the only children, 6 in number. Plats of the tracts of lands and division is given here-

322- thru 324- Feb. 22, 1838- proved Nov. court 1838-
William **Puryear** -----wills to son Daniel a negro boy; to daughter Rebecca **Ligon**, a negro slave; to son Randal, a negro, to daughter Polly **Wagstaff**, a negro and the $200.00 due me from her husband, John **Wagstaff**; To daughter Letty **Halliburton**, a negro; to daughter Letty **Wilkerson**, a negro; to grandson Peyton **Puryear**, a negro; All remaining to be divided between my daughter Elizabeth **Melton**, grson Peyton **Puryear**, son Daniel, son Randal, daughter Polly **Wagstaff**, daughter Lethy **Halliburton**; To William P. and Alexander **Ligon** in trust for daughter Rebecca **Ligon** and her children; If any one of legatees die without issue to be divided to others or go to their issue if there are any.
Exrs: sons Daniel and Randal **Puryear** and grson Peyton **Puryear**.
Wts: Semore **Puryear**, Lemuel **Smith**, Wm. **Amis**.

324- Sept. 18, 1838- proved Nov. court 1838.
Fielding **Kittrell**---- willed to wife Abagail for life or widowhood then to my children:
Exrs: John S. **Eaton**, James **White** (renounced and Abagail **Kittrell** was appointed admstr.)
Wts: Wm. **Blacknall**, Simon G. **Hayes**.

325- Oct. 29, 1838- Sale of property of David **Chandler** Sr., deceased, by Littleberry and Thomas **Chandler** excrs.- covers page 325 to 333.

333- thru 335- Inv. of estate of John R. **Sneed** by Elijah **Hester** Oct. 31, 1838.

335- thru 337- Inv. of estate of Mary **Somerville**, deceased, by Wm. A. **Somerville**, Aug. 17, 1838.

337 thru 341- Nov. court 1838- Inv. and sale of estate of Anderson **Baley** deceased, by Dorris **Canaday**- admstr. and among buyers were: Mrs. Cyntha G. **Baley**, Israel **Bailey**, Solomon **Bailey**.

341- thru 343- Inv. of property of Samuel **Brummit**, deceased, by Wyatt **Cannaday**, admstr. Sept. 18, 1838- Sold Oct. 5, 1838 and among buyers were Mrs. Mary **Brummet**-

344- Inv. and acct of sales of estate of Jesse C. **Dean**, deceased, sold Sept. 12, 1838 by William **Dean**, admstr. and also the property allotted to Sarah **Dean**, widow, of Jesse **Dean** deceased, sold Dec. 11, 1837.

360

346, 347- Acct. sale of estate of David **Parker**, deceased, by John **Shearman**, admstr. Sept. 8, 1838.

347, 348- Sale of estate of John **Rice**, deceased, by Fleming **Rice**, admstr. Sept. 22, 1838- mentions as buyers Mrs. Betsey and Thomas **Rice**.

348- Sale of notes of estate of John **Lyon** by excrs. Elkanah and C. Clement **Lyon** June 19, 1838 -settlement by order of court.

348, 349- Acct. of estate of Lydia **Lyon** by excrs. C. and E. **Lyon** June 19, 1838.

349, 350- Power of attorney Aug. 7, 1838 from Peyton **Madison** to William **Forsythe**, to receive from Thomas B. **Littlejohn**, Clk of Equity court, all due me from estate of Radford **Gooch**, deceased, coming to me as guardian of William **Madison's** orphans.
Wts: Saml. **Redmon** and Saml P. **Forsythe**.

350, 351- May term 1838- Petition of Mason **Bass**, widow and relict of Moses **Bass**, deceased, who died Jan. 1838, possessed of 60 acres in northwest part of Granville Co. She asks for dower in land. The only survivors of said Moses **Bass**, deceased, are: Amey, Chesley, Woodson, Maria and Hilliard, all minors. Allotted 1/3rd-20 1/4 acres with the dwelling house Oct. 31, 1838.

352, 353- Feb. term 1838- Petition of John D. **Bullock** and wife Sophia and of John A., Anna, James, Edward and Penelope **Dolby**, minors, by their guardian John D. **Bullock** against Prudence **Bolby**..... state that Dick H. **Dolby** died in 1831, intestate, and William **Fleming** became admstr. of estate and took into his possession the negroes of the estate. **Fleming** closed his administration 1836 and delivered negroes to John D. **Bullock**. With consent of Prudence **Dolby**, widow of Dick H. **Dolby**, and **Bullock** in right of his wife and as guardian to minor children of Dick H. **Dolby**, hired the negroes out until the present time. He now asks to have negroes divided to each heir. Granted and allotted Nov. 3, 1838.

354, 355- Feb. 10, 1839— William B. **Taylor** of Tennessee by his agent and attorney Lunsford A. **Paschall** of Granville Co., N. C., to William H. **Wheson** of Northampton Co., N.C., for $350.00 sell 10 shares of stock in the Roanoke

Estate Records of Granville Co, NC Volume 13-16   57

Navigation Co.
Wts: R. H. **Kingsbury**, Jeremy **Hilliard**.

355, 356- Power of Attorney July 8, 1839 from Alexander H. **Nuttall** to Wyatt **Cannaday**, to collect for him the money in hands of George C. **Eaton** for land sold to **Eaton** where sd. **Nuttall** formerly resided, also all right coming to me from my father's, John **Nuttall**, estate and to collect all debts due me and to pay to Elizabeth **Peace**, H. G. **Pittard**, John **Blacknall**, Dr. Joseph W. **Hawkins** of Warren Co., and to Joseph **Kearny** that which I owe them.
Wts: George **Burns**.

356 thru 359- Sept. 25 1828- proved Feb. term 1839.
John G. **Smith**---- wills to Trustees of Female Humane Society of Richmond, VA. for benefit of Institution, 5000 acres of land in Harrison Co., formerly Monongahala Co., VA, which was conveyed to me by Robert **Campbell**. To friend William **Ford** of Richmond VA. $500.00 as small mark of my respect and esteem for him; To Dr. **Nelson**, a negro man; To sister Ann **Smith**, 20 shares of stock in Farmers Bank of VA. and my gold watch; To brother Maurice **Smith**, a negro woman, and my horse, and he may have my Mineral collection at residence of Mrs Ann A. **Smith** to give to his son Samuel William **Smith**, also all my library to his son John B. **Smith**. To Samuel G. **Smith** Esq. of Tennessee, in trust and benefit of his sister Frances **Smith** 15 shares of stock of U.S. Bank, and her heirs to have it; To Samuel S. **Downey**, in trust for sister Jane **Smith Downey** and heirs of her body, 15 shares of Farmers Bank Stock of VA.; To Samuel S. **Downey** in trust for my niece Sally P. **Smith** 15 shares of stock in U.S. Bank; To Dr. Thomas J. **Williamson** of Ohio in trust for his sister Jane **Smith Williamson** and her heirs 5 shares of stock in U.S. Bank; To Col. Joseph **Amis**, a negro and whatever he owes me; To nephew Alexander, son of my

361
brother James W. **Smith**, a gun which carries a screw driver and knife in it's breech, when he is of age; to nephew, Samuel Smith **Downey**, my double barrel gun in a mahogany case and chest of cabinet makers tools; To nephew Richard J. **Smith** my collection of Minerals now in Richmond VA.; To all nieces living when will probated, one dozen silver table and tea spoons, to mark with initials of my name; to sister Ann and brother Alexander's widow, Mrs. Ann **Smith**, all my household furniture tools, carriages, live stock except that given away heretofore each an equal interest; (the one who outlives the other to have all); To legal heirs of my brother Samuel **Smith**, one negro; All remainder of negroes either divided equally or. sold and divided among my legatees named in residuary clause of this will. To Ann, widow of my brother Alexander, 5 shares of stock in Bank of VA.; To friend William **Webb** $500.00 in case he acts as my excr.; To excr. 20% for settling this estate of the whole; to my two living brothers Maurice and James W. **Smith** all that remains of my estate.
Exrs: my nephew Samuel Smith **Downey** and if he does not qualify then my friend William **Webb**.
Wts: Lewis **Webb**, Saml. L. **Graham**, James **Young**.

A caveat entered by Richard J. **Smith** and others but withdrew.

359- thru 372- Sale of estate of Mary **Somerville**, deceased, by Wm. **Somerville**, admstr. Dec. 18, 1838- mentions among buyers, James **Somerville**, Joseph B. **Somerville**.

372- thru 382- Inv. and sale of estate of William **Puryear**, deceased by Randal and Peyton **Puryear** excrs.-Feb. court 1839.

382- thru 384- Commissioners ordered to divide negro estate of Mrs Mary **Somerville**, deceased, value of same was $26,800.00 to be divided into four parts- Lot 1 to James **Somerville**– Lot 2 Mrs Susan **Eaton**,- Lot 3- to heirs of George C. **Somerville**- Lot 4 to John **Somerville**. The children of John **Somerville** were: George **Taylor** and wife, William A. **Somerville**, Willis L. **Somerville**, Nathaniel M. **Green** and wife, Thomas S. **Somerville**, Richard **Somerville**, Joseph J. **Somerville**, Robert P. **Somerville**.

384- thru 389- Sales of estate of Randole **Miner**, deceased, by Thomas H. **Willie**, admstr.- Nov. 3, 1838- mentions among buyers: John, David, Henry, Sally, Henrietta, Mary F. **Mine** [sic] - Feb. court 1839 -

389- thru 392- Estate of Thomas **Daniel** deceased by Washington H. and Thomas G. **Thomas** excrs. Dec. 5, 1838- Inventory and sales of estate.

393- Inv. of estate of Chesley **Daniel**, deceased, by Henry M. **Daniel** admstr. Aug. 10, 1838.

393- thru 399-.Estate of Mrs. Nancy **Daniel**, deceased, by Henry M. **Daniel** admstr. Aug. 10, 1838- Inv. and sales of perishable property Oct. 22, 1838 mentions among buyers: P. S., N. S., Nancy S. **Daniel**, Chesley **Daniel** -

399, 400- Sale of estate of Keziah **Yancey**, deceased, by Charles **Yancey**, admstr. Dec. 17, 1838- mentions among buyers: Hezekiah, Lewis, Richard **Yancey**, Charles, Richard Jr., Robert Sr., Samuel **Yancey**.

401- Feb. court 1839- Money paid by Isham **Cheatham**, admstr. of James **Cheatham**, deceased- mentions amt. received of Isaac **Cheatham** as agent of Prudence **Cheatham**, and mentions James **Cheatham**, Jr.

401- thru 404- Inv. of estate of Mary **Daniel**, deceased, by William H. **Webb**, Nov. 7, 1838- also sale Dec. 1838.

404- thru 406- Inv. and sale of estate of William **Jinkins**, Sr. deceased by William **Jinkins** Jr. admstr. June 30, 1838-among buyers were Margaret **Jinkins**, Bennett **Williams**, William **Weaver**.

Estate Records of Granville Co, NC Volume 13-16   59

407- thru 409- Inv. and sale of property of A. **Hayes** deceased, by William P. **Smith** admstr. Feb. court 1839-

409-410, 411- Inv. and sale of property of Henry **Emery** deceased by Clemeny **Wilkins**, special admstr. mentions Polly **Emery**, widow, John **Emery**-

362
411, 412- Estate of Richard **Blanks** deceased, by Samuel **Blanks**, excr Dec. 8, 1838- from 1831 forward.

412-413- Sale of estate of James **Haskins**, deceased, by Aron and Geo. **Haskins**, excrs. Nov. 30, 1838.

413, 424-- Acct. of sales of estate of Claborn **Parrish** deceased, by Alfred **Jones**, excr. Feb. 2, 1839 from 1836 forward- mentions pension -

414-415- Nov. court 1838- David K. **Glover** receives his share of the negroes of estate of his father Daniel **Glover**, deceased, his brothers and sisters having received theirs Feb. 1, 1839.

415, 416- Estate of Thomas **Husketh**, deceased, by John **White**, admstr. Sept. 8, 1838- mentions Archiby, Ann, William Jr. **Husketh** as buyers and mentions dower and years support of widow.

416- thru 418- Estate of William **Roberts**, deceased, by Benjamin **Bullock** excr. - mentions widow, Christian **Roberts**- Feb. court 1839.

418-419- Inv. and sale of estate- of Fielding **Kittrell**, deceased, by Abagail **Kittrell** admstr.- Dec. 8, 1838-

419- 420- Inv. and sale of estate of Henry **Wilson**, deceased, taken Nov. 16, 1838 by James M. **Heggie** Admstr.- among buyers were Amy, Robert Pomfret and Mason **Wilson**.

421-Sale of estate of Henry **Woodworth** by Benjamin **Norwood**, Jr., admstr. Dec. 1, 1838.

422- Hire of negroes of estate of Thomas **Jones** for 1839 by L. A. **Paschall** admstr.-

422, 423- Sale of negroes of estate of Simeon **Cozart**, deceased by Allen **Cozart**, admstr. Dec. 22, 1838.

423, 424- Joseph **Blanks** makes bond to secure title to land to James L. **Ramsey**, after death of his mother Elizabeth **Blanks**, or as soon as will of Richard **Blanks**, deceased, will give it to him for all lands devised to me by said Joseph

Blanks, by Richard Blanks, deceased, and also all right he has in negroes belonging to estate.
Wts: J. R. Gregory, Tomas S. Sandford, Jos. A. Norwood.

424- Maury County, Tennessee- William B. Parrish and wife Eliza, former Eliza Cheatham, and Mary Hicks, formerly Mary Cheatham, assign all our rights and interests to Thomas Cheatham, that we have in estate of James Cheatham, deceased, of Granville Co., N. C. in hands of Isham Cheatham, admstr. to wit: Wm. B. and Eliza Parrish 1/9th part, Mary Hicks (feme sole) 1/9th interest as heirs of James Cheatham deceased. Mar. 9, 1839.
Wts: Lewis and John Amis.
William Erwin, clerk of court of Maury Co., Tazwell S. Alderman, chairman.

425-426- Mar. 9, 1939 - Thomas Cheatham of Maury Co., Tenn., appoints Isham Cheatham of Granville Co., N. C., attorney, to receive all that money or legacy coming to me from estate of James Cheatham, deceased, that is #/9ths (sic- probably 3/9ths) of estate- 1/9th in my own right and 1/9th to Wm. B. and Eliza Parrish assigned to me, and 1/ 9th to Mary Hicks which I purchased.

426, 427- Prudence Cheatham of Maury Co., Tenn. appoints Isaac Cheatham of Granville Co., N. C. to receive all due her from estate of James Cheatham deceased, in hands of Isham Cheatham,-admstr. of estate. Mar. 11, 1839-
Wts: John and Lewis Amis.

427, 428- Negroes of Randol Minor deceased, divided to heirs -namely: Sally Miner, Henry Miner, Mary Frances Miner,- Henrietta Miner, Joseph Miner, Rachel Miner,- Ann Miner, David Miner--legatees. Mar. 19, 1839.

428, 429- Division of negroes of estate of George Somerville, dec'd to heirs: John Y. Taylor and wife; Francis O. Markham and wife, Mercer Booker and wife, William B. Somerville Feb. 15, 1839.

430- thru 431- Inv. and sale of estate of Gideon E. Gill, deceased, by Wyatt Cannaday, admstr. Aug. 17, 1838- mentions Widow Gill, William A. Gill, John M. Gill as buyers at sale.

432-May court 1839- additional sale of David Parker's estate, dec'd by John Shearman admstr.

363
432- Additional Inv. of estate of Jesse Dean, deceased, by Wm. Terry Apr. 22, 1839-

432, 433- Inv. and sale of estate of Thomas York, Sr. by William Beck, admstr. Mar., 2, 1839- mentions widow and Thos. A York.

Estate Records of Granville Co, NC Volume 13-16   61

433- thru 435- Estate of Joseph **Barnett** Sr., deceased, by T. B. **Barnett** acting excr. Feb term 1837 to 1839- mentions board for Elizabeth, Mary, Martha, J. W. **Barnett**, Jane, Robert **Barnett** and the widow **Barnett**-

436- Estate of Jesse **Dean** by John **Shearman** admstr. settled Feb. Ct. 1839-settles May 1839.

437 thru 439- Inv. and sale of estate of Mary **Buchannon** by William D. **Allen**, excr. Nov. 28, 1838-

439- 440- Acct. of Board of Wardens of Granville Co. for Poor- 1839.

440, 441- Mar. 4, 1837- proved Aug. court 1839.
Francis **Dean**---- wills to Sarah **Dean**, widow of Jesse **Dean** deceased, for her lifetime, negroes then to J. **Dean**s heirs; To son Daniel **Dean** 2 negroes, bed and furniture and $5.00 to make the bed as good as one I gave Jesse **Dean**, deceased; All land divided between the heirs of my son Jesse deceased and son Daniel **Dean**.
Exrs: son Daniel **Dean**.
Wts: William L. **Tippett**, Isaac **Slaughter**, H. W. **Jones**.

441, 442, 443- Mar. 4, 1833- proved Aug. court 1839.
Anderson **Paschall** ----wills to wife Mary, negro, bed and furniture, all household furniture she brought with her at our marriage and during her lifetime, I lend her 100 acres of land, a negro, horse, live stock, household and kitchen furniture necessary for keeping house for her small family; To daughter Betsey **Bennett**, the 2 negroes in her possession; To son John the negro now in his possession; to son Daniel, negroes he now has in possession; to son Donaldson Potter, negroes now in his possession; to son Isaiah Mitchell the negro in his possession; to dau. Mildred, 2 negroes a bed and furniture, chest and horse; to daughter Lucy the same as given Mildred; to son Zebulon Montgomery, a negro; To son William Henry, a negro; I have not willed negroes to sons Edwin, Dennis and Lunsford for they have already received their share of estate. To wife a years support for herself and family at my death, out of estate and all else sold and after debts paid, to distribute to my children: $50.00 to Zebulon and Isaiah; to William Henry $100.00 for education and remainder to be divided to my 12 children. codicil 1836-unimportant.
Exrs: wife Mary and sons Dennis, Lunsford, Daniel and Potter **Paschall**.
Wts: Leslie **Gilliam**, Thomas L. **King**, Abner **Hicks**.

444- Estate of Long **King**, deceased, by L. P. **Forsythe**, admstr. Aug. 1, 1839- mentions widows allowance for year and her dower.

445- Further Inv. of Millington **Blalock**, deceased by Thos **Blalock** Aug. court 1839.

445- thru 449-, Estate of John R. **Sneed**, deceased, including Inv. and sales by Elijah **Hester**. Excr. beginning Oct. 5, 1838- Sale Nov. 1838.

449- Granville Co. in Account with Leslie **Gilliam**, sheriff- for 1839.

456-457- Sept. 28, 1838- proved Feb. court 1839.
Abraham **Lawrence**--- wills to wife Leannah, all I possess for her lifetime and at her death or if she re-marry, to children of my son, William **Lawrence**, deceased, certain negro slaves; To daughter Anna **Cardwell**, certain negroes; to son Abraham **Lawrence** certain negroes, a featherbed and furniture and a chest; All remaining of property at wife's death, to be sold and to Abraham **Lawrence**, my son, I give $100.00, the remainder divided between my children.
Exrs: grson John P. **Lawrence**, son Abraham **Lawrence**.
Wts: William C. **York**, Henry **Sikes**, William A. **Mitchell**.
Exrs. renounce right to exrxship--

364
457, 458- Apr. 12, 1839- proved Nov. court -1839.
Vinam **Ball**---- wills to wife Temperance, all I possess for her lifetime and at her death to be sold and the proceeds divided into 7 parts. To daughter Elizabeth **Newton**, ½ share; to son Hinton Hall, ½ a share; All else which is 6/7ths divided between Joseph, James, John, Alexander **Ball**, and Martha Rasmus(?).
Exrs: son Joseph **Ball**.
Wts: J. M. **Stone**, Jas. **Blackley**.

458-459- Oct. 24, 1838- proved Nov. court 1839.
Ephraim **Fraizer**--- wills to wife Elizabeth, during her life or widowhood the plantation whereon I live and the tract adjoining whereon, my brother lived that I bought of sd. brother William **Fraizer**, all furniture, stock negroes, to be kept together as long as children need or while she is a widow, or living then to be equally divided between them, my wife having a childs part if she re-marry; As children come of age or marry I wish my wife Elizabeth to give them what she can spare.
Exrs: wife Elizabeth and her brother Stephen **Blacknall** (**Blackwell**?).
Wts: Elijah **Medows**, Ransom **Fraizer**.

459, 460-Aug. 29, 1837- proved Nov. court 1839-
Susan **Phillips** ----wills to Mary Ann **Abbet**, Salley Weaver **Abbet**, Lucy Butler **Abbet**, Betsey Luceean **Abbett** and my money between the children of Bennett **Abbett** and Rowland **Perdue** and all property loaned to Bennet and Sally **Abbett** for their lifetime and then divided as above.
Exrs: Lewis and Samuel J. **Reavis**.
Wts: James **Ball**, Lewis **Reavis** Jr.

460, 461- June 6, 1839- proved Nov. court 1839.
Matilda **Barnett**---- wills to have executor sell her land on Island creek adjoining Nathaniel W. **Norwood**, Thomas D. **Barnett** and others and all other property excepting one large trunk which is to be given my son James **Barnett**. All money held by my executor who is Elijah **Barnett** for my son until he is of age.

Wts: Thos. B. **Barnett**, William **Davis**.

461 thru 463- Mar. 29, 1839- proved May court 1839.
James **Hart** Sr.--- wills to daughter Nancy **Hart**, 3 negroes and if she die leaving no issue then to return the negroes to my estate; to daughter Polley **Barnett** 2 negroes and if she die leaving no heirs then to come back to my estate; to son John G. **Hart**, the land whereon I live, two negroes and anything else he has had of my estate; To the living children of my daughter Rebecca **Strom**, all I have lent daughter and 3 negroes she to have use of same for her single life then to the **Strom** children. To the lawful issue of my daughter Elizabeth **Hutson**, 4 negroes, for the use of my daughter for life then to her children; To son Pleasant **Hart** 2 negroes, and bed and furniture and if he die without lawful issue, to return to my estate; to son Maurice S. **Hart**, 2 negroes and the land whereon I live understanding that daughter Nancy is to live in house for as long as she live or until married; To son James **Hart**, negroes and all else he has received; to grson Pleasant **Strom**, a negro and if he die under age or without issue then to James **Hart** son of my son John G. **Hart**; to grdau. Amy **Hart** daughter of my son John G. **Hart**, a negro but if she die without heirs then to Ann, her sister; To dau. Rebecca **Strom**, I loan the plantation whereon son Maurice now lives for her life time and to clear what land necessary for herself and children and at her death or re-marriage to be sold and divided with rest of estate; My daughter Nancy and Rebecca to have a years support off my provisions and all else sold and divided to all my children.
Exrs: son John G. **Hart** or Maurice S. **Hart** or Pleasant **Hart**.
Wts: Jno. R. **Hicks**, Jas. **Young**, Jas. B. **Daniel**, Thos. B. **Barnett**.

464- thru 471- Inv. and sale of estate of Anderson **Paschall**, deceased, by D. A. **Paschall** excr.-The **Paschalls** bought most of property Nov. court 1839.

365
471- thru 474- Inv. and sale of property of Richard H. **Bullock**, deceased, by B. F. **Bullock**, admstr. Nov. court 1839---sold Oct. 29, 1839-a great deal of property bought by **Bullocks**.

475-Acct of estate of John **Eastwood**, deceased, by Thos. **Gooch**, admstr. Nov. 5, 1839--mentions widow unnamed.

475-476- Oct. 24, 1839- James **Hart** of Henderson Co., Tennessee, John G. and Maurice S. **Hart** of Granville Co., N. C. for love we have for our brother Pleasant **Hart** of Granville Co., N. C. give him all our interest in the estate of our father that came to us or will come to us, of our father, James **Hart** Sr. deceased. and also anything that would be ours at death of Rebecca **Strom** or her re-marriage, of Polly **Barnett** or Nancy **Hart**.
Wts: L. B. **Barnett**, Margaret **Barnett**.

477- thru 480- Inv. and sale of estate of- Micajah **Bullock**, deceased, Aug. 27, 1839- by Edward **Bullock**, excr.

481- 482- Inv. and sale of property of William **Akin**, deceased, by Elijah **Hester** Oct. 30, 1839- Mrs. Polly **Akin** and John **Akin** buyers at sale also William **Akin**.

482- thru 490- Estate of Capt. Benjamin **Hester**, deceased, by Bennett **Hester**, admstr. at house of Mrs. Mary **Hester** Dec. 31, 1831--that is hiring of negroes, rentals accounted for to Nov. court 1839.

490- thru 492- Acct of estate of Daniel **Gooch**, deceased, by Amos **Gooch** excr. and pay to legatees: Joseph, Thomas, William, Dudley S., Daniel T., Hannah, Nancy; Samuel(deceased), Amos, James **Gooch**, William **Clements**, Rachel **Howard**, Oct. 9, 1839- also Thomas **Howard**-

492-493- Dec. 5, 1839- proved Feb. court 1840.
John **Barker**---- wills to wife Sarah for lifetime, since has already given to children, then at her death to divide land to three sons: John G., Charles and Davy **Barker**; The slaves sold at death or remarriage of my wife and divided to Thomas R., William, James, Wilson, Ambrose **Barker** and Martha wife of Samuel **Wilson**, Washington **Barker**, Polly wife of Stephen **Currin**, my children.
Exrs. sons John G. and Charles **Barker**.
Wts: Jno. R. **Hicks**, Absalom **Hunt**..

493-494- Apr, 24, 1839- proved Feb. court 1840--
James **Powell**---wills to wife Harriet All I possess for life or widowhood, but if she remarry she receives nothing of my estate. My son William, when of age the land adjoining Caroline **Blacknall**, Wm. **Blacknall** and Geo. **Eaton**s; to son James when 21 the other part of land; to daughter Mary Ann **Powell**, when of age or marries, 2negroes. All to be given my children at death of wife or remarriage of wife and she excrx.
Wts: Thos. L. **King**, Benj **Philops**.

495-496- June 6, 1828- proved Feb. court 1840.
John **Suit**---- wills to wife Susannah, the land whereon I live for her life or widowhood and at either eventually to son William **Suit**; to son William a featherbed and bedding and a horse; to dau. Susannah, at death of wife a featherbed and bedding; to grdau. Harriet **Suit**, daughter of my son William, a cow; All else to wife for life or widowhood and at her death to all children: Mary, wife of James Walker; Sarah, wife of John **Clark**, Nancy wife of Francis **Clark**, Susannah and William **Suit**.
Exrs: son William **Suit**.
Wts: Clement B. **Lyon**, James **Brogden**.

495-Feb. 9, 1839- proved Feb. court 1840-
Anne S **Pittard**-- wills to my two sisters: Rebecca and Letty **Pittard**, all my property of every description, and any property that comes to me in any way and the one who survives the other to receive all, and they excrxs.

Wts: Samuel S., John A. **Downey**.

497- Dec. 9, 1839- proved Feb. court 1840.
Rebecca **Pittard** wills all to her two sisters Anne and Letty **Pittard**-
Wts: Saml S. and John A. **Downey**.

366

497- Estate of Henry **Woodworth** deceased, in acct with Benjamin **Norwood** Jr., admstr. from Nov. 1837- mentions John **Read** as special admstr. accounted to Feb. 1840-- was a merchant-

505- Nov. 1839- Inv. of property of James **Hart**, deceased, by M. S. **Hart** excr. sold Nov. 14, 1839-

509- Inv. and sale of estate of Mary **Weaver**, deceased, Dec. 25, 1837 returned to court Feb. 1840 by A. E. **Henderson**, excr. and states at end of transaction that is estate of Mary **Perkinson**, deceased-

511, 512- Inv. of estate of Susannah **Prewitt**, deceased, Nov. 11, 1839 by Allen **Bridges**, admstr. among buyers at sale were Thos. Y. and C. H. **Cooke**, Elisha **Prewitt**.

513- Inv. of all estate of Ann **Smith**, deceased, by Samuel S. **Downey** Feb. court 1840.

514- Estate of Thomas **Jones**- mentions negroes recovered of Moody **Fowler** and acct. of hire of negroes for 1839.

515- Inv. and sale of estate of Vinam **Ball**, deceased, Dec. 9, 1839 by Joseph **Ball**, excr.

515- Hire of negroes of estate of Capt. Benjamin **Hester** for 1839 by Bennett **Hester** -excr.

517- Property sold by Elijah **Barnett**, excr. of estate of Matilda **Barnett**, deceased- Dec. 6, 1839-

518- Nov. 8, 1839- Negroes of estate of James **Hart** deceased, divided according to will- Miss Nancy **Hart** got the three old negroes as they chose her as mistress, John G. **Hart**, James Har[t]y Jr., Pleasant **Hart**, Maurice S. **Hart** and Joseph **Barnett**, Cephos **Hutson**, Mrs. Rebecca **Strum**-

519-Estate of John **Champion**, deceased, by Wm. **Huskey**, admstr. settled.

520- Nov. court 1839- Estate of Willie **Grisham**, deceased, by Anderson H. **Walker** admstr- from June 1837.

521- Inv. of property of Ephraim **Fraizer**, deceased, by St. **Blackwell** excr. Feb. court 1840.

522- Estate of Nathan **Bass**, deceased, by Anderson H. **Walker**, admstr. from June 22, 1838-

522, 523- Estate of Thomas **Blacknall**, Jr., deceased, by Geo. **Kittrell** admstr. from Feb. 1838- to Jan. 30, 1840-

523-Estate of Mrs. N. **Daniel** by L. H. **Hare** from Oct. 1837 to Feb. 1840.

525- Current acct. of estate of Millington **Blalock** with Thomas **Blalock** admstr. Jan. 29, 1840 at house of Mrs. Rebecca **Blalock**.

527- Estate of Jonathan **Davis** by commissioners, to divided to Sarah S. **Davis** and James W. **Davis**, their share of negroes- Nov. court 1839 and also shares of stock, etc. as per will-

528 thru 530- Vinson **Vaughn**, late of Granville Co., N. C., deceased, bequeathed to Jonathan G. **Vaughn** of New Madrid county, Missouri, certain legacy to be paid me by executors, John **Bowden** of Warren Co., N. C. and Martha **Vaughn** of Granville Co., N.C.,- and I appoint John **Vaughn** of Warren County, N.C., to collect my legacy for me-Jan. 16, 1839.
Wts: Richard **Barklet**, clerk of court of New Madrid, Arabel **Smith** J. P.

529- Woodson **Vaughn** of **Henderson** county, Tennessee, appoints John **Vaughn** of Warren Co., N. C. agent and attorney to collect that due him from estate of Vincent **Vaughn**, deceased, of Granville Co., N. C. May 1838.
Wts: Jeese **Taylor**, clerk of Henderson Co., court, Saml L. Edwards, chairman. This name is spelled both Woodson and Woodward **Vaughn**.

530, 531- Feb. 27, 1839- proved May court 1840.
Jacob **Vincent**--- wills that all land and other property be sold and money divided to his children: daughter Mary **Straton**; son Jacob **Vincent**; son John W. **Vincent**; daughter Ann **Vincent**; son William is dead so his part to his children; son John M. in trust for daughters Amey **Craft** and Elizabeth **Parrish**; son Henry H. **Vincent**-
Exrs: son John M. **Vincent** and friend Jno. **White**.
Wts: Lemuel **McGehee**, Hooker A. **Mitchell**, Benjamin **Moss**.

532- Sept, 24, 1827- proved May court 1840.
Temperance **Blackwell**---- wills to son James **Blackwell**, the land whereon I live so as to include the settlement made by Thomas **Handley** Sr., and at his death to the heirs of his body but if none then to daughters Sarah **Clopton** and Rosey **Blackwell** and they all the remainder of my property; I have given in my husband's lifetime to the other children.

Estate Records of Granville Co, NC Volume 13-16   67

Exrs: Sarah **Clopton** and Rosey **Blackwell**.
Wts: Jno. P. **Lemay**, Henry L. **Martin**.

532, 533- Feb. 23, 1840- proved May court 1840.
Alfred **Hester** wills to wife for life or widowhood then to all his children.
Exrs: Samuel **Hunt** Jr. -
Wts: L. **Huddeston**, Woodson **Carne**, Lewis **Parham**.

533, 534 Feb., 1839- proved May court 1840.
Sarah **Hedgepeth**---- wills to sons Carter and Richard B. **Hedgepeth**, all my land divided so that Richards land will adjoin that willed him by his father and they to have all personal property divided between them in they can agree on division and if not to be sold and money divided between them by excrs.
Exrs Dennis T. **Paschall** or Lunsford A. **Paschall**.
Wts: Lot **Watson**, Mary **Critcher**.

534- Inv. of personal estate of William **Mays**, deceased, by Lunsford A. **Paschall** admstr. Feb. 27, 1840 and sale thereof– Among buyers were Lucrecia **Mays**, Francis **Mays**, John and Margaret **Mays**, Eliza **Mays**, John B. **Mays**, Augustin **Landis**, Robert A. **Jones** and others.

540- 541- Estate of Solomon **Philpott** deceased, by W. A. **Philpott**, admstr; returned to May court 1840.

541- May court 1840- Inv. and sale of property of James **Powell**, dec'd by Harriot **Powell** excrx. mentions William, Honor **Powell**, Jonathan **Davis** as buyers at sale among others.

543- Estate of Henry H. **Dedman** deceased, by M. D. **Royster**, admstr., Feb. term of court 1840 mentions Amanda **Deadman**, widow- property sold Feb. 29, 1840- Mrs. **Deadman** bought at sale.

545, 546- Property of Francis **Dean** deceased, Inv. and sale by Joseph H. **Gooch** -Feb. 29, 1840-

547- Henry **Hamme** (?) and wife Elizabeth allotted their share of estate of Jonathan **Davis**, deceased-as per will of sd. **Davis**- Feb court 1840.

547- 548- Estate of negroes of Leonard **Bullock**, deceased, by William F. **Flemeing** admstr. Feb. 27, 1840- mentions those advanced to son Philip P. **Bullock** in lifetime and that advanced to Willis B. **Mitchell** in lifetime, to Obediah **Winston** in his lifetime-

548, 549- Inv. of estate of John **Barker**, deceased, May 4, 1840, by John and Charles **Barker**, excrs, and acct. of sale Feb. 27, 1840.

550- Additional Inv. of property of M. **Blalock**, dec'd, by Thomas **Blalock**, admstr. May court 1840.

550, 551- Sale of estate of John **Suit**, deceased, by William **Suit**, excr. May court 1840.

551-552- Estate of Thomas **Huskey** deceased by John **White** admstr., gives years allowance to Mrs. Ann **Huskey**- May 1840.

552-553- Estate of John **Wiggins** by John **Jordan**, admstr. from Jan. 21, 1838- paid $10.60 for coffin- returned to May court 1840.

553-554- Estate of John **Rice**, deceased, by Fleming **Rice** admstr.- paid $6.00 for coffin, returned May court 1840.

554 thru 556- Estate of Charles P. **Glover** deceased, with Mary **Glover** admstr. May court 1840.

557-Estate of Col. B. **Kimball**, deceased, by W. P. **Kimball** admstr. from Dec. 9, 1836- to Feb. 1840-

562- thru 564- Oct. 19, 1830- proved Aug. court 1840.
Courtney **Ingles**----wills to Fanny **OBrien**, eldest daughter of Dennis **OBryan**, now wife of Thomas **Wortham**, 10 shares of stock in Bank of N. C. left by my husband Col. John **Ingles**; To friend Nancy **Jones**, wife of Daniel **Jones**, chests, a family bible; To friend Joseph **Gales** Sr. of

Raleigh, for the many kindnesses rendered myself and husband, 7 shares of Capitol stock in N. C. Bank and a note which he said Joseph owes me for $280.00; To John Ingles **Falconer**, son of Nancy **Jones**, 4 shares of stock in Bank of N. C. of Newbern for his education; To Courtney Ingles **OBrien** (**OBryan**), daughter of Dennis **OBryan** of Warren Co., 5 shares of Stock in Newbern Bank; to friend Daniel **Tanner** of Warren Co., N. C. 12 shares of stock in State Bank of N. C.; to friend Thomas **Tanner** of Granville Co., N.C. 12 shares in bank of N. C. and 10 shares in Newbern Bank, 3 negroes and all else of my estate.
Exrs: Daniel and Thomas **Tanner**.
Wts: Agnes **Hare**, Wm. **Robards**.

564- thru 566- June 19, 1836- proved Aug. court 1840.
Elizabeth **Marrow**-- states that her late husband Daniel **Marrow** left her by will, the estate to divide as she wished among his children and my children. First to my daughter Nancy **Lewis** during her natural life, with no claim thereof of her husband and at her death to all my children and should Nancy have issue then to the issue; To daughter Easter **Lemay** and then to her children and if no issue to return to my other children; To Elizabeth **Marrow**, negroes, furniture and half stock and

provisions; to son Thomas F. **Marrow**, a half the stock and provisions, negroes, and furniture; As per will of my husband sons Thomas, Drury and Alexander received land and my daughter Nancy **Lewis** to have sufficient to equal this bequest; To daughter Elizabeth **Marrow** a like amount; all else and my old negroes may choose which of my children they wish to live with.
Exrs: three sons Thomas, Drury and Alexander.
Wts: James **Lewis**, Howel L. **Read**, Jno. A. **Burwell**.
James **Lewis** is dead and Howel S. **Read** resides outside jurisdiction of court, so their handwriting attested to by others.

567- 568- July 20, 1840- proved Aug.- court 1840.
Joseph **Amis**--- to wife Elizabeth and my son-in-law Lewis **Amis** and son Lewis **Amis**, executors of this estate; My negroes in Mississippi to be left there or brought back as they see fit for interest of my family; Each of children as come of age or marry to be given enough to make equal with daughter Betsey **Amis** which she has in her possession; My son Lewis to remain in college and my other two sons James and Joseph given like education and my daughters a good English education.
Wts: Jno. R. **Hicks**, John **Amis**, S. S. **Downey**.

568-Mar. 27, 1840- proved Aug. court 1840-
Howell G. **Pittard** ---- To sister Elizabeth **Pittard** of Carroll Co., Tenn. $200.00, my gold watch and breast pin; To sister Nancy **Moore** of same place all my wardrobe and to-them all else I own or will own.
Exrs: Robt. B. **Gilliam**, Latney **Montague**.

569-570- July 27, 1837- proved Aug. court 1840.
William **Washington**---- wills to wife Elizabeth for lifetime or widow-hood, a wagon, set of smiths tools, the land whereon I live called The Indian Grave tract, all household and kitchen furniture, tools, stock, all provisions and to sell sufficient crop to pay debts; to sons Woodson, William, George and Ephraim when of age a cow and calf a horse and furniture out of what I loaned my wife; to daughters when either marry to have bed and furniture, cow and calf out of what is lent my wife; At death of wife the land to son William and he to let my daughters live in house as long as single; My sons to have other lands and at death of my wife the property left loaned her sold and divided to all my children equally.
Exrs: son Woodson **Washington**.
Wts: William **Suit**, Elijah **Hester**.

570- 571- June 16, 1837- proved Aug. court 1840.
Abraham **Slaughter**----wills to wife all he possesses after debts paid and at her death or remarriage to be equally divided to children she taking a childs part; The land whereon Thomas **Slaughter** I lives to be his

369
and land whereon I live to belong to son Abraham, the youngest son, to son Jacob G., William P. B., James H. and Abraham S. **Slaughter**, each an equal share of personal estate; To son Thomas, after his death to his children; I lend to Elizabeth

wife of Anderson **Dunkin**, to Franky, wife of Alfred **Dunkin**, to Ailsey G. wife of Jacob L. **Slaughter**, to Susanna wife of James **Terry** Jr, to Sally P. wife of John **Bryant** each their share of my estate and at their death to their children and if any die then to the survivors of them without interference of their husbands; to daughter Charity, if she marry, her share is as others; -
Exrs: sons Jacob G, and William P. B. **Slaughter**.
Wts: D. J. **Young**, S. **Terry**.

572-573- Nov. 25, 1839-- proved Aug. court 1840.
William **Lawrence**--- wills to daughter Mary G. **Furguson**, all she has already received and $1.00; to daughter Elizabeth **Lawrence**, $340.00 and a horse to make her equal with that given children that have left me; to son Henry B. $100.00 and that already given him; to daughter Leanah, land whereon I live 111 acres, all cattle, $100.00, a horse; to son William, $76.00 and all given him; to daughter Margret P. **Garner Gramer**(?) $110.00 and all given her; to son Lemuel J. $300.00 and all given him; to son Robert $1.00 and all given him; All else sold and divided as above.
Exrs: Henry B. **Lawrence** and William **Fleming**.
Wts: Clement **Wilkins**, John **Wilkins**, Benjamin B. **Hester**.

574- Inv. of property of John G. **Hart**, deceased, taken by T. B. **Barnett**, admstr. May 25, 1840 mentions that portion to widow for her support and that of children from estate of Col. John G. **Hart**, deceased, and that sold May 26, 1840- mentions Rebecca, Ann, Susan, Edward, Pleasant, Joseph **Hart**, Maurice S. **Hart** as buyers- Susan bought most.

577- Inv. of estate of Sarah **Hedgepeth**, deceased, by Dennis T. **Paschall** excr. Apr. 16, 1840- and sale thereof Apr. 16, 1840.

583- Estate of Jesse C. **Dean** by William **Dean**, admstr. May court 1840.

584- Inv. of estate of Lewis **Green** by Ann L. **Green** admstr. Aug. 1840.

584- Inv. of estate of Elly **Higgs**, deceased by Lewis **Parham**, admstr. Aug. 1, 1840.

585- Feb. 8, 1840- Harriot **Powell** appoints James **Fuller**, attorney to be acting administrator of estate of her late husband James **Powell**.
Wts: Geo. **Kittrell**, Thos. L. **King**..

585- Aug. court 1840- Sale of estate of Wills **Tayloes** estate by Wm. P. **Forrest** special admstr.

586- 587- Acct. of Wardens of the Poor of Granville Co. for 1840.

588- Estate of Mary **Perkinson** by A. E. **Henderson**, audited and settled from

Estate Records of Granville Co, NC Volume 13-16   71

Feb. 1839- to July 24, 1840.

589- Inv. of estate of Mary **Nuttall** deceased, by George **Barns** admstr. Aug. court 1840.

589- thru 592 Estate of Jacob **Vincent** by John **White**- Inv. May 7, 1840 and property of deceased sold May 27, 1840-

593- thru 595-Estate of Mary **Somerville**, deceased, by William A. **Somerville** admstr. from Aug. 1838- to Aug. 1840.

595- thru 597- Estate of Alfred **Hester** deceased, by Samuel **Hunt** Excr. Aug. court 1840.

597- thru 599- Estate of William **Cozart** deceased, by James C. **Cozart** admstr- from Aug. 25, 1836 to Aug. 1840.

599- Bonds in hands of Charles **Smith** belonging to estate of Alfred **Hayes**, deceased- Aug. 1840.

600- In Acct. with Leslie **Gilliam**, sheriff of Granville Co. from Feb. court 1837- Jan. 1, 1839 to Jan 1, 1840--

604-605- Aug. 7, 1822- proved- Nov. court 1840.
Lewelen **Jones**---wills to wife Ann Alston **Jones**, 14 negroes, and all else I am possessed of and she executorix.
Wts: Wm. and Geo. **Floyd**, Thomas **Mann**.

370
605- Jan. 20, 1840- proved Nov. court 1840.
Benjamin **Merritt**--- wills to son Joel **Marrett**, 50 acres of land; To wife Celia for lifetime, all rest of land except that deeds given for; To wife the property I have at James **Overtons** and at her death to go to Jane **Overton's** children I give all; to daughter Abagail W. **Merritt** a cow and calf and a bed and furniture; All else to wife and at her death divided between my sons Joel and John G. **Merritt**, the land and daughters Amy H. **Powell** and Abagail W. **Merritt** the remainder except that given my daughter Jane **Overton's** children.
Exrs: none named. Amdtrx was Celia the wife.
Wts: John and John G. **Merritt**.

606- Nov. 4, 1821- proved Nov. court 1840-
William H. **Searcey** ---wills to wife Dorcas all I own for her life and at her death to Sally **Hudspeth** $1.00 and all remaining on hand; to grson William L. **Fletcher** the land whereon I live; to him all else.
Exrs: Joseph **Fletcher**, James **Jinkins**.
Wts: Claborn H. **Cooke**.

607- Estate of Zachariah **Hester** by Hamilton **Hester** excr. Oct. 3, 1839.

608- Inv. of estate of William **Washington**, deceased, by Woodson **Washington** excr. Nov. 5, 1840.

609- Estate of Francis **Dean** by Joseph H. **Gooch**, admstr. Aug. 1840-

610- Aug. 31, 1840- Inv. of estate of Rebeckah **Blackwell**, deceased by Abner **Currin** and sales of same; Among buyers were John, James, Stephen **Blackwell**.

611- Inv. and sale of estate of Vinum **Ball** deceased, by Joseph **Ball** excr.- Oct. 13, 1840.

612- Sale of estate of William **Jinkins**, deceased, by William **Jinkins** admstr- Nov. 3, 1840- mentions support of Margaret **Jenkins**.

614- Aug. 3, 1840- Inv. of estate of Abraham **Slaughter**, deceased taken by William P. B. **Slaughter** excr.

615- Inv. of estate of Joseph **Amis** deceased, by Lewis **Amis** Sr., excr and Elizabeth **Amis** Exrx. Aug. 22, 1840.

James M. T. **Wiggins**, clerk of Court
End Book 14

Estate Records of Granville Co, NC Volume 13-16   73

371
1 thru 5- Aug. 29, 1840- Sales of estate of Mills **Tayloe** deceased by William P. **Forrest** admstr.

5 thru 8- Inv. of estate and acct. of sales of estate of William **Lawrence** Sr. deceased, by William **Fleming** excr. Oct. 1, 1840.

8 thru 11- Inv. and acct. of sales of Phebe **Morris**, deceased, by Stephen **Morris**, special Admstr. Oct. 8, 1840- among buyers at sale were Stephen **Morris** Jr., Thomas G. **Morris**, Asa **Morris**, Phebe **Morris**.

12-13- List of property of James **Lewis** Sr., deceased, by James M. **Bullock** admstr. Nov. court 1840- owned 68 slaves.

14- Estate of Zachariah **Hester**, deceased, by Hamilton **Hester** admstr. Nov. 2, 1840.

15-16- Acct. of sales of estate of Abner **Boothe**, by William **Fleming** admstr. Oct. 24, 1840 mentions as buyer Eliza **Boothe** among others.

16- Feb. 8, 1840- proved Feb. court 1841.
John **Bailey**---- wills to wife Penelope for her lifetime, my house and furniture, plantation tools and all else while she is living; To dau, Polly **Bailey** to live on plantation as long as she lives; to Thomas **Due**, 5 shillings; daughter Elizabeth **Bailey** 5 shillings; to daughter Glaffry (?) $50.00; to the rest of my children and Glaffry are to divide my estate equally.
Exrs: William **Bailey**.
Wts: Israel F. **Dillard**, Samuel **Bailey**.

17, 18- Nuncupative Will-Nov. 1, 1840--Feb court 1841--
Thomas **Harris**, deceased--wills that all debts paid and rest of estate to wife Elizabeth and at her death to my nephew James **Harris**.
Wts: John **Jenkins**, Patsy **Fowler**, Daniel **Fowler**.

18-19- Apr. 4, 1840- proved Feb. court 1841.
Nathan **Haswell**--- wills to wife Nancy, land and as much live stock as she need for support of self and the children for her widowhood; To Julia Adaline and Sabilia **Hawkins** do not choose to live with their mother or if they marry, then to each a bed and furniture and a cow and calf; All rest of my estate sold, my debts paid, and remainder used for educating my children and support of family; My wife to advance to any one of my children who marries or leaves home that which she can. If wife marry all to be sold and divided between her and all children.
Exrs: Thomas T. **Cooke**.
Wts: Thomas **Hicks**, James **Blackly**, John **Davis**.

20- Jan. 1, 1841- proved Feb. court 1841.

Peter **West**----- wills to wife Susan, all estate for her lifetime, and at her death, all to be sold and divided to my legal heirs. To Miss Judith **Edwards**, my young bay horse. My wife's mother Mrs. Mary **Edwards** and my wife's sister Miss Judith **Edwards** to remain on my land for their lifetimes and then to my legal heirs.
Exrs: Wife and Fleming **Beasley**.
Wts: James and Stephen **Beasley**, David W. **Knott**.

21, 22- Dec. 4, 1839- Feb. court 1841.
Charles **Heflin**---- wills to son Lewis and daughter Elizabeth for their lifetime, 534 acres whereon I now live on Ford creek, and at their death to the legal heirs of Lewis **Heflin**; Exr. to sell that necessary to pay debts and the legacies I hereafter specify; To son William, to daughter Cary, wife of Edward **White**, Susan wife of Buckhorn William **Heflin**, Mary wife of James **Mann**, Ava wife of Thomas J. **Smith**, Nancy wife of Green **Fuller**, Heirs of daughter Phebe, deceased wife of James **Cawthorn** 5 shillings each; to son Lewis and daughter Elizabeth, my live stock furniture, tools, and after their deaths to heirs of Lewis **Heflin**. Also to them negroes for lifetime then to heirs of Lewis **Helfin**.
Guardians and agents and also exrs: grandson Rufus T. **Helfin** and son Lewis **Heflin** (Lewis to be guardian for Elizabeth for her lifetime).
Wts: John **Walker**, Joseph **Walker**.

372
22, 23- May 6, 1839- proved Nov. court 1840.
Joseph **Lumpkin**- - - - wills to wife Frances, all property for her lifetime or widowhood, and at her death to each of my grandchildren 50¢; The rest divided between my daughter Martha **Lumpkin** and daughter Nancy **Hudson's** two children: Nancy and Susan **Hudson**.
Exrs: none appointed (Marcus D. **Royster** admstr) Henry H. **Deadman** is dead now at time of probate.
Wts: H. H. **Dedman**, Richard H. **Richards**.

23, 24- Current acct of estate of Alfred **Hayes** by Charles **Smith** admstr Feb. court 1841-

25- Acct. of Capt. Benjamin **Hester's** estate - - negroes hired for 1841 by Bennett **Hester** admstr.

26- Sale of estate of Lewis **Green**, deceased, by Ann L. **Green** admstr. Dec. 22, 1840- - William **Green** bought a book.

27, 28- Acct. of estate of Henry **Emery** deceased by Clement **Wilkins**, admstr.- mentions paying widow an allowance. Feb. 2, 1841.

28- 29- Estate of Henry **Wilson**, deceased, by James M. **Heggie**, excr. mention paying Masa **Wilson** a yrs. provisions- Feb. court 1841.

29- thru 31- Acct. of sale of estate of Sarah **Roffe**, deceased, by James **Gooch**, Nov. 24, 1840.

31- thru - 36- Sale of estate of Judith **Bradford**, deceased, by William D. **Allen**, admstr Aug. 26, 1840- mentions John **Bradford** Jr., William and Davis **Bradford**, Jacob **Bradford**, John **Bradford** Sr., Hardy **Bradford**, Benjamin **Bradford** among buyers at sale.

36- 37- Acct. of estate of Samuel **Brummett**, deceased, by Wyatt **Cannaday** admstr. Feb. 1841.

38- thru 40- Acct. of estate of Thomas **Daniel** deceased, by William P. **Thomas** excr. Feb. court 1841.

41, 42- Estate of William **Puryear** deceased, by Randal and Peyton **Puryear** excrs., Feb. court 1841- - Accounting.

42- thru 48- Estate of Abraham **Lawrence** Sr., deceased, sale of estate by William **Fleming** admstr Nov. 3, 1840- mentions among buyers John P., A., Leanner, Lydia, Turner **Lawrence**, E. O. **Lawrence**, and others.

48- Estate of Thomas **Jones**, deceased, with Jane **Jones** the widow being allotted her share of slaves, Nov. 28, 1840- She received 1/5th part.

49. thru 51- Acct. of sales of estate of Phebe **Morris** deceased, by Stephen **Morris**, admstr. - Feb. court 1841.

51- thru 53- Estate of William B. **Williams** by John B. **Moore** admstr. May 30, 1840- sale of estate, and years allotment to widow Elizabeth **Williams**.

53 thru 55- Estate of Leanner **Lawrence** deceased, by William **Fleming** admstr Nov. 30, 1840- Sale of estate.

55- Nov. 14, 1840- John P. **Lemay**, John J. **Lemay**, Susanna F. **Phillips**, Margret **Strother** agree to a division of six slaves belonging to estate of their deceased mother Lucy **Lemay**.
Wts: R. T. **Heflin**.

56- Estate of Jacob **Vincent**, deceased, by John **White**, Oct. 29, 1840 mentions as buyers at sale: Anna **Vincent**, among others.

58, 59- Sale of estate of John **Bradford**, deceased, by William **Bradford** executor- Feb. court 1841- -

59- Estate of Abner **Boothe** deceased- Negroes sold Jan. 2, 1841 -

60- Feb. court 1841- Lewis **Amis** and Elizabeth **Amis**, execrs. mention negroes brought from Mississippi, 10 of them, on Jan. 1, 1841- -

60- Inv. of estate of Mary **Hayes** deceased, by Henry **Hobgood**, admstr. Feb. court 1841- no estate unless small amt from estate of Alfred **Hester** estate deceased, and much from admstr of estate of Benjamin **Hester**, dec'd.

61- In. of bonds of Alfred **Hester** deceased, by Samuel **Hunt** Jr. excr. Nov. 21, 1840- mentions Stephen **Hayes**.

62- Acct. of sales of estate of Martha **Floyd**, deceased by Pleasant **Floyd**, Feb. court 1841- among buyers were Charles, Stephen, Pleasant, Buck **Floyd**.

373

64 thru 68- Sale of estate of William **Floyd** by Samuel **Duty**, excr. Oct. 13, 1838- and Nov. 20, 1840- among buyers were Charles, George, Pleasant, Stephen, Rachel **Floyd**.

68, 69- Jan. 30, 1841- proved May court 1841.
Elizabeth **Peace**- - - - wills to daughters Mary, Margaret, Charlot, son John, $130.00 each; This makes them equal with my other children to whom I have given, Ann **Macey** (Mary) Catherine **Peace**, Joseph **Peace**, Elizabeth **Maconily** who have already received $130.00 each: To my five children in this county namely: Mary, Margaret, Charlotty, John and Catherine jointly to have the land whereon I live, all stock, tools furniture and my children living in the West, Ann **Masery**, Elizabeth **Malconily**, Joseph **Peace** to each $25.00; anything left divided to all.
Exrs: All my children since they are all of age-
Wts: Lewis and James P. **Montague**, Latney **Montague**

69 thru 74- Acct. of sales of estate of William A. **Hamilton**, deceased by P. **Hamilton**, admstr. mentions among debts some in Tennessee.

74- Estate of John **Bailey** deceased, by William **Bailey** excr. Feb. 26, 1841- delivered to widow that willed to her.

76, 77- Estate of Thomas **Harris**, deceased: sale of- by L. A. **Paschall**, admstr. May court 1841.

77, 78- Estate of David **Chandler**, deceased, by Littleberry and Thomas **Chandler**, excrs. - gives amt. paid legatees (not named).

78- Sale of estate of James **Powell**, deceased, by Harriot **Powell** axcrx and by her agent James Fuller.

79- 80- Account of Wardens of the Poor of Granville Co. for 1841.

80- 81- Estate of Reuben **Smith**, deceased, Inv. of and sale- by Stephen **Dodson** admstr. Nov. 23, 1839- - mentions negroes sold to heirs of Joel **Smith**, heirs of Bennett **Smith**, to Stephen **Dodson**- Feb. court 1841.

81- 82- Estate of Mary **Daniel**, deceased, by Wm. H. **Webb**, admstr. from 1838 forward- to May term 1841.

83- Estate of Nancy **Daniel**, deceased, by Henry M. **Daniel**- from July 7, 1838- to May 1841-

84, 85- Current acct. of estate of David **Parker**, deceased by John **Shearman**, admstr. Nov. 22, 1839-

86- Sale of estate of Jonothan **Stone** deceased, by Jonathan M. **Stone** excr. mentions J. M. **Stones**' legacy paid him, mentions receipt of heirs Nancy **Thompson**, Claborn **Stone**, Averilla **Russ**, Wiley E. **Jones** admstr of Polly **Jones** deceased, John **Bobbitt**, Delphia **Washington**, J. M. **Stone**, Judy **Simons** (she out of State resident).

87- Leslie **Gilliam**, Sheriff in Account with county of Granville 1841 covers pages thru 92- Aug. court 1841.

92- 93- Estate of William **Lears**, deceased, sold by Daniel A. **Paschall** admstr May 21, 1841- Jane **Lears** bought furniture at sale.

94- 95, Sale of estate of Leonard **Williams** deceased, by Daniel A. **Paschall**, admstr. Mar. 2, 1841.

95- thru 97- Estate of Robert **Hester** deceased, by D. F. **Gooch**, admstr Aug. court 1841- mentions suit in court on estate of B. **Hester**, from which an amt. due here. Nancy **Hester** bought at sale and Francis G. **Hester**. Nancy bought furniture-

98- thru 100- Acct of Inv. and sale of estate of Thomas J. **Sandford** Oct. 1840. by Lucy P. **Tuck** excr.

100- 101- - Estate of Micajah **Bullock**, by Edward **Bullock** excr. Aug. court 1841.

101- 102- Acct. of estate of Thomas **York** Sr, deceased by Wm. **Beck** admstr. mentions money to widow- - July 14, 1841.

102- Estate of Solomon **Bailey** deceased, by John **Davis** admstr. Aug. court 1841- mentions board for Louisa, Angram and Prudence.

104- Inv. and sale of estate of N. **Haswell**, deceased, by Thomas Y. **Cooke**, excr. Aug. court 1841.

374

104, 105- May 12, 1841- proved Aug. court 1841.
John C. **Thompson**- - - wills that executors pay to Dr. Jno. F. **Price** of....., Maryland $30.00 and also Dr. William **Harper** of Alexandria $30.00; To father James **Thompson**, for his lifetime, my interest in a house in Port Tobacco, Maryland and at his death to my brother, James **Thompson**: Jenny and Edward, my servants who have cared for me so well during my illness to be paid what is just and right by my excrs. to my father all else remaining of my estate: To excrs. my wardrobe and two trunks and excrs. to sell my property that may come to his possession as he sees fit.
Exrs: John **Bullock**.
Wt s: John W. **Hicks** Jr., Fred **Wales**.

105- thru 107- May 12, 1841- proved Aug. court 1841.
Edward **Jones** - - - - wills to eldest daughter Leanah **Fletcher** wife of William **Fletcher**, $250.00; to daughter Rebecca **Robards** wife of James **Robards**, $250.00- to daughter Hannah wife of John **Shearman**: $250.00, To Polly **Parrish** wife of William **Parrish**: $250.00: to daughter Ailey **Gooch** wife of William **Gooch**, $250.00: To grandson Allen **Jones**, and grandson Alfred N. **Jones**, each $33 1/3 dollars: to Ralph **Jones** son of Polly **Jones**, 33 1/3 dollars: To granddaughter Polly **Jones** a cow and calf: to granddaughter Elstada **Jones** $10.00; to grson Marion **Jones**, $10. - The residue of estate to be equally divided between daughters:
Exrs: John **Shearman**, William **Parrish**, Edward **Jones** Jr.
Wts: William and Abner **Jones**.

107, 108- May 6, 1841- proved August court 1841.
Mary **Jones**- - - - wills to Ann **Edwards**, wife of Washington **Edwards**, a negro to sister Amy **Hunt**, ½ the balance of estate after debts paid: to James **Hunt** in trust for support of brother Robert **Jones** and family the other half of my estate.
Exrs: James **Hunt**.
Wts: William **Hicks**, John **Fuller**.

108- June 30, 1841- proved Aug. court 1841.
Anderson **Dunkin**- - - wills to wife Elizabeth, all estate for her life or during widowhood but if she marry then she to have a childs part with all my children; To son-in-law John W. **Dixon** 1.00 dollar.
Exr: brother-in-law William **Slater**.
Wts: Portius **Moore**, Abraham **Slaughter**.

109, 110- Mar. 9, 1841- proved Aug. court 1841.
Sally **Smith** - - - - wills to granddaughter Mary S. **Hunt**, without prejudice from any other source, 10 negroes and their children and at her death to her heirs by her husband Thomas P. **Hunt**: namely Sally Anderson and Elizabeth Taylor **Hunt**: to grandchildren namely (Mary T. **Hunt** excepted) William A., William P., James A., Edward T., Sally T., John H., Samuel T. **Taylor**- 22- negroes divided between them, also beds and furniture, with Mary S. **Hunt** have a share in furniture: to niece Mary A. **Rawlings** a negro and $1000.00 which she has received from me.

Estate Records of Granville Co, NC Volume 13-16   79

Exrs: none named.
Wts: William M. **Walker**, William N. **Blackwell**.

110, 111- Nov. court 1838- Petition of Mary **York** widow of Thomas **York** states that he died possessed of 118 acres on Robertsons creek and asks for her dower right in land. She received 39 ½ acres Jan. 29, 1839.

112-113- Petition of Ann **Husketh** widow of Thomas **Husketh**, deceased Nov. term 1838- states he died possessed of 60 acres of land and asks her dower in land. Received 20 acres Jan. 17, 1839.

113, 114, 115- Petition Nov. term 1838- Massey **Wilson** states that she widow of Henry **Wilson**, deceased, who died possessed of 2 tracts of land and asks her dower in land- Received 89 acres Nov. 26, 1838.

115, 116, 117- Petition of Caroline G. **Blacknall**, widow of Thomas **Blacknall** who died in 1833, possessed of 209 acres of land, leaving three children George, Henry and Charles **Blacknall** of whom I am guardian- - asks for dower in land. granted 69 acres Jan. 14, 1839-

375
117- 118- Clarissa B. **Woodworth** widow of Henry **Woodsworth** who died in 1837 possessed of several tracts of land adjoining lands of Spotswood **Burwell** and Hartwell W. **Hargrove** and also another tract adjoining, asks her dower in lands. Henry **Woodworth** left surviving him the children here named: Henry, Mary E., Benjamin, Clarissa, Samuel **Woodworth** who are all minors. Petition Nov. 1, 1838- Allotted Nov. 21, 1838, 63 ½ acres.

119- 120- Nov. term 1838- John B. **Smith**, Men R. **Smith**, Ann Rebecca **Smith** minors, by their guardian Richard J. **Smith** - against Samuel W. **Smith** state that Maurice **Smith** died in 1835 leaving surviving him the widow Amy **Smith** and children: Mary G. wife of Richard J. **Smith**, Francis S., James A., Thomas M. and your petitioners and Samuel W. **Smith** who is a minor- They ask that the division of estate divided to them their share of the negroes as was done for the widow and other children. Division was made Dec. 1838.

121 thru 125- Nov. term 1837- Petition stating that Millington **Blalock** died in 1837, leaving widow Rebecca and children: Sally, wife of Woodson **Washington**, John P. **Blalock**, Nancy wife of Joseph D. **Hobgood**, Luetta **Blalock** (minor, by her guardian Samuel **Philpott**), Milly wife of Edward **Boswell**, Thomas **Blalock**, and Milly & F. [sic*], daughter of a deceased daughter Martha **Philpott**, who died prior to her father, Millington **Blalock**, and the Milly and F.[sic*] **Philpott** was an only child of sd Martha. Robert, William, Millington and Etna **Blalock** are children of William **Blalock**, deceased, a son of Millington **Blalock** Sr., deceased, and died prior to the death of his father, whose children are all minors. Milly and Edward **Boswell** live in Tennessee. The negroes of the estate of Millington **Blalock**,

deceased, were divided to the widow (she taking a childs part) and all the heirs with the grandchildren of Millington **Blalock** receiving their parent's share, divided amongst them. Divided into 9 parts and distributed. [*Because of the wording in the abstract list, these were compared with the original Liber & page.}

125- thru- Nov. term 1838- Petition stating that Leonard **Bullock** died leaving land on Ledge of Rocks adjoining Dick H. **Dolby's** heirs and Edward **Bullock** which land is subject to the dower right of Pamelia, widow of Leonard **Bullock**, deceased, and children: Phillip P., Susan wife of Williss **Mitchell**, Pamelia wife of Obediah **Winston**, Weldon E., Francis C., Mildred A., Sara and Mary L. **Bullock**. Ask petition of land, excluding the dower of the widow. Division was made dividing into 6 lots- Thus:.
Lot 1 to Willis B. **Mitchell** and wife Susan 45 acres-
Lot 2- to Obediah **Winston** and wife Pamelia.
Lot 3- to Agnes **Bullock**.
Lot 4 to Francis C. **Bullock**.
Lot 5- to Sarah **Bullock**.
Lot 6 to Mary L. **Bullock** See Plat on following page.
Lot 7- to Mildred A **Bullock**.
Lot 8- to Weldon E. **Bullock**.
See Plat on following page

129- thru 130- Division of negroes of estate of Leonard **Bullock**, deceased, to heirs- - same persons as above.

130- thru 133- Aug. Term 1838- Chesley **Daniel**, late of Charlotte county, Virginia, died in the year 1821, having published his will and probated in Charlotte county, VA. and the executor of said will died in Granville Co., N. C. (where she had lived some years, our mother now decd) in April 1838, and Henry M. **Daniel** became admstr of his estate. And we, Henry M. **Daniel**, Elizabeth M who married Charles L. **Read**, Nancy S. **Daniel**, Priscilla S **Daniel**, Chesley B., and John J., and William N, and Stephen R. **Daniel** (the last two minors) with their brother Henry M. as guardian are the only living children of testator to whom the estate Is given at death of testator and mother of your petitioners. Ask negroes divided to them, since their father and mother are now deceased, and we are only heirs as per the will. Sept. 24, 1838.

376
Land division to heirs of Leonard **Bullock** deceased Dec. 11, 1838. 430 3/4 acres.

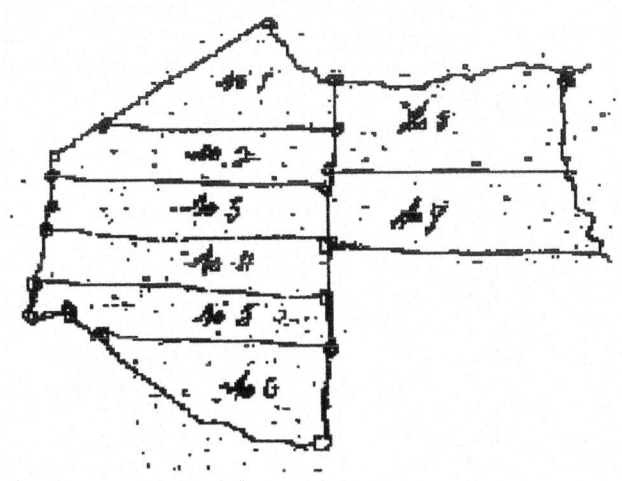

133- Aug. court. 1839- Martha **Bullock**, widow of Richard H. **Bullock**, deceased, died leaving the widow Martha, and the following children: Thomas J., James M., Adeline, Frances, Sarah and Micajah **Bullock** (minors). Richard H. **Bullock** was possessed of land adjoining that of the late Micahah **Bullock**, Leonard **Bullock** and Edward **Bullock**- Asks for dower in land, granted 52 ½ acres Oct. 16, 1839.

135- 136- Nov. term 1839- Mary **Gill**, widow of Gideon **Gill**, deceased, who died in 1838 possessed of land adjoining that of Mekins **Bledsoe**, Anderson and James **Cash**, and William **Lyon** containing 307 acres. He left survivors widow Mary and children: Francis, William, James, Joseph, Robert, Gideon, Benjamin and Samuel **Gill** all minors. She asks dower right be allotted her in land. She was given 102 ¼ acres Jan. 16, 1840.

137- 138- Nov. term 1839- Henry C. **Ray** and wife Cynthia J. **Ray**, ask for dower in the land of Anderson **Bailey**, deceased, since Cynthia J. is the former wife of the deceased, who died possessed of 2 tracts of land one of 576 acres and the other 20 acres adjoining William **Qualls**, Hanson **Harris**, Obadiah **Winston**. The following persons are heirs of this land: Nancy H., Flavius Josephus **Bailey** both minors. She was allotted 198 acres Jan. 14, 1840.

138- 139- 140- Lucretia **Mayes**, widow of William **Mayes**, who died Dec. 24 1839, - leaving widow Lucretia and the following children: Mary Ann, wife of Robert A. **Jones**, Jno. B. **Mayes**, E. R. **Mayes**, Martha N. **Mayes**, William W., Francis E., and Virginia C. **Mayes** (the last three minors). Lucretia **Mayes** asks dower in lands. Allotted 287 acres Feb. 26, 1840.

140- 141, 142- - Feb. term 1839- Elizabeth **Blanks**, widow of Richard **Blanks** deceased, who died leaving wife and the following children: Samuel, Mary A., Jane who married Thomas **Stokes**, Sarah who married James **Watson**, Richard **Blanks**, Nancy who married James **Winfree**, Elizabeth who married James L. **Ramsey**, Susan who married Logustin P. **Pool** and Joseph **Blanks**. Widow asks dower in lands of deceased husband- given 336 ¾ths acres Feb. 19, 1840.

377

142- thru 144- Feb. term 1833- Eliza **Kittrell** widow of Benjamin **Kittrell** deceased, who died Mar. 1836, in Oxford where he lived and died and was possessed of that house and lot and other land in Wake Co. 300 acres and the widow does not want the land in Wake but asks as dower the lot and mansion house in Oxford, N. C. - Benjamin **Kittrell** is survived by children named: Melissa, Joseph, Benjamin and Louise **Kittrell**, minors. She was given the lot and house in Oxford. May 2, 1838.

144- thru 146- Nov. term 1837- Dorcas **Searcey**, widow of Hargrove **Searcey**, deceased, who died May 1836 leaving a widow and daughter Mary wife of Joseph **Fletcher**, Sally another daughter, and widow of ----- **Hedgepeth**. **Searcey** died possessed of 200 acres of land at line of Wyatt **Canaday**, John **Davis** and James **Jenkin** lands. The widow asks dower and was given 54 acres. June 24, 1840.

147- 148- Aug. court 1840- Jinsey **Dean**, widow of Jesse C. **Dean**, deceased who died in 1838 possessed of 60 acres adjoining Wm. Joseph **Dean** and others, asks dower and is given 20 acres Sept. 29, 1840.

148- 149, 150- Mary A. **Lewis** widow of James **Lewis**, deceased, and who died possessed of 1800 acres of land, asks her dower in land. She was allotted 742 acres being 1/3rd of all land. Oct. 1, 1840.

150- thru 152- May term 1840- Susan **Hart**, widow of John G. **Hart**, deceased, who died in April possessed of 440 acres of land. Asks her dower in land and was allotted 144 acres May 25, 1840.

152- 153- Elizabeth **Williams** widow of William B. **Williams**, deceased, who died in 1840 possessed of land bought of Adnah **Robertson** June 18, 1835. Asks dower right in land. William B. **Williams** has heirs at law namely a sister Phebe **Williams** and a sister Elizabeth who married Harvey **Harris**. Widow allotted 572 square yards. Dec. 16, 1840.

154- thru 156-, Nov. term 1840- Mary A. **Lewis** widow of James **Lewis** who died June 1840 leaving the widow Mary A. **Lewis** and children: Edward A. **Lewis** (minor) and Sarah Ann wife of James M. **Bullock**: Widow asks division of the 68 negroes left by deceased, that she may have her share for her lifetime. Negroes divided and allotted Feb. 1841.

157- Nov. term 1840- James **Farrow** and wife Lucy, Madison **Daniel** and wife Argen, James H. **Wiggins** (minor) state that Theophilus H. **Wiggins** died in Washington Co., Georgia in 1839 and excr. of estate became John B. **Debriana**-Petition for division of negroes to them. Granted.

158- thru 162- Nov. term 1840- William **Flemming** and wife Frances, Pamelia **Bullock**, wife of Leonard **Bullock** (deceased), Phillip P. **Bullock**, Willis B. **Mitchell** and wife Susan, Obadiah **Winston** and wife Pamelia, Agnes **Bullock**, Sarah **Bullock**, Weldon E. **Bullock**, Christian **Bullock**, Mildred **Bullock**, and Mary L. **Bullock** (last 4- minors) against Edward **Bullock**, Eliza, widow of Benjamin **Bullock**, Albert **Sneed** and wife Maria, Walter **Mangum** and wife Eliza, Erasmus D. **Bullock**, Alexander H. **Bullock**, Walter A. **Bullock** (minor), Robert **Harris** and wife Catherine, Ann A. **Bullock** and Robert **Lee** and wife Jane, Ann **Dolby**- - Micajah **Bullock** had five children to survive him, namely Frances F. **Fleming**, Leonard **Bullock** (who had died since death of sd Micajah), Edward **Bullock**, Ann **Dolby** and Benjamin **Bullock** (who has died since the death of Micajah **Bullock**)- Leonard **Bullock** left survivors: his widow Pamelia and children, Phillip P., Agnes, Sarah, Weldon E., Christian, Mildred, Mary L. **Bullock** and Susan who married Willis B. **Mitchell**, Pamelia who married Obadiah **Winston**, the minors represented by their guardian Clement **Wilkins**.
Benjamin **Bullock** left survivors: Eliza, his widow and children Maria, wife of Albert **Sneed**, Eliza, wife of Walter **Mangum**, Erasmus D. **Bullock**, Alexander H. **Bullock**, Catherine, wife of Robert **Harris**, Jane, wife of Robert **Lee**, Ann A. **Bullock** and Walter A. **Bullock**- Ask division of two tracts of land to them, in five equal parts. Allotted to them Apr. 28, 1841. Plat on next page- -

378
84¼ acres in left tract—143 in right plat- - divided to heirs of Micajah **Bullock**, the elder, deceased. Apr. 28, 1841 -

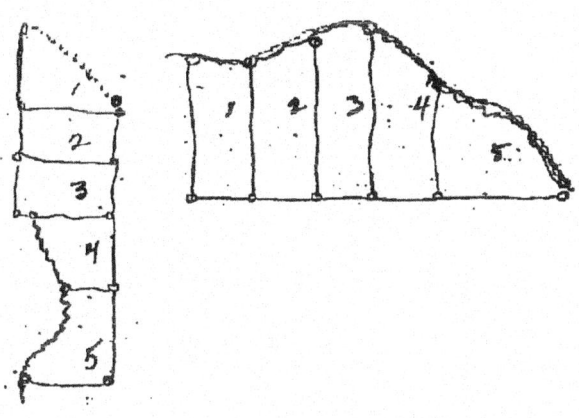

163- 164- Reuben **Smith** die in Granville Co., N. C. in 1820 - leaving a will bequeathing to his wife Elizabeth, for her lifetime, certain negro property and at her death was to go to son Joel **Smith** and dau. Nancy **Smith** who married Bennitt **Smith** and Polly who married Stephen **Dodson**. Elizabeth **Smith** is now dead. Joel **Smith** is also dead leaving as survivors: Reuben **Smith**, Catherine **Smith** who married Henry T. **Smith**, Alexander **Smith**, Joel R. **Smith**, Caroline **Smith** who married W. J. G. **Baynham**, his children and heirs at law. Stephen **Dodson** has been appointed admstr of estate. We petition the court to divide negroes to us as heirs of Joel **Smith** deceased and Bennitt **Smith** who married Nancy sister of Joel **Smith** and daughter of Reuben and Elizabeth **Smith**, and to Stephen **Dodson** who married Polly, daughter of Reuben and sister of Joel **Smith** both deceased as is the mother of Polly, Elizabeth **Smith** deceased. divided and allotted Nov. 24, 1840.

165- May term- 1841- - Daniel T. **Gooch** and wife Nancy. Robert **Hester** died in March 1841 leaving widow Nancy **Hester** and a daughter Nancy who married Daniel T. **Gooch**- - - Ask that dower in land be allotted to the widow Nancy **Hester** in lands belonging to Robert **Hester** deceased. She was allotted 104 acres June 1, 1841.

167- 168- John C. **Taylor** and James H. **Taylor** ask division of negroes left them by their father John **Taylor** Sr., deceased, who died in 1837- willing to them all negroes since he had already allotted to his dau. Agnes B. **Taylor** in his lifetime- Will: was probated May 1837- Allotted to them Aug. 1841.

169- Aug. 1841- Amos T., Ruffin T., and Duffy **Jones** minors by their guardian Daniel A. **Paschall**, ask that the land upon which their father Thomas **Jones**, now deceased, lived and died and which they own jointly as per will of Amos **Gooch** as may be determined by reference to his will on probate in Granville Co., N. C. - Divided and allotted them Oct. 28, 1841 See next page for plat- - -
Lot. 1- to Amos T. **Jones**- - lot 2 to Ruffin **Jones**- - lot 3-to Duffy **Jones**.

379
  Land of Amos **Gooch**, deceased, given to Amos T., Ruffin and Duffy **Jones** sons of Thomas **Jones** Decd. Divided to them Oct. 28, 1841

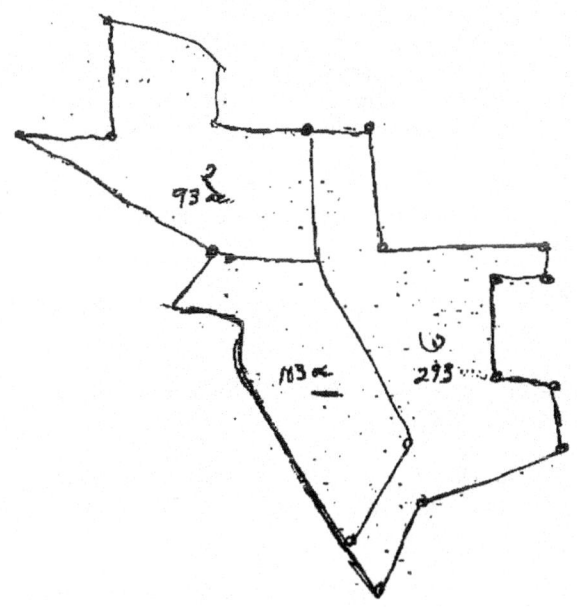

  171, 172- Dec. 9, 1840- proved Nov. court 1841
George **Wood**- - - - wills to wife Nancy, all estate for lifetime or her widowhood, then to be sold and divided between my four children: William C., A. S., Mary A. E., Richard S. **Wood** and the last two named to have a horse also.
Exrs: William **Terry** and my son Wm. C. **Wood**.
Wts: Stephen **Terry**, Yancey **Oakley**.

380
  172- 173- Apr. 20, 1841- proved Nov. court 1841
Charles **Bullock**- - - - wills to daughter Nancy **Goss**, in addition to that already given, a negro slave; to daughter Mary **Forsythe**, the negro I have already given her and the half of two others; to son James, 2 negros; to son Jerimiah, 2 negroes, the land whereon I live, 200 acres, a bed and furniture and live stock: to son Joshua, the other half of negroes given daughter Mary **Forsythe** and the negro he already has; to son James in trust for daughter Susan **Laws** and her children, in addition to that already given her, $250.00 and a negro slave; To granddaughter Louisa **Laws**, 2 negroes, a bed and covering; to son- in- law Jonathan **Laws**, $1.00; Anything left and not herein willed away or been given away to be sold and money divided between all my children.
Exrs: sons James and Jeremiah **Bullock**.

Wts: Wm. A. **Gill**, George **Bullock**

174- thru 178- Inv. of debts due and money of estate of Sarah **Dean** deceased, and articles sold Oct. 27, 1841- mentions money due from the heirs of Jesse C. **Dean**, deceased- by Hamilton **Hester**, admstr.

179- thru 185- Inv. and sale of estate of Edward **Jones**, deceased, June 18, 1841- mentions among buyers William, Edward Jr., Littleton Y., Thomas, Alfred, Allen, Henry W., Abner N. M. **Jones**- returned to Nov. court 1841.

185- 189- Inv. and sale of estate of Lucrecia **Mays**, deceased, by Lunsford A. **Paschall**, admstr. Oct. 8, 1841- among buyers were Eliza, John B., Martha, Virginia, Francis, William **Mays**, Robert **Mays**.

189- thru 193- Inv. of estate of Edward **Burton**, deceased, May 7, 1841 by P. E. **Jones** admstr. - sold May 29, 1841.

194- thru 195- Acct. current of Benjamin F. **Bullock** admstr. of Richard H. **Bullock**, deceased, Oct. 27, 1841.

195- thru 197- Sale of property of Jonathan **Tippitt**, deceased, Aug, 28, 1841- mentions among buyers Mary, Thomas, John, Betsy, Eli **Tippett** by John H. **Tippett**, admstr.

198- May 31, 1841- Inv. of estate of Mrs. Margaret **Daniel**- cash from W. G. **Thomas** excr. of estate of late Thomas **Daniel** decd. to D. J. **Young**, admstr.

198- Estate of John C. **Thompson** by Jno. **Bullock** excr. Nov. court 1841.

199- Estate of James **Lewis**, deceased, by James M. **Bullock**, admstr.-from July 1840- Paid J. C. **Thompson** for preaching funeral sermon. Nov. 1841.

203- thru 210- Inv. and acct. of sales of property of estate of Sarah **Smith**, deceased, Dec. 1, 1841- by John **Lewis**, admstr. returned to February court 1842.

211- thru 215- Sale and negroes of estate of John **Minor**, deceased, by Robert **Longmire** and Wm. **Clement**, admstrs. Nov. 29, 30, 1841- mentions Jo, Mrs. Massa **Minor** and Joseph **Minor** among buyers, also David **Minor**, Henry **Minor**.

216- thru 222- Oct. 13, 1841- Inv. of estate of Charles **Bullock** by James **Bullock**, excr. and that sold Nov. 8, 1842.

223- thru 225- Inv. and acct of sales of estate of Hezekiah **Hobgood** deceased, Nov. 28, 1841 mentions among buyers William, Sarah, William, Thomas, Henry, Fowler **Hobgood**. By James B. **Hobgood**, admstr.

Estate Records of Granville Co, NC Volume 13-16   87

226- 227- Sale of Property of George **Thomason** Sr. deceased, Oct. 4, 1841 by Jas. **Thomason** admstr.

228- Dec. 10, 1841- Sale of estate of Samuel J. **Harris** (perishable goods) deceased, by Benj. F. **Harris**, admstr.

229- 230- Leonard **Bullock**, deceased, estate in acct. with William **Fleming** admstr- from Nov. court 1837 and settlement made for year Nov. term 1841 returned to Feb. court 1842.

231- 232- Sale of estate of Peter **West**, deceased, by Susan **West** and Flemeng **Beasley** exctrs. Oct. 20, 1841- mentions James, Thomas and Joseph **West** among buyers.

233- Sale of property of Edward **Jones**, deceased, - Sept. 1, 1841- by John **Sherman** and William **Parrish**.

381

233 thru 235- Sale of estate of Martha **Philpott**, deceased, by Samuel **Philpott**, admstr. Dec.- 3, 1841- mentions Simeon, W. A. **Philpott** among buyers.

235- Inv. of estate of Charles I. **Wilkerson**, deceased, by David J. **Young** Dec. 16, 1841-

235- Inv. of Judy **Lemon**, Deceased by Joseph M. W. **Smith** admstr. - Feb. term 1842.

236- Nov. court 1841- Petition- Henry C. **Ray** and wife, Dorris **Canaday** admstr of Anderson **Bailey**, deceased, and Duncan **Cannaday** guardian of Nancy G. and Flavius J. **Bailey**- - ask division of negroes of estate of Anderson **Bailey** deceased, among the legatees above. Dec. 23, 1841.

237- Estate of Gideon **Gill** deceased, by John **White** and Lemuel **McGehee** admstrs. Feb. 1, 1842 mentions years support for Polly **Gill**.

238- Estate of John **Suit**, deceased, by William **Suit**, excr. Feb. 3, 1842.

238, thru 240- Sale of estate of Elizabeth **Blackwell**, deceased, by William M. **Blackwell** admstr. Nov. 12, 1841- mentions among buyers, John P. **Blackwell**, Benj. C. **Cooke** and others.

240 thru 241- current acct. of estate of Richard **Wood**, deceased, by Shadrack **Parrish**, admstr. Nov. 1841- mentions trip to Tennessee.

241, 242- Inv. and sale of estate of Robert **Sandford**, deceased, by Robert **Harris** and Robert **Sandford**, excrs. mentions property left to wife Mary **Sandford**, deceased. Returned Aug. 1841 mentions as buyers John Y. **Sandford**.

243, 244- Estate of Sally **Smith** - deceased- division of negroes- - To Mary Eliza **Lewis** daughter of Col. John **Lewis**, William A. **Taylor** son of Capt. John **Taylor**, James A. **Taylor** son of William **Taylor**, William R. **Taylor** son of William **Taylor**, Samuel **Taylor** son of William **Taylor**, to Sally daughter of William **Taylor**, Edward son of William **Taylor** and heirs of John H. **Taylor**- John H **Taylor** son of Major William **Taylor**, died before will of Mrs. **Taylor** was recorded and shortly after Mrs. **Smith** died, and we aren't sure he is entitled to a share.

244 thru 246- Acct of estate of Simeon **Cozart**, deceased, by Allen **Cozart** admstr. Aug. court 1840- lists the amount paid by Simeon **Cozart** deceased, for other shares of estate of Hubbard **Cozart** deceased, over his share of estate. Cash paid for horse for Mary **Cozart**-

246- 247- Negroes of estate of Thomas **Jones** deceased, divided among his children, Dec. 27, 1841- Widows portion allotted to her and rest of negroes to Amos T. T., Riffin and Duffy **Jones**, also Lotus and Thomas **Jones**.

247- May court 1841- Estate of Kesiah **Yancey**, deceased, by Charles **Yancey** admstr.

249- Mar. 4, 1839- proved Feb. court 1842-
Eady **Adcock**- - - wills to Nicholas G., son of Henry W. **Jones**, a bed and furniture, a chest, 7 chairs, a pot and an oven and all livestock; To David P. **Jones** a horse and $20.00- ; to Solomon W. **Jones**, $20.00; to William H. **Jones**, a bed and furniture; To Sary, wife of Henry W. **Jones** a horse, earthenware, knives and forks and clothes; To Nancy, daughter of Henry W. **Jones**, my side saddle; To Henry W. **Jones** all my crop and residue of property at my death.
Exrs: Henry W. **Jones**.
Wts: William **Clement**, L. **Bennett**.

250- Estate of William **Hockaday**, by James **Wyche** Nov. 7, 1837.

251- thru 261- Estate of Richard **Bullock**, deceased, and sale of property which came to William **Russell**, admstr, Nov. 24, 1841. He had $740.00 of railroad script on Western and Atlantic Railroad of Georgia- John **Rudd** bought a great portion of property, Thomas **Parrish** also, also Minerva who bought a piano, and Martha bought beds etc also Joshua B. and George **Bullock**, Capt. James **Bullock**.

262 Inv. of estate of Thomas **Coghill** deceased, by Lucy **Coghill** and Robert P. **Hughes**, excrs. Feb. 8, 1842.

382
264 thru 268- Sale of estate of Thomas **Cogbill**, deceased by Lucy **Cogbill** and Robert. P. **Hughes**- Mar. 4, 1842- by excrs.

Estate Records of Granville Co, NC Volume 13-16

269 thru 273- Inv. and sales of estate of N. N. **Southall**, deceased, by W. W. **Voss**, admstr. Feb. 10, 1842- Mrs. **Southall** refused to turn over a gold watch and was sued for same, among buyers were Mary **Southall**.

274, 275- Acct of sales of estate of Israel **Estes** by Jeremiah **Estes** admstr. May court 1842.

275- thru 277- Estate of Anderson J. **Duncan**, deceased, by Wm. H. **Webb** admstr- - Inv. and sale - mentions disputed interest in George **Duncan** estate and land whereon John B. **Duncan** lives- Buyers included Sterling H., Elizabeth **Duncan**- sold Mar. 10, 1842.

277 thru 279- Sale of estate of Alfred **Hester**, deceased, Mar. 4, 1842- by Samuel **Hunt** Jr., Admstr. Hamilton, Mary, Francis G. **Hester** among buyers at sale.

279- 280- Estate of Jacob **Vincent**, deceased, by John **White** excr.

281- 282- Negro hire of estate of Capt. Benjamin **Hester** deceased, for 1842- by Bennett **Hester** admstr.

282- Hire of negroes of estate of Phebe **Morris**, deceased, by Stephen **Morris** admstr May court 1842.

283 to 285- Estate of Anderson **Bailey**, deceased by Dorris **Canaday** admstr- Sale Dec. 22, 1837 thru May 1842- mentions Cynthia G. **Bailey**.

285- Inv. of estate of Sally **Ford**, deceased, by Wm. H. **Webb** Admstr May court 1842- and sale of property.

285- Inv. of estate of Nancy **Williams**, by Wm. H. **Webb** May court 1842 and sale of property.

287- 288- May 14, 1838 proved May court 1842- John **Minor**- - - - wills to daughter Clary **Johnson**, all estate real and personal which I have in my possession and 11 negroes she has in her possession. At my death negroes sold and money divided between my wife Massey **Minor**, Marshal **Minor**, Clary **Johnson**, John **Minor**, Lazerus **Minor**, Polly **Bledsoe**, Francis **Wilkins**, Elizabeth **Beardan**, Annie **Wood**, Tabitha **Blackwood**, Jinsey **Williams**; heirs of son Randal **Minor**- $100.00 and what they have already had from me; To Robert **Longmire** and Wm. **Clement** $50.00 each and they executors.
Wts: Thomas **Reeks**, William W. **Craft**.
Objection to probate by Henry **Minor** and others- Nov. term 1841- - Jury decided in favor of will and probated May court 1842.

289- Sale of negroes of estate of John **Minor** deceased, by Robert **Longmire** and Wm. **Clement** excrs. May court 1842.

290- thru 291- May court 1842- Acct. of Wardens of Poor of Granville county for the year.

291 thru 294- July 10, 1838- proved Feb. court 1842
Thomas **Coghill** - - - - wills to wife Lucy, negroes, live stock, 3 horses, harness and carriage, furniture, years support from produce but in case she marry then all returns to my estate. I lend her the land whereon I live and at her death or if she re- marry then to my daughter Mary and son- in- law Lewis **Reavis**; To Robert **Hughes** in trust for support of daughter Sally **McGraw** and her children, certain negroes. The live stock and furniture I have given my daughter and also 400 acres and also 250 acres I bought of **Haywood**, and Robert to hold land and negroes for my said daughter Sally; At death of my daughter Sally that left in trust divided to her children or sold and money divided between them, and each child to have their portion as come of age; to- son- in law John **Dedman** & dau. Damsel, certain negroes, and land I bought of Thomas **Brain**, and at her death to her children and if she die without children then to son- in- law; To son- in- law Robert **Hughes** and my dau. Lucy his wife, certain negroes, and land and at her death to her children or her husband do with it what he think best; To son- in- law Lewis **Reavis** and dau. Mary, negroes and land I lent my wife at her death and small tract bought of Cearn **Clark** and at her death to her children. To grson Lafayette **McGraw** a horse.
Exrs: wife Lucy, son- in- law Robt. **Hughes**.
Wts: William **Robards**, William T. **Vaughn**.

383
294 thru 296- June 2, 1842- proved Aug. court 1842
Susan **Eaton**- - - - wills to son Thomas R. **Eaton**, negroes, land whereon I live which formerly belonged to my mother, Mrs. Mary **Somerville**, and at his death to go to his children; to son Thomas R., all crop, live stock, plantation tools, household furniture and my son is to pay anything due on purchase price of the land I am giving him, and he to waive any claim he has against his father, for this is in addition to that given him by the will of his father; To son John S. **Eaton**, the residue of my estate and he to pay all my debts except that mentioned above and all debts of estate of my deceased husband.
Exrs: son John S. **Eaton**.
Wts: William **Eaton** Jr., John **Bullock**.

296 thru 298- June 16, 1842- proved Aug. court 1842.
William **Robards** - - - - wills to have his son Horace L. **Robards** as executor of this will (he to sell enough negroes to pay debts); To. daughter Jane **Royster**, wife of Stephen S. **Royster**, ½ of my *LaGrange* tract and the other half to my son Henry J. **Robards**, and To Jane and her husband several negroes; To Jane **Royster** furniture, ½ of stock and of crop except tobacco, a carriage and a pr. of horses; To son Henry J. **Robards** several negroes. Thomas **Miller** and I have divided the negroes but our account is not confirmed and is not binding on my legatees, and if any loss in name of **Robards** and **Miller** for work done on Railroad and James River and Kanawaha Canal Co., it is be accounted equally for all interested; to son Horace L. **Roberds**,

land called "Horseshoe" on Tar river and he to pay the last bond due on land, also several negroes; To son George W. **Robards** of Williamsborough, all the mill tract on Littel Nut Bush excepting 40 acres with dwelling house which I give my son Henry James **Robards** ; If Horace L. **Robards** die, I appoint Thomas **Miller** and William H. **Robards** Jr., Stephen Sampson **Royster** husband of my daughter Jane as executors. My son Horace may sell the land I am entitled to on Mattamuskeet Lake and divide money among my children, also sell my right in 30,000 acres called "*The South Mountain Speculation*" being ¼th of 1/3rd of the acreage, also sell the gold mine called *Hard Bargain* and the one called *Edwards Place* and one called **Robards** *Castle* and land on which Dr. **Satterwhite** now resides, also sell or lease 1/3rd of the *Moores Mine* including 4 acres which I hold individually; balance of tract 200 acres with **Hodges** heirs and Nathaniel **Robards**, also lease or sell the *Bryanville Gold mine*, and any tract I may own an interest in of gold or copper mines which have not already been mentioned.
signed Col. William **Robards**.
Wts: John R. **Hicks**, Thomas **Turner**, Benjamin **Best**.

299, 300- Mar. 4, 1838- proved Aug. court 1842.
Mary D. **Hester** - - - wills to Lewis and Robert **Parham**, sons of the late Samuel R. **Parham**, negroes; To Mary **Crews** wife of Capt. Meredith **Crews** and daughter of Benjamin **Thomason**, certain negro slaves, featherbeds and furniture and a chest; to Bennet **Hester**, negro slaves; to Mary wife of Joseph **Howard**, negro slaves; To Robert **Tally** son of Reuben **Tally** deceased, $200.00; All else to Mary **Howard** wife of Joseph **Howard** after debts and legacies paid.
Exrs: Joseph **Howard**, Lewis **Parham**.
Wts: John R. **Hicks**, James **Cooper**.
Apr. 9, 1839- To daughter, Mary **Howard** negroes I recently bought of H. **Hester** and at her death to heirs of her body.
Wts: James **Cooper**.

301, 302- Nov. 13, 1840- proved Aug. court 1842.
Elizabeth **Royster** - - - - wills to daughter Martha **Farrow** $1.00 and to lawful female heirs of her body namely; Elizabeth, Emily, Mildred, Matilda, Martha and Fanny **Farrow** and any other born, my negro and its increase and remainder of my estate after debts paid- To lawful males of her body namely; Absalom, Cicero and any other born $1.00 each; my property

384
kept together for support of my daughter Martha and until courts think best to appoint trustees.
Exrs; Banister and M. D. **Royster**, my sons.
Wts: Henry **Yancey**, Willis A. **Royster**.

302- Nov. 11, 1841- proved Aug. court 1842.
Linsey **Butler**- - - - wills to her two beloved sisters Nancy and Elizabeth **Butler**, after debts paid, all I possess.

Wts: M. D. **Royster**, Richard H. **Richards**.

303- July 7, 1842- proved Aug. court 1842.
Pompret **Edwards**- - - - wills to wife Betsey, land whereon I live, all live stock, furniture, crop and other property for her lifetime and at her death equally divided to all my children except my daughter Dilly married to Littleton **Forkner** and that loaned to them be returned to my wife unless he or they pay the $50.00 he owes and for which I am security.
Exrs: wife Betsy.
Wts: John S. **Eaton**, R. M. **Chapman**, H. J. **Robards**.

304- June 18, 1842- proved Aug. court 1842.
Edwin **King**- - - - wills to Mary, daughter of Col. P. E. A. and Mary F. **Jones** all my possessions which consists of house and lot in Henderson, N. C. a negro with sister in Northampton Co., N. C., 263 acres in Halifax County which I bought of E. **Drumgold**, live stock, furniture which I bought of Samuel **Westray's** sale and he still has; After all is sold the money is to buy negroes for her, for her and her heirs forever and not be contracted by her husband if she marry.
Exrs: P. E. A. **Jones**.
Wts: William J. **Hawkins**, William **Abbott**, H. T. **Royster**.

305, 306- Inv. and sale of estate of Howel **Briggs**, deceased, by J. M. **Satterwhite** admstr. June 24, 1842- mentions among buyers Solomon **Satterwhite**, Henry and Lucy **Briggs**.

306 thru 309- Sale of estate of Robert **Wilson**- deceased, by Samuel P. and Solomon G. **Wilson** admstrs. June 4, 1842- mentions Ritter **Wilson** and Rebecca **Wilson** as buyers at sale, lists negroes and stock.

310 Estate of John **Bradford**, deceased May 12, 1842- acct. made by excr.

311- Current acct. of estate of Daniel **Parker**, hiring negroes- by John **Sherman** admstr Feb. 28, 1842.

311 thru 313- Current acct. of estate of John **Barker**, deceased by John G. and Charles **Barker**, excrs. Aug. 2, 1842.

312- thru 314- Estate of Judith **Bradford**, deceased, acct. by William D. **Allen**, admstr. Aug. 2, 1842.

315- Estate of William A. **Norwood** deceased, by William **Barnett**, admstr. Aug. court 1842- says he received nothing of estate.

315- thru 318- Petition of William **Dean**, Moses **Carnal** and wife Margaret, John **Carnal** and wife Elizabeth, Joseph R. **Dean** by guardian Hamilton **Hester** against Jesse **Dean**, minor child of Jesse C. **Dean**, deceased- - - Stating that: Jesse

Dean, minor child of Jesse Colin **Dean** and the petitioners are heirs of Jesse C. **Dean**, deceased who died possessed of 137 acres of land, being the dower land of Sarah **Dean**, widow of late Jesse C. **Dean**, deceased. They ask division of land to them all. Granted and divided into 5 parts-
No.1. to Elizabeth **Carnal** Wife of John **Carnal**, formerly Elizabeth **Dean**-
No.2- to - Joseph R. **Dean**-
No.3- to Margeret wife of Moses **Carnal** formerly Margaret **Dean**-
Lot 4 to Jesse C. **Dean**s heirs-
5 to William **Dean**- See Plat of land division on page following, no 293 (sic)

318- thru 321- Petition of Woodson, John, Ephraim (minor) **Washington**, George **Washington** (minor) ask that guardian be appointed for two minor children and state that William **Washington**, father of them all, died after having bequeathed certain property that is 3 tracts of land and they the sons above to whom he bequeathed the land, are to pay to the daughters of their father (their sisters) each their rateable part of the value of land- ask that land be valued and allotted to them-

385
Division of land of Jesse C. **Dean**, deceased, to his children and heirs, Feb. 15, 1842 and Sarah **Dean**, widow of Jesse **Dean**.- See P.292 [sic].

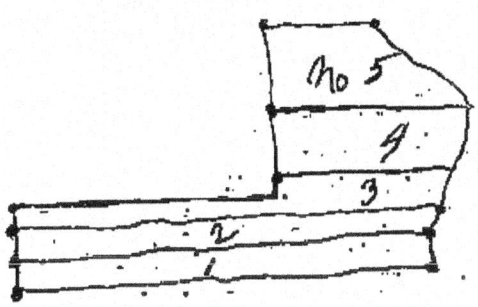

Page 318 continued-- The land of William **Washington**, deceased, divided and allotted to his heirs, his children-
Lot No. 1 to George **Washington** and he pay to sisters Alsey and Emant **Washington**.
Lot No. 2 to John **Washington** and he to pay to sisters Demaris, Elizabeth and Roan **Washington**.
Lot No. 3 to Ephraim **Washington** and he to pay to sisters Celestia, Roane and Emant **Washington**.
Lot No 4- to Woodson **Washington** and he pays his sisters Mary Ann and Alsey **Washington**.

321 thru 324- Petition of Triplett **Estes** and wife Elizabeth against Horace T., William J., Indianna E. and Horace T. **Royster** Jr. the last three named being minor children of Horace T. **Royster** Sr. above named- - - State that William **Jones** died in 1829 and will was proved with Thomas W. **Norman** and William **Sneed** excrs, of will. **Sneed** alone qualified- probated Nov. 1829- In Feb. 1830, the petitioner Elizabeth entered dissent and filed for dower and distributive share of her husband, William **Jones**, deceased, estate. There were 3 tracts of land and Elizabeth, then widow of William **Jones**, was allotted the tract with the mansion house thereon and her right in lands. There was also another tract of land on Ruin Creek containing 925 acres subject to life estate of Mrs. Sarah **Norman**; Elizabeth, the widow of William **Jones** now Elizabeth **Estes**, asks for her dower right in the 925 acres, since she was allotted land only in the three above said tracts but is due to have dower right also in the other land- - Remainder of land was devised by William **Jones** to his daughter Indianna wife of Horace T. **Royster**, who has since died and left surviving her, her husband and the following children; William James **Royster**, Indiana E. W. **Royster** and Horace T. **Royster** Jr.- Sarah **Norman** is also dead, and the land is now held by Horace T. **Royster** as tenant by courtesy of wife Indianna- - deceased- - Elizabeth **Jones**, widow of William, has married Triplett **Estes**- - and asks her dower right in the 925 acres. She was given 238 acres of land.

325- Estate of Thomas **Coghill**, deceased, -negroes valued and allotted to legatees; John B. **Stedman** and wife, Lucy **Coghill**, Lewis **Reavis** and wife, to Frank **McGraw's** children, Robert P. **Hughes** and wife- Mar. 1842.

325- thru 227- Petition Feb. term 1842- Petition of Sarah **Hobgood** widow of Hezekiah **Hobgood**, deceased- - - states that Hezekiah **Hobgood** died in 1841 possessed- of 454 acres on Mill Creek, and asks for her dower in land. Allotted 151 acres.

327 thru 329- Petition of William **Blackwell**, John P. **Blackwell** and William **Wortham** and wife Fanny A. **Wortham**- - - stating that during the present year, Elizabeth **Blackwell**, mother of the petitioners, departed this life, leaving estate and William **Blackwell** became admstr as she left no will, and part of estate are slave that can be divided between them without sale and the perishable property is ordered sold - - -

386
Petitioners ask that slave be divided between them, and also to divide to them all other property not sold. Granted and allotted to them by commissioners appointed for that purpose, Nov. 11, 1841.

329 thru 332- Petition Nov. term 1841- by Susan **Hart**, James A. **Hart**, James **Shotwell** and wife Rebecca, John and Amy **Hart** (minors) by their guardian Maurice S. **Hart**, against Thomas **Bennett** admstr of estate of John G. **Hart**, deceased, and William **Royster** and wife Ann, Susan G. **Hart**. State that John G. **Hart** died intestate, leaving Susan **Hart**, his widow and the following children; namely: James

A. **Hart**, Rebecca who married James **Shotwell**, John **Hart** and Amy **Hart** (minors) and under guardianship of Maurice S. **Hart**, Ann, wife of William **Royster**, and Susan G. **Hart**- - Ask division of negroes- - division made and allotted them. There were seven lots- - Dec. 24, 1841.

332, 333- Nov. court 1841 - Petition of Margaret H., Mary S., Elizabeth B. and John E. **Freear** (minors) by their guardian John S. **Eaton** who are all tenants in common of negro slaves, and ask division of same. Division was made and allotted to each of the four children Dec. 1841.

334- Aug. 5, 1842- Joseph H. **Gooch** elected, Sheriff of Granville Co. with bondsman; William **Clement**, Elijah **Hester**, Samuel **Philpott**, McVey **Chandler**, Fleming **Beasley**, William H. **Lyon**, Lyndon S. **Philpott** and Carter **Waller**-

335 - same as above- - also 336

337- July 16, 1842- proved Nov. court 1842.
John A. **Norwood**- - - Wills to wife Penelope, 1/3rd of all land I die possessed of, also a childs part which is 1/7th of my personal property for life, and at her death divided to my daughters: Harriett, Mary, Parthena, Catherine, Arabella **Norwood**; to brother Benjamin **Norwood** Jr. 1/6th part of balance of my personal property to hold in trust for my daughter Pheby **Wilson**; To above name daughters all balance of my property, also the property which will fall as my portion of my father's estate at his death.
Exrs: brother Benjamin **Norwood** Jr.
Wts: Robert A. **Jenkins**, Elijah **Barnett**.
Benjamin **Norwood** relinquished- right as excr. and Robert A. **Jenkins** became admstr.

338- Oct. 31, 1842- proved Nov. 1842.
Mary A. **Hargrove** ----to sister Nancy J. my negro Jesse; To the heirs of my sister Nancy J. when she is dead that which I have left her;
Exr: Israel W. **Hargrove**.
Wts: Samuel W. **Smith**, Charles **Sturdivant**.

339, 340- May 17, 1839- proved Nov. court 1842.
Polly **Mallory**- - - - wills to have my debt to my brother James paid which is with interest for 10 yrs, which would have been paid long ago but I did not know who to pay it to, the sum with interest is the principle $24.67 and interest 14.50 and the debt I owe my brother John, he has my bond for 118.89 ½ bearing interest from May 1, 1839; My brother John told Father in his life time that he would never call on me to pay and he tell me the same thing but I want it paid; When all is paid I want the rest to be put in hands of sister Betsey; The negro man that father left me a half of, I wish to have liberty to choose his master. If my sister Betsey wastes this left her, then the executors to sell it and divide the money among all my sisters and brothers and their children that is the children they had by their first wives or first husbands. Brother Williams part to his daughter Mary Ann; sister Aggy is dead, but I want her children

to have her part;
Exr: my brother John **Mallory**
Wts: Meredith **Crews**, William B. **Crews**.

340, 341- Sept. 22, 1842- proved Nov. court 1842
Lucy **Bullock**- - wills to sister Susan **Jiggetts**, my bureau and $600.00.

387
To my sister Lucy **Lewis** my new imported carpet and $600.00; to son John **Bullock**, in trust for my son William H. **Bullock**, my mahogany bedstead and $1200.00; to son James M. the land I bought of John **Bullock** and my locker and to him in trust for my daughter Fanny Ann **Hunt**, during her life so as not to be liable for her husbands debts or his able to sell it, that is her husband John T. **Hunt**, my easy chair, and negro woman with her three children and all their increase and at death of my daughter, to go to her daughters; to grandson William B. **Inge**, $600.00; All else divided to my living children namely; John **Bullock**, Susan **Jiggetts**, Lucy **Lewis**, James M. **Bullock**, William H. **Bullock** and Fanny Ann **Hunt**; That to the last two be kept in trust for them by James and John **Bullock**.
Exrs: son John **Bullock**.
Wts: Fanny A. **Lewis**, John J. **Speed**, William M. **Walker**.

341, 342- Estate of William B. **Williams** by admstr. John B. **Moore** from Sept. 1842 - listing sale Feb. 10, 1841- and years support for Elizabeth **Williams**- Sept. court 1842.

342- 343- Aug. court 1842- Estate of Sarah **Roffe** deceased, by James **Gooch** admstr- mentions sale of Nov. 24, 1841.

344 thru 346 - Inv. of personal estate of William **Robards**, deceased by Horace L. **Robards** excr- - mentions note of Julian **Haylander** now Mrs. **Dewey**- and one large bible lister among Inv. Nov. court 1842.

347- Nov. court 1842- Inv. of personal estate of George **Wood**, deceased by William C. **Wood**, excr.

347- Aug. 4, 1842- Inv. and sale of estate of James M. **Estes**, bought by Jeremiah **Estes**.

348- Nov. 2, 1842- Inv. and sale of estate of Pomphret **Edwards**, deceased, by Elizabeth **Edwards**, excrtx.

349- Aug. 4, 1842- Inv. of estate of Edwin **King** by Protheus E. A. **Jones** excr. returned Nov. 11, 1842.

350- Inv. of Mary **Hester's** property by Joseph **Howard** excr. Nov. 1842.

Estate Records of Granville Co, NC Volume 13-16

351- 352- Aug. term 1842- Petition of Rebecca **Wilson**, widow of Robert **Wilson** deceased- Stating that Robert **Wilson** is dead and left a widow surviving- that he possessed 2 tracts of land; one of 1,024 acres adjoining lands of Pleasant **Rowland**, James T. **Starke**, Charles E. **Hamilton**, William **Wilson**, Robert **Wilson**- and Howel and James **Satterwhite**, whereon stands the mansion house, and a tract of 413 acres- - Asks her dower right and that the heirs at law namely; Ritter, Benjamin and wife Lethe, Temperance who married ..... **Usery**, Stephen, Samuel, Jemima who married Ambrose **Barker**, Mildred who married John C. **Lemay**, Solomon, Lundy who married David **Knott**, Susan and Julia who married Kysar J. **Stark**- She was allotted 501 acres and dwelling etc on property Aug. 26, 1842.

353- thru- 356- Petition stating that William **Mays**, husband of Lucretia **Mays**, and father of Mary Ann who married Robert B. **Jones**, John B. **Mays**, Eliza R. **Mays**, Martha N. **Mays**, Virginia C., William W., and Francis E **Mays** (minors) died and Lunsford A. **Paschall** became admstr of his estate and ask, the petitioners, ask for separation of the negroes of sd William **Mays** who died Dec. 24, 1839- The negroes were separated and divided between them.

356- thru 370- Inv. and amt. of sale of estate of Robert **Anderson**, deceased Sept. 1, 1842- by R. **Anderson**.

371- A list of open accts. of Robert **Anderson** deceased, rendered to court by R. **Anderson** excr.

371- thru 376- Inv. of estate of Howel G. **Pittard**, deceased, by James T. **Littlejohn**, admstr. mentions George W. **Hawkins** of Warren City and Charles H. K. **Taylor** of Person City, Alexander B. **Hawkins** of Warren City, Jas. B. **Littlejohn** of Franklin City, Edmund **Hester** of Clarksville Va., Thos. **Harris** of Halifax, Va., Jno. O. **Taylor** of Connecticut, Wm. D. **Amis** and Wm. **Hunt** of Miss., This is list of accounts due estate.

388
375- 376- Oct. 8, 1842- Sale of property of estate of Howell G. **Pittard** deceased, by J. A. **Littlejohn**, admstr.

376- 377- Hire of negroes of estate of Capt. Benjamin **Hester**, deceased Dec. 31, 1842 by Bennett **Hester**, admstr.

378- thru 385- Inv. and sale of the estate of Mrs. Lucy **Bullock**, dec'd by John **Bullock**, excr. Dec. 1, 2, 3 1842- Sept. 1, 1843.

385- Inv. and acct. of sales of estate of William **Bullock**, deceased, by John **Bullock**, excr. Dec. 1, 2, 1842. The negroes and bedding was divided between the 6 heirs. The negro bought by Mrs. Lucy **Bullock** is due the estate of William **Bullock**.

389- Inv. of estate left by Mrs. Susan **Eaton** to Thomas R. **Eaton** Feb. court 1843.

390- Estate of George **Thomason** by James **Thomason** from Feb. 1836 to Nov. court 1843 when the examiners speak of the death of Mrs. Martha **Thomason** and sale of her estate added to that of George **Thomason** by excr. and disbursements as per will of George **Thomason**.

392- 393- Feb. term 1843- Estate of John **Norwood**, deceased, by Robert A. **Jenkins** - Inv. and sale at which Mrs. **Norwood**, Harriette **Norwood**, Benjamin **Norwood** Jr., John M. **Norwood** were buyers among others.

393- thru 400- Sale of estate of Robert **Wilson**, deceased, Nov. 24, 1842 at which Mrs. **Wilson**, J. P. **Wilson**, Stephen and Benj **Wilson** were buyers among others.- by Solomon G. **Wilson** admstr.

400- Estate of Hezekiah **Hobgood**, deceased, by James B. **Hobgood** admstr Feb. court 1843.

400- Sale of property of Peter **West**, deceased, Dec. 7, 1842 by Fleming **Beasley**, Susan **West** excrs.

401- 402- Sale of property of estate of Alfred **Hester**, deceased, sold Dec. 31, 1842 and is that not before found by Samuel **Hunt** Jr. excr. and hiring of negroes for 1843-

402- thru 406- Estate of Leanner **Lawrence** deceased, by William **Fleming** amstr. property was sold Nov. 30, 1840 and accts. to Feb. court 1843.

402- thru 406- Estate of William **Lawrence**, deceased, by William **Fleming** excr. property sold Oct. 1, 1840, paid clerk for recording will of dec'd mentions acct. on Leannah **Lawrence** and special legacies delivered. Accounting made Feb. court 1843.

406- Inv. of property of James R. **West**, deceased, Nov. 14, 1842.

406- 407- Feb. 6, 1843- Estate of Mary A. **Hargrove**, deceased, by Israel W. **Hargrove**, excr.

407- 408- Feb. 4, 1843- Estate of John **Bagley**, deceased, by William **Bayley**, excr. mentions and pays for Funeral expense and coffin 11.45.

408- 409- Nov. 17, 1842- proved Feb. court 1843.
Abner **Adcock** ----wills to wife Rachel, the land whereon I live for her lifetime or widowhood and then to my four children; David Y., Rowlen, Susannah, Thomas H. **Adcock**. To wife Rachel all stock, furniture, tools to support children not married;

and at marriage of any one of them to give them a bed and furniture, cow and calf. After death of wife all stock, furniture sold and divided to children.
Exrs: Dr. James **Russell**.
Wts: Wm. A. **Gill**, Wm. **Adcock**.

Dec. 17, 1842- I have, at request of my wife, allowed my son John C. **Adcock** to build a house on my land, but nothing more is to be built on the land for it is willed to the minor children.
Wts: Wm. A. **Gill**

410- 411- Mar. 14, 1840- proved May court 1843- -
William **Allen**- - - - wills to son Archibald, a bed and furniture; to daughter Susannah P. **Allen**, a horse and a cow and calf; to son James, 5 sheep; to daughter Mary B. **Allen**, land whereon I now live, a horse and colt, a cow and calf, 5 sheep, 2 beds and furniture, a secretary and folding table, a dressing table, 2 trucks, 2 bedsteads, all sitting chairs, kitchen furniture and crop enough for support for one year; To daughter Permela W. **Johnson**, a china press, folding table, blue chest formerly belonging to

389

my daughter Judith J. **Allen** I give to grandson James **Allen** and if does not come forth to receive it then to granddaughter Virginia P. **Johnson**; all else sold and money divided to all my children.
Exrs: William A. **Johnson**.
Wts: W. S. **McClanahan**, M. A. **Smith**.

411 thru 413- Jan. 28, 1834- proved May court 1843.
James **Weathers**- - - - wills to have gifts of land to sons William, Edward, and John P. **Weathers** confirmed and also the gifts of negroes to daughters Elizabeth **Buchannon**, Gilly **Winston**, daughter Mary **Winston**, daughter Piety **Morgan**, to daughter Charity **Moss**, daughter Catherine **Lile**, daughter Penny **Freeman**; And to son John P. a negro; to daughter Prudence, widow of Dick H. **Dolby**, deceased, the negro I gave her; to son William, a negro; son Edward, a negro; to friend Thomas **Husketh** $30.00 and to each negro living with me $4.00 each; All else sold and debts and legacies paid; That which remains to go to children; To children of deceased daughter Elizabeth **Buchannon**, and of daughter Piety **Morgan**, deceased, and Penny **Freeman**, deceased, her children; Benjamin **Lile**, late husband of my deceased daughter Catherine, shall have no further part of my estate but may keep what he has.
Exrs: friends James **Wyche**, Thomas **Winston**.
Wts: Eaton J. **White**, Pleasant **Floyd**.

413- 414- Apr. 11, 1843- - - - - Proved May court 1843.
James **Boswell**- - - - wills to wife Lueta, 3 negroes, ½ land where on I live, all stock, all furniture, all tools and a years support; to daughter Rebeccah **Boswell** and the child my wife is pregnant with if lives, if not the property divided between daughter and wife.

Exrs: brother- in- law Thomas **Blalock**.
Wts: John **Sherman**, Jas. D. **Hobgood**.

414, 415- 416- 417- Feb. 22, 1843- Proved May court 1843.
Solomon **Perry**- - - wills to wife Rodey, 122 acres whereon I live, all house hold and kitchen furniture, 12 hogs, a filly, 4 sheep, a cow and calf, 2 plows, 2 axes, hoes, all fowls, all cash and debts due me, a saddle, and all provisions, for her natural life; to daughter Elizabeth **Emry** and daughter Nancy **Guarner** all heretofore given them; to son John, all given him and ½ land given my wife at her death; to daughter Polly **Sherrin** all heretofore given her; to granddaughter Elizah Adaline **Sherrin** all property now in possession of John M. **Sherrin** which I hold under a constable sale deeded to me Mar 22, 1836 by John H. **Robertson**: to daughter Salley **Arnold**, all given her; to son Thomas, the other half of land after death of my wife, my saddle, and all he has had from me; to daughter Rebeckar **Harris**, all she has had from me; to son Peter, all he now has, my shoemaker tools, my clock; to son Sollomon all he has had from me and my coopers tools; to sell all else and divide between all children and also that left my wife excepting the land.
Exrs: John **Guarner**, Clement **Wilkins**.
Wts: James **Brogdon**, David **Brogdon**, J. **Robertson**.
Codicil I wish my son- in- law John **Guarner** to superintend the placing of someone to live with my wife and if no one does then the land rented out for her benefit, and my daughter Polly **Sherrin** to have her part kept by excrs. for benefit of her children. Feb. 22 1843.

417- May court 1843- - Inv. and sale of estate of John **Walker**, deceased, by Burnis **Walker**, admstr. Mar. 22, 1843 mentions among buyers, R. D., C. W., Wm., Nancy, T. J. **Walker**- - no one else bought at sale.

418 thru 432- May court 1843- Sale Feb. 28, 1842- Estate of Benjamin G. **Long**, deceased, by Stanford **Long**, admstr. mentions note on Robert **Jeffreys** of Franklin Co., N. C., S. B. **Huggins** and Jas **Newbold** of Obslow Co, Joseph **McKinney** of Green Co., N. C., Em. P. **Ferrand** of Swansboro, N. C., Isaac **Ramsey** of Beaufort, N. C., Kinchen **Kearney** of Franklin Co., N. C. and notes and due bills of Benja G. **Long** and George **Cattlett**, partners- note on J. C. **Patrick** and Solo **Carmick** of Lenoir Co., N. C., Alexa **Miller** and Jonothan **Blaney** of Craven Co., N. C., Wm. P. **Moore** of Newbern N. C., A. E. **Gill** of Edgecombe

390
Sale of estate of B. H. **Long**, Feb. 28 and Mar. 1, 2, 3, 1843 is mostly hardware and furniture, lumber etc- and hire of negroes for 1843, of grist and saw mills, houses and lots- - William P. **Long** was clerk of court of Halifax county, N. C.

432- 433- May 2, 1843- Estate of Rebecca **Blackwell**, deceased, by Abner **Currin** admstr.

433- Estate of Robert **Hester**, deceased, by Daniel T. **Gooch** Apr. 1843.

434, 435- Estate of Joseph **Amis** deceased, by Lewis and Elizabeth **Amis** excrs. from Aug. 1840- to Apr. 27, 1843.

438- Estate of D. **Parker** by John **Sherman**, admstr. with will annexed mentions money for disbursement My court 1843.

439- thru 441 Estate of Edward **Jones** deceased, by John **Sherman** and William **Parrish**, May court 1843.

441- Inv. of estate of Collins **Winfree**, deceased, May 1, 1843 by Edward **Tucks**, excr. paid by John Y. **Sandford** excr of Gabriel **Jones** dec'd. Inv. of estate of Charles **Winfree**, deceased, May 1, 1843 by Phaltial **Turk** admstr - dued from Edward **Tucks** admstrs. or executors to this estate.

442- Debts due estate of Dr. Benjamin **Bullock**, deceased, by D. C. **Parrish** admstr. and property sold Dec. 12, 1840- to May court 1843.

443, 444, 445- Dec. 5, 1842- Rent of plantation and sales of property of Sally **McCram's** estate by trustee Robert P. **Hughes**- estate of Sally **McCram's** children and hire of negroes May court 1843.

446, 447- Estate of Willie **Jones** by John **Jones**, admstr. Mar. 8, 1843 sold.

447 thru 449- Feb. 18, 1843- Estate of Abner **Adcock**, deceased, by Jas. A. **Russell**, excr. Inv. and sale- John C., Rachel, Mary W., David Y., Susan and Ann **Adcock** bought at sale.

450- Wardens of the Poor of Granville Co- - account to May 1843.

452- Aug. term 1842- Petition of Saml **Wilson**, Ritter **Wilson**, Benjamin **Wilson** and wife Lethe, Temperance **Usery**, Stephen **Wilson**, John C. **Lemay** and wife Mildred, Ambrose **Barker** and wife Jemima, Solomon **Wilson**, David **Knott** and wife Lundy, Susan **Wilson**. and Kysar J. **Stark** and wife Julia- state that Robert **Wilson** died leaving the above named children surviving him and that he possessed two tracts of land on Flat Creek, one of 1024 acres and the other 413 acres. That Rebecca **Wilson**, widow of Robert **Wilson** has her dower right in land and they ask the remainder divided between them, the children. The land was divided to them in 11 parts, one tract to each of them excluding the widows dower Feb. court 1843- Plats here

457- Jan. 1843- John **Bullock** by order of court, reports that at Williamsborough Jan. 2, 1843, he sold three negroes at public sale and were bought by James M. **Bullock** and Thomas L. **Williams**.

458- Rebecca **Wilson** widow of Robert **Wilson** and children Ritter, Lethe wife of Benjamin **Wilson**, Temperance **Usery**; Stephen **Wilson**, Milderd wife of John C.

Lemay, Jemima, wife of Ambrose **Barker**, Lundy wife of David **Knott**, Susan **Wilson**, Julia wife of Kysar J **Stark**, Samuel and Solomon **Wilson**- ask division of negroes of estate of Robert **Wilson** deceased.12 shares.

461- thru 464- Dec. 8, 1842- Joseph **Sims** and Betsy **Jeffreys** against Sidney **Jeffreys**- - Petition states that William **Jeffreys** died leaving a tract of land to has wife Dorcas, for her lifetime adjoining **McGehee**, **Levister** and others on both sides of road leading from Dickersons Bridge to Raleigh, N. C. containing 300 acres. The wife Dorcas is now dead and the children ask division of land. James **Bullock** became the owner and held all rights of the children in land except Betsey and the minor grandchild, Sidney, and only devisee of Sally **Jeffries** one of the children of William **Jeffreys** of 10 acres of the land. All children deed right to James **Bullock** except Betsey and he therefore held 4/5ths of the 10 acres and at an execution against James **Bullock**, Joseph **Sims** became he purchaser of the interest. Betsey **Jeffreys** is entitled to 1/5th or 2 acres of the 10 acres and 1/5th of all the balance of the land and Sidney **Jeffreys** entitled to 1/5th exclusive of the 10 acres being the child of Sally, the daughter of William **Jeffreys**, deceased.

391
The land was divided to the heirs, and Joseph **Sims** bought the two acres remaining of the 10 from Betsy **Jeffreys** and he drew lots 1, 3, 4; Betsy **Jeffreys** No. 2 and Sidney **Jeffreys** no 5 -

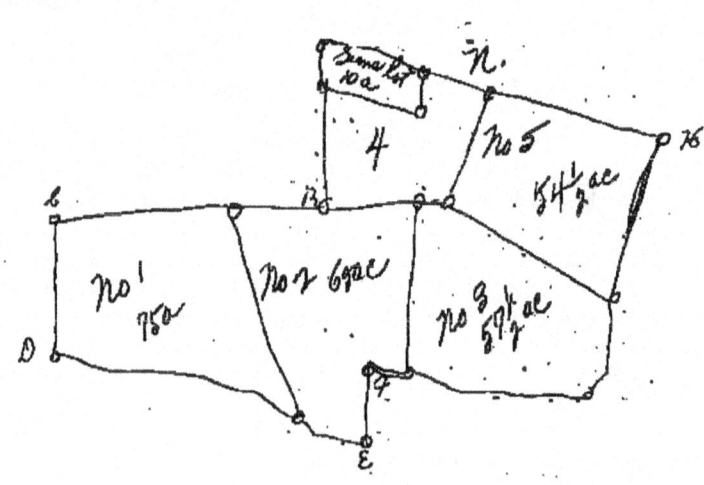

Dec. 8, 1842
Plat of land of William **Jeffreys** deceased, allotted to heirs.

464- thru 466- Clement **Wilkins** against Moses **Winston**- - - petition that they are tenants in common of land on Beaverdam creek in Granville Co. which contains 186 acres, 1/3rd of which is the dower of Dorcas **Searcey** widow of Hargrove **Searcey**, deceased, heretofore allotted her. Ask that land be divided between them excluding the dower. Division made Apr. 17 1843- Lot 1 to Moses **Winston** and Lot 2- to Clement **Wilkins**.

392
466, 467, 468- Feb. term 1843- James **Minis** and Wife Mary against Martha J. **Johnson**, Sarah A. **Johnson**, Celestia R. **Johnson**, Drusilla T. **Johnson** and Lucinda **Johnson**- State that Stephen **Johnson** deeded by deed of gift to the above named Mary **Minis**, then Mary **Johnson** and the others herein named as tenants in common, certain negroes. Mary and James **Minis** ask for their share of negroes and since others are minors they, are herein represented by their guardian William R. **White** Feb. 25, 1843.

468 thru 470- Abner **Adcock** died January 1843, leaving Rachel, his widow and possessed 200 acres adjoining Wm. A. **Gill**, Nash **Jones** and others, that James A. **Russell** was appointed admstr of will to which will the widow dissented and asked for her dower in land. She got 66 2/3rds acres.

470- Accts of Leslie **Gilliam**, sheriff, of Granville Co. for 1842- 1843 gives list of jurors for Feb. court 1841, thru 1842- and taxes and cost of New court house. There were 4934 polls in 1841 and 5079 in 1842, also gives pay of jurors thru 1343-

485- July 26, 1839- proved Aug. court 1843.
Rowland **Bryant** Sr. very advanced in age----wills to wife Mary all estate for life then the land whereon I live sold and money divided to sons James, Rowland, John and Robertson or they may keep the land and divide it; My sons Edward, Robertson, Rowland and James and John to have all I have given them and all else divided between them excepting my daughter Elizabeth **Summerhill** is to have $200.00; My

daughter Martha **Woodlief** is to receive nothing as I have boarded her and her children for many years-
Exrs: son James A. **Bryant**, James **White**.
Wts: Thos L. **King**, George **Kittrell**.

486- Aug. 22, 1837- proved Aug. court 1843.
Joseph **Proctor**- - - - wills to wife Nancy the 200 acres I live on for as long as she is my widow and all cattle, the crop, furniture, money, bonds and accounts and all else belonging to me; At her death or re- marriage the whole estate divided to the children she has by me and she to be executrix.
Wts; John T. **Hunt**, Thomas B. **Barnett**.

487- Nov. 1, 1833- proved Aug. court 1843.
Lucy **Jones**- - - - wills to son Everad S. **Jones**, 2 featherbeds and 6 silver spoons; to grandson Frederick Jones **Carter** in trust for benefit of my daughter Louisa A. **Carter** for life, all rest of my silver spoons, 6 beds and furniture, a negro, furniture and 1/3rd of money coming from the sale of the land whereon I formerly lived in Virginia and which Everard S. **Jones** is to collect and at her death to go to my grandson Frederick Jones **Carter**, her son, and he also to have a negro, and to be executor of this will.
Wts: James **Wyche**, H. W. **Peace**.

488- thru 490- Estate of James **Hart** Sr., deceased, by Maurice S. **Hart** excr. from Feb. 11, 1840- to Aug. court 1843.

490- 491- Feb. 6, 1843- Estate of Theophilus H. **Wiggins** deceased, by John B. **Debnam** from Oct. 1839 to Feb. 1843 mentions legatees (not named).

491, 482- Inv. of estate left by Solomon **Perry** Sr. to his wife Rody which she refused to give excr. receipt for. Aug. 7, 1843- by Clement **Wilkins**.

492, 493- Sale of property of Sollomon **Perry** Sr., deceased, May 25, 1843 by John **Guarner**, excr.

493, 494- Estate of Matilda **Barnett**, dec'd by Elijah **Barnett**, excr. refers to sale of Dec. 6, 1840-

495- Feb. 22, 1841- Inv. of estate of Joseph **Lumpkin**, deceased, by M. D. **Royster**, deceased, and sale of same Feb. 22, 1843.

497- Estate of Sarah **Dean**, deceased, by Hamilton **Hester**, admstr mentions sale of Oct. 27, 1841 and judgement against heirs of Jesse **Dean**, deceased Nov. 15, 1838- this acct. Aug. 7, 1843.

498- Apr. 27, 1843- Acct. of sale of personal estate of Dorcas **Jeffreys**, deceased, by John W. **Jenkins**, admstr.

Estate Records of Granville Co, NC Volume 13-16   105

499- Joseph H. **Gooch** appointed Sheriff of Granville Co., N. C. with Wm. **Clement**, Elijah **Hester**, Fleming **Beasley**, James C. **Cooper**, Lindon S. **Philpott**, Horace L. **Robards** and Samuel **Philpott** as bondsmen, Aug. 8, 1843.

393
502- Sept. 27, 1843- proved Nov. court 1843.
Samuel **Cottrell**- - - - wills that all debts paid and then that remaining of estate divided between his six children; Mathew, James, David, Solomon, Samuel **Cottrell** and daughter Amey **Sears** and each to make acct. of all already given them so as to equalize the division; My sons Solomon and Mathew to have a bed and furniture each. My negroes treated well as they have been good and faithful;
Exrs: James A. **Crews**.
Wts: Williamson **Parham**, James **Satterwhite**.

503- Aug. 24, 1343- proved Nov. court 1843.
Cannon **Parham** (also spelled Canaan) Sr.- - - - wills to have estate divided into 7 parts and given to eldest daughter Tabitha, daughter Martha **Harnett's** 2 children Wially and Thomas; children of Elvira **Powell** namely, Robert and Elizabeth; To three children of Thomason **Parham**, namely Lucindy, Elizabeth and James; To son Canaan; to grson Ruffin **Fuller**; to the three children of Elizabeth **Purkinson**, namely: Whitfiel, Seth and Permealey.
Exrs: sons Thompson and Canaan **Parham**.
Wts: Lewis **Parham**, Alfred **Knight**

504- 505- Sept. 6, 1843- proved Nov. court 1843
William **Kittrell** (very aged)- - - - wills to ten children; - Martha, Egbert, and Lucy Frances by my first wife; Mary, Rebecca, Maria, Loretta, Tabitha, Eugenia and John William by my present wife; I gave my daughter Martha **Wright** of Tennessee a negro and hereby confirm gift; gave to Egbert **Kittrell** a negro; to William **Young** a negro; To Mary **Young** a negro; to Rebecca **White**, a negro; To Maria Jane **Kittrell** a negro; To Loretta Y. **Kittrell** a negro; to Tabitha Ann **Kittrell**, a negro; to Eugenia Elizabeth a negro; to John William **Kittrell**, a negroes; to my wife Martha B. **Kittrell** the 500 acres of land and a negro slave, and if she marry she is to have only 1/3rd of land and the remainder sold and money divided to all my children; Rebecca **White** $52.00; and to each; Maria, Loretta, Tabitha, Eugenia E. and John William $115.00 when each are married. My excr. to sell certain furniture and wife to dispose of other as she see fit.
Exrs: John W. **Young** and my wife Martha B. **Kittrell**.
Wts: John **O'Brien** Jr., John **Young**.

506- July 14, 1840- George **Burns**- - - wills to daughter Mary H. **Bullock** and heirs of her body all my property and her husband John H. **Bullock** to be executor- Proved Nov. court 1843.
Wts: Blair **Burwell**, Robert B. **Gilliam**, Lunsford A **Paschall**.

506- 507- Nov. 12, 1838- proved Nov. court 1843.

Seth Petty **Pool**- - - - wills all to his wife Elizabeth for her lifetime and at her death divided between my sons Seth and Alexander; To sons each a bed and furniture; to daughter Dosha, bed and furniture; to dau. Patsey Tailor Petty **Pool** a bed furniture and saddle; son Thomas $1.00 To granddaughter Elizabeth **Daniel** $1.00; The remainder of estate to my other six children: daughter Sally **Avrets** and children; to daughter Elizabeth **Melton** and two sons Stephen and William **Melton**; son Seth; daughter Dosha; daughter Patsey T.; son Alexander.
Exrs: sons Seth and Alexander Petty **Pool**.
Wts: Gabriel **Jones**, William P. **Ligon**.

507, 508- June 22, 1843- proved Nov. court 1843.
Isaac **Huskey**- - - - wills that debts be paid; to son Isham, $25.00; to son Archeley, $185.00; to son James, if alive, $185.00; to son John, $200.00; All else sold and divided to the children equally after paying above legacies; To Elizabeth **Kittrell**; to Mary **Wheelas**; to Isham **Huskey**; To Archeby $185.00; To James **Huskey** $185.00; To John **Huskey** 185.00.
Exrs: John **White**.
Wts: William A. **Bobbitt**, Allen **Thompson**.

509- thru 511- Inv. of property of estate of Lewis **Amis**, dec'd, Nov. 3, 1843 by Wm. **Amis**, admstr. Nov. court 1843.

394
511- Dec. 25, 1843- Inv. of estate of James **Weathers**, deceased, by James **Wyche**. excr. Oct. 28, 1843- Thomas Y. **Cooke**, late guardian of testator assigns bond on Thomas B. **Moore** and Richard **Coley**, also one on William A. **Bobbitt** and Allen **Thompson**, Elijah **Winston** and Booker A. **Mitchell** and hire of negroes for which some is due.

512- Estate of Mary A. **Hargrove** by Isrt W. **Hargrove** excr. from Nov. 1842 to Nov. 1843.

513- 514- Estate of Hezekiah **Hobgood**, deceased, by James B. **Hobgood**, admstr. Nov. 1, 1843.

514- 515- Inv. of estate of Rowland **Bryant** Sr., deceased, by James H. **Bryant**, excr, and Inv. of that left his widow, Mary **Bryant**, for lifetime Nov. 8, 1843.

516- Estate of Peter **West**, deceased, by Fleming **Beasley**, excr. 1843.

517- Estate of Elizabeth **Blackwell** deceased, by William M. **Blackwell** admstr. Aug. 1842 to Oct. 1843.

518- 519- Estate of Jonathan **Tippett**, deceased, by John H. **Tippett**, admstr Aug. 1843 mentions sale of Feb. 25, 1842 and widows support for 1841.

Estate Records of Granville Co, NC Volume 13-16   107

519, thru 526- Sale of property of Estate of Lewis **Amis**, deceased, by William **Amis**, admstr- Nov. 3, 1843- list among buyers Warren **Amis**, Alex. **Amis**, Lewis **Amis**, James **Amis**, Thomas **Amis**- Feb. court. 1844.

527- thru 529- - Feb. court 1844- Inv. of property of John P. **Butler**, dec'd and acct. of sales Mar. 30, 1843 by James C. **Cooper**.

529- thru 532- Sale of property of estate of Seth Petty **Pool**, deceased, Nov. 30, 1843 by Seth Petty **Pool**, excr. and Inv. of personal property.

532- Inv. of property left the widow Martha B. **Kittrell**, delivered to her, mentions land in Franklin and Granville Co.- 500 acres, by John W. **Young**.

533- Inv. and sale of estate of William **Kittrell**, deceased, Dec. 6, 1843 mentions Harbira H. **Hight** as a buyer at sale of many, many things by John W. **Young**.

537 thru 539- Inv. of property of Samuel **Cottrell**, deceased, by James A. **Crews** excr. and sale of property, Feb. court 1844.

540- Estate of S. J. **Harris** deceased, by Benj F. **Harris**, admstr, from Dec. 10, 1841 thru Feb. 1844.

541- Inv. of cash and judgements of James **Boswell**, deceased, by Joseph D. **Hobgood**, admstr mentions years support for Luetty **Boswell**- Feb. 1844.

End Book 15

Estate Records of Granville Co, NC Volume 13-16

395

1- Inv. of property of Mary **Hayes**, deceased, received in division of estate of Benjamin **Hester**, deceased by Henry **Hobgood**, admstr Feb 1844.

2- thru 5- Inv. of property of William G. **Ellixson**, deceased, by S. **Beasley** Nov. 1843- and sale Nov. 29, 1843- by Stephen Beasley mentions Mrs. Sally **Ellixson** as a buyer.

6 thru 10- Feb. court 1844- Inv. of money, bonds, accts. of James R. **Roberts** by Presly **Roberts** admstr, and Inv. of property sold Dec. 6, 1843 mentioning among buyers Rebecca **Roberts**, Mark **Roberts**, Wesley and Thomas **Roberts**, Mark **Roberts** Sr., and Alsey **Roberts** and giving list of property given Mrs. Rebecca Roberts., widow of James T. **Roberts**.

10- thru 18- Estate of Thomas **Blalock** deceased, by John **Sherman** admstr. Inv. of personal estate Dec. 2, 1843 mentions cash belonging to heirs of William **Blalock** and notes due that estate and Sale on Dec. 1, 1843- at which Rowan **Blalock** was a buyer and John P. **Blalock** and Inv. of property given to Rowan **Blalock**, the widow of Thomas **Blalock**.

18- thru 24- Estate of Kannon **Parham**, deceased, by Kenan **Parham** Jr. Inv. and sale of property- Feb. court 1844.

28- 29, 30- [sic; ladies this is out of order] Estate of Joseph **Lumpkin**, deceased, by D. **Royster**, admstr. from 1841- for Feb. 1844- -

24- 25- 26- Estate of Martha **Philpott**, deceased by Samuel **Philpott**, admstr from sale Dec. 3, 1842 to Feb. 2, 1844.

26- Inv. and sale of estate of James **Lyon** Deceased, by John **White**, admstr mentions widows allowance Feb. court 1844.

28- Estate of Joseph **Lumpkin**, deceased, by W. D. **Royster**, administrator, on 23rdday of Feb 1843; Feb Court 1844.

29- Estate of H. H. **Dedman**, deceased, by M. D. **Royster** from 1840- to Feb. 1844.

30- Estate of Joseph **Lumpkin**, deceased, by M. D. **Royster**, admstr from 1841 to Feb. 3, 1844.

32- A years provision set off to Luetta **Boswell**, widow of James **Boswell** deceased, Nov. 1844.

33- Hire of slaves of estate of Benjamin G. **Long**, deceased, by Stanford **Long** admstr Dec. 29, 1843, mentions William P., Pharimono T. **Long** 1844.

Estate Records of Granville Co, NC Volume 13-16

34- Estate of Anderson J. **Duncan** by Wm. H. **Webb**, admstr. from Feb. 10, 1842 to Feb. court 1844.

35- Additional Inv. of estate of Alfred **Hester**, deceased, by Samuel **Hunt** mentions bonds from estate of the late Benjamin **Hester** and also D. J. **Young** as agent for Alfred **Hester**, and negroes to legatees (unnamed) Feb. court 1844.

36- Inv. of Isaac **Husketh**, deceased, and sale Dec. 30, 1843, by John **White**, excr.

37- Additional Inv. of estate of Robert **Hester**, deceased, by Danl T. **Gooch** admstr. Jan. 30, 1844.

37- Sale of property of estate of John A. **Norwood**, deceased, Jan. 4, 1844 by Robert A. **Jenkins**.

37- Inv. of estate of James **Daniel** Sr. by Joel T. **Watkins**, admstr, in Granville Co., N. C., mentions suit in court against John G. **Daniel** excr of Beverly **Daniel**, deceased, for large sum. Feb. 6, 1844.

38- Sept. 12, 1842- proved Feb. court 1844.
Patience **Anderson**- - - - wills (she is a widow) - - Anderson **Chavass**, son of John **Chacass**, deceased, a cow and calf and a bed and furniture; To Joyes **Mayhoe**, children Varnal W. **Mahoe**, Tamazer **Juliner** all rest of estate at death of their mother, being in possession of William **Mayhoe** and wife for lifetime.
Wts: William H. **Paschall**, Lewis **Parham** Sr.

39- 40- Dec. 29, 1841- proved May court 1844.
Lemuel **Curren** Sr. (**Currien**) - - - - wills to wife Betsey, all land I own on Grassy creek and 4 negroes for her lifetime or widowhood, and as much stock as she wishes to keep. and of household furniture as she wishes, a wagon, cart, tools and all provisions on hand; At death of wife, all to be divided between all my children; Elijah, James, Davis, Mary, Lemuel, Elizabeth, Lucy Ann -
Wife Elizabeth, admstrx.-
Wts: Edward **Hunt** Jr., James **Blackwell**.

396
41- Feb. 7, 1844= proved May court 1844.
Susan **Willis**- - - - wills to brother Edward **Royster**, all her slaves; to all my brothers and sisters all left from sale of remaining property and debts are paid, and brother Edward **Royster**, excr-
Wts: J.T. **Hunt**, Henry **Yancey**, William **Strum**.

42- thru 53- Estate of Lemuel **Goodwin**, deceased, by Samuel W. **Smith**, admstr. Inv. of cash and notes Mar. 8, 1844, rent of lands and hire of negroes, sales May court 1844.

53- thru 55- Estate of Joseph **Barnett**, deceased, by T. B. **Barnett**, excr from 1840- to May 1844.

55- thru 57- Estate of William **Huskett**, deceased, by Jno. **White**, admstr. Mar. 4, 1844- Sally and Archeby and William R. **Husketh** were buyers at sale.

58- Estate of Margaret **Butler**, deceased, Feb. 26, 1844, by D. J. **Young** admstr. and sale Mar. 1, 1844.

59- Estate of Samuel **Briant** by Washington H. **Thomas**, gives receipt to William A. **Philpott** admstr. of Solomon **Philpott**, deceased, for money paid Oct. 28, 1840-

60- Estate of Robert **Wilson**, deceased, by Solomon G. and Samuel P. **Wilson** excrs. May court 1844.

63, 64, 65- -
Benjamin **Hester** - - - - wills to wife Mary Dyer **Hester**, for her lifetime or widowhood, all property real and personal estate and $500.00 and 12 negroes to do with as she please; to Robert **Hester**, the land bought of William **Shoer** and wife adjoining Col. **Ridley** and **Hesters** line; To Francis **Hester** son of Francis land after death of my wife; To Benjam **Currin** land whereon he lives 200 acres; to Alfred **Hester** land whereon he lives at death of my wife; to William **Hester** son of Francis, 200 Acres; To Nancy **Huddlestone** a negro for her lifetime and then to heirs of her body; to wife a half of household goods and furniture; To William B. **Wirrel** $100.00; To Thomas **Crocker** $100.00; To brother Huggins of Warren Co., $100.00; To Nancy **Thomason**, a bond; to Elizabeth **Parham** a bond; All remaining money and bonds collected and put to interest for my wife's lifetime then divided. Some of my brothers heirs owes me money and this to be taken out of the 100 pds; to Francis **Goodman**, a horse; to Alfred **Haze (Hayes**?) a horse; To Baptist Society one acre and spring as long as used for meeting house and no longer; to sell all else not given away and give the children of my brothers and sisters jointly 100 pds. I except John, Jeremiah, and Benjamin **Hester** sons and Patrick **Obriant** and John **Bat** for they are good for nothing and I give them 5 shillings; (John Jeremiah and Benjamin sons of Zachariah **Hester**); $500.00 given a young Baptist man of good talent; All else to children of my brother Francis **Hester** and my old negro set free. (This will is unfinished and undated.)

66- thru 68- Oct. 10, 1843- - proved Aug. court 1844.
Samuel **Moss**- - - wills to son Banja **Moss**, ½ of money- arising from sale of land on which I live; and also 5 negroes and increase, and the money and negroes taken by Jno **Ellis** and invested in land anywhere wise to buy and not permit it to be used for debts of said **Moss**, and at his death to divided to his children; To Drury R. **Turner** and wife Elizabeth land east of his house and five negroes. for their lifetime then to their children; To Jas. T. **Stark** and wife Sarah, 6 negroes for their lifetime then to their children; To children of Jno. **Ellis** and his wife Fanny 7 negroes and Jno. nor

Sarah exercise any claim to negroes; To granddaughters Priscilla **Wilson** wife of Solomon **Wilson** and Elizabeth **Stark**, both daughters of James T. **Stark** and wife Sarah, a negro girl; To granddaughters, children of Drury and Elizabeth **Turner**, Izabellah and Puss, a negro girl; Jas.T. **Stark** may sell negroes if he moves away. To three sons of Johns **Ellis**, to each $100.00; To Drury R. **Taimer** $200 To son Benjamin ½ and other half to children of John and Fanny **Ellis**; Jno. T. **Stark** and wife Sarah; 1 acres for graveyard;
Exrs: Daniel A. **Paschall**, James T. **Stark**.
Wts: John H. **Wright**, J. M. **Hare**.

397
Codicil Sept. 10, 1843- - - A negro sold and the $200.00 given Drury R. **Tamer** to be equally divided to children of Benjamin **Moss**, Drury R amd wife Elizabeth **Tailer**, James T. and wife Sarah **Stark**, John and wife Fanny **Ellis** Oct. 10, 1843.
Wts: Len. H. **Hare**, John H. **Wright**.

69- 70- Dec. 24, 1838- proved Aug. court 1844.
Rigdon **Volentine**- - - - wills to daughter Elizabeth **Howell** and Dilley R. **Sturdivant**, all land west of Gaston and Raleigh railroad adjoining Luke **Solomon**, Robert **Jones** and Jonathan **Fullers** land- ½ of this land to him; and To Elizabeth **Howell** ½ this land, 4 servants, 2 horses, cattle and stock, a cart and 2 beds and furniture, 6 chairs, 20 barrels of corn, 1000 pds. of pork; To daughter Nancy **Mann**, 4 servants; To four sons of daughter Mary Ann **Reed** (**Rud**?)- namely William **Rudd**, Thomas, John and Daniel **Rudd** and granddaughter Dilley R. **Sturdivant**, $1000.00 divided between them when they come of age; to son John W. **Volentine** land where I live east of Gaston and Raleigh railroad. 4 servants, cart, sheep.
Exrs: son John W. **Volentine**, William B. **Mann**.
Wts: Wm. **Robards**, Samuel **Edwards**.

71, 72- June 12, 1844- proved Aug. court 1844.
Ann A. **Jones**- - - - wills to son Eaton S. **Kittrell**, blacksmith pointer tools; to daughters Sally H. **Brodie** and Parthena E. J. W. **Marrow**, and Demetrias E. **Young**, in trust for the use of my daughter Ann H. **Jones** and to my son Eaton H. **Kittrell**, an equal share of all my estate real and personal; To Solomon L., son of Thomas F. and Parthena E. J. W. **Marrow**, a colt for the use of negroes purchased by Thomas F. **Marrow** in 1837 of my husband Lewellen **Jones** and left as said **Marrows** property to be delivered to him when called for.
Exrs: son Eaton H. **Kittrell**, son- in law Thomas F. **Marrow**, Demetries E. **Young**.
Wts: Wm. **Holmes**, Wm. F. **Henderson**.

72, 73- Inv. of estate of Benjamin **Williams**, deceased, by Thomas T. **Hester** admsrt Aug. term 1844- -

73, 74, 75- Estate of Thomas **Coghill** deceased, by Lucy **Coghill** and Robert P. **Hughes**, excrs. mentions Lucy **Coghills** allowance.

76- Estate of Lewis **Reavis**- Inv. of estate by Peter L. and George J. **Reavis**, admstrs.- Mrs. **Reavis** bought at sale a great deal of estate. A. **Reavis** also a buyer, and C. W. **Wynn**, Thos. **Reavis** Aug. court 1844.

83- thru 86- Estate of Col. John G. **Hart** by Thomas B. **Barnett**, admstr beginning May 5, 1841 to May 1844 mentions Maurice, Nancy **Hart**.

86, 87- Acct. of estate of Lemuel **Currin** Sr. deceased, by Elizabeth **Currin** excrs or admstr. Aug, court 1844.

87- thru 90- Inv. and sale of estate of Susan **Willis**, deceased, by Edward **Royster**, excr. June 1844.

90- thru 92- Wardens of the Poor, acct with County– Aug. court 1844.

92, 93- Sale of estate of Joseph **Champion**, deceased, by William **Champion**, admstr, June 29, 1844 and among buyers were Elizabeth **Champion**.

93- 94 Aug. 2, 1844- Estate of Robert **Hester** deceased, by Daniel T. **Gooch**, admstr. - Inventory and acct.

94- Estate of Miss Martha E. **Ballard**, deceased, by L. **Gilliam**, admstr June 4, 1844- -

95 thru 97- July 9, 1844- proved Nov. court 1844.
Joseph **Lewis**- - - to wife Nancy, land, live stock, furniture, crop except tobacco which is to be sold to pay debts, 20,000 tobacco hills now laid off by my son James and privilege of using her negroes on land, for her natural life in lieu of her dower in my real estate, and after her death all property divided among my children; To son John 500 acres now in his possession and $3. 00; To Sally Ann and Henrietta $700. 00 each. All children made equal in proportions of my estate and negroes divided into 8 lots and drawn by Thomas, Emily, Polly, Martha, Susan, Charles, James and Eliza **Lewis**; That left my deceased daughter Emily, to her children and her husband do as he please with it; also daughters Susan and

398
Henrietta, their part to their husbands to do as they please with; namely James **Speed**, Alexander **Amis**, William G. **Thomas**. Estate left to daughters Polly, Martha, Sally, Eliza, and Ann be entailed and kept for them for life time then to their children free from control of their husbands; At death of wife land sold and all children made equal in their shares of estate.
Exrs: My wife and Thomas B. **Lewis**.
Wts: Was. H. **Thomas**, Joseph A. **Norwood**.

97, 98- June 1, 1844- proved Nov. court 1844.
John **Washington**- - - - wills to wife Nancy **Washington**, 30 acres including house where I live and remaining 45 acres sold to pay my debts, also one negro and the

property left by my father William **Washington** sold and debts paid; to wife Nancy furniture, stock, utensils and. crop.
Exrs: Carter **Waller**.
Wts: Calvin **Waller**, John **Nance** Jr.

99, 100, 101- Aug. 3, 1843- proved Nov. court 1844.
George **Floyd** Sr. wills to wife Rosey and two deaf and dumb daughters Nelly and Juda **Floyd**, the land whereon I live for their life time then to the other children, also to wife for her lifetime, negroes and at her death sold and divided to my children; To two deaf and dumb daughters Nelly and Judy, 3 negroes, a cow and calf, featherbed and furniture, horse, bridle and saddle, tools and a years provision for wife and daughters. To daughter Elizabeth **Rud**, a slave; to daughter Martha **Turner**, a slave; to daughter Susanna **Cardin**, $300.00 to her and her children; To daughter Polly **Grisham** $1.00 to her and her heirs; To sons Henry (or his heirs), Lewis **Floyd** $1.00 each as they have received their share; to son William **Floyd**, my still as he has also received his share. All else sold and debts paid. All else divided to my nine children above named.
Exrs: Samuel and James **Fuller**.
Wts: William R. **Hicks**, Charles **Floyd**, John **Higgs**.

101- 102- Jan. 16, 1841- proved Nov. court 1844.
David J. **Young**---- wills to have all accounts charged against his children, to be added up and whole estate be divided equally among my wife and all my children; the home place and dwelling must be kept for a home for wife and children and Mrs. **Hutchinson** and the boys may continue to carry on store and factory but must do so free of rent and all to have education equal to James and girls equal to Harriet free of charge.
Exrs: Wife Julian and son James **Young**.
Wts: Dr. John R. **Hicks**, Thomas B. **Barnett**, James C. **Cooper**, A. W. **Venable**.

102- thru 108- Inv. and acct. of sales of estate of Warren **Amis**, deceased, by William **Amis**, admstr. Aug. 13, 1844- buyers at sale included James **Amis**.

108- thru. 111 Sale of estate of John B. **Mays**, deceased by L. A. **Paschall** admstr. Oct. 3Q, 1844- Virginia **Mays**, William, Frances, Eliza **Mays** bought at sale.

111- thru 113- Estate and accts. of estate of John A. **Norwood**, deceased by Robert A. **Jenkins**, admstr. beginning Dec. 5, 1842- recorded will in Nov. 1842, paid widows allowance, to Nov. court 1844.

113- thru 115- Acct. of estate of William **Allen** deceased, by Wm. A. **Johnson** excr., mentions pension certificate and county seal for same.

115- thru 119- Inv. and acct. of sales of estate of N. L. **Hill**, deceased by Walter A. **Bullock**, admstr. Nov. 5, 1844.

120- Inv. of Thomas **Blalock** by John **Sherman**, admstr. Nov. 5, 1844.

120- Estate of Lemuel **Currin** deceased, and sale of same- Nov. court 1844 by Elizabeth **Currin** excr. mentions Wyatt and James **Currin**.

121- Current acct. of estate of James **Levister**, deceased, and sale of property by George **Levister**, admstr. Oct. 11, 1844 - Ann **Levister** bought entire property.

123- Sale of property Benjm G. **Long** by Stanford **Long**, admstr. Dec. 29, 1843-

399
123 thru 129- Thomas J. **Hicks**, County Trustee, accounts of county. Aug. 1, 1844.

129, 130- Oct. 5, 1840- proved Feb. court 1845.
Isaac **Duncan**- - - - wills to wife Affa **Dunkin**, for life or widowhood, all estate real and personal for her support and that of family and after her death all sold and money divided among my children and if any of them die leaving issue they to have their parent's share.
Exrs: Wife Affa **Duncan**.
Wts: James H. **Young**, D. A. **Young**.

130, 131- Nov. 8, - 1844- proved Feb. court 1845.
John **Royster** - - - - wills to daughter Mary **Moody**, a slave and property worth $200.00, now in her possession; To daughter Julia **Moore**, a slave and $200.00 worth of property in her possession; To daughter Panthia **Chandler** land worth $200.00 now in her possession; to heirs of daughter Elizabeth **Overby** $1.00; to heirs of daughter Nancy **Brame**, $1.00; to son Clark **Royster**, land whereon I live and all else sold and divided among my living children.
Exrs: son Clark **Royster**.
Wts: Lewis M. **Jiggers**, David **Overby**.

131- thru 139- Acct. of sales of property of Thomas **Coley** Sr. by R. H. **Coley**, admstr, Dec. 3, 1844- mentions W. J. G. **Coley**, William **Coley**, Thomas B. **Coley**, John **Coley**, Wm. **Coley** Sr., Mary **Coley** and others bought at sale, sold by Richard H. **Coley** admstr.

139 thru 146- Estate of William A. **Hamilton**, deceased, by Patrick **Hamilton** from Aug. 1840 to Feb. court 1845 mentions P. **Hamilton** surviving partner of Mercantile Co.

146- thru 152- Sale off estate of Ann A. **Jones** deceased, by Eaton H. **Kittrell**, excr. Oct. 31, 1844- S. L. **Kittrell**, J. H. **Kittrell**, bought at sale.

152- thru 154- Yalabusha Co., Mississippi- Robert **Blalock** went before Hon.

Estate Records of Granville Co, NC Volume 13-16

John W. **McLemore**, Judge, David **Mabry** sheriff and Davidson M. **Rayburn**, clerk of court of Yalabooshe Co., Miss. and ask that Robert **Dallahite** be appointed his guardian, and at same time **Dallahite** asks for letters of guardianship of William, Etna, Rebecca and Millington minor heirs of William **Blalock** deceased, late of Henry Co., Tennessee. He was bonded for $12,000 with John A. **Wilson** and Hugh B. **Johnson** securities.
Wts: D. M. **Rayburn**, Samuel **Pool**- Dec. 3, 1844.

154- thru 161- Acct. of sale of estate of Samuel **Moss** deceased, by D. A. **Paschall** and James T. **Starke** excrs. Feb. court 1845.

161- 162- Sale of property of Wyatt **Currin**, deceased by Fleming **Beasley** special admstr. mentions Mrs. Elizabeth **Currin**, Ansil and Abner **Currin**, Feb. court 1845.

162, 163- Inv. of estate of Anthony **Sale** deceased, by Thomas A. **Sale**, admstr. Feb. court 1845 mentions 10 negroes in Tennessee and note of William M. **Sneed** of Mississippi and Peter **Epps** of Tennessee.

163- 164- Current acct. of estate of Collin **Winfree** deceased, by Phaltick **Tuck**, admstr. Dec. 20, 1844.

164- 165- Inv. and sale of estate of Benjamin **Overton**, deceased, by Jas. **Fuller** admstr. mentions Harriet **Overton**. Feb. 1845.

165- Sale of negroes of William **Kittrell**, deceased, by John W. **Young** excr. Jan. 1, 1845.

166- Sale of estate of heirs of William **Elixson**, deceased, by James M. **Satterwhite** admstr. Feb. court 1845.

167- Current accts. of estate of Willie **Jones** deceased, by John **Jones** admstr. -from Dec. 9, 1843- to Feb. court 1845- widows support given.

168- thru 170- Acct. of sales of estate of Benjamin **Williams** dec'd by Thomas T. **Hester**, admstr. Nov. 13, 1844 mentions Mrs. **Williams**, John S. **Williams**, Person **Williams** Feb. court 1845.

170 Sale of negroes from estate of John **Mays** deceased, by L. A. **Paschall** Dec. 1844.

400
171- Hire of servants and mill and fixtures of estate of B. G. **Long** deceased, by Stanford **Long** admstr. - Dec. 31, 1844.

171- 172- Acct. of estate of Cannon **Parham**, deceased, by Cannon **Parham**

Jr. Dec. 4, 1844.

172- 173- Inv. and sale of estate of S. **Parrish**, deceased, by H. J. **Parrish**, admstr- Nov. 29, 1844 and sale of property.

173 thru 223- Inv. of money, Bonds and accounts and sale of estate of Warren **Amis** deceased, by [blank space-no name] from Dec. 19, 1842- mentions Miss Ann **Amis**, Thomas **Amis**, William **Amis**, John **Amis** Jr., Alexander **Amis**, Estate of Lewis **Amis**, estate of Joseph **Amis**, James **Amis**, Elizabeth **Amis**, William **Amis** admstr of Lewis **Amis**, dec'd (Warren **Amis**. was a merchant)- sale Oct. 4, 1844- was goods of the store. Dr. Lewis **Amis**, Lewis **Amis**- bought at sale here - Feb. court 1845.

224- thru 235- Inv of estate of David J. **Young**, deceased, taken Nov. 13, 1844 by James H. **Young**, excr. had 54 negroes, land and negroes in Mecklenburg Co, 1/7th of slaves and 50 acres Mecklenburg Va. and lot in Clarksville, Va. 1/7th of personal estate of late Wm. **Hester**, 2 ½ shares of personal estate of late Mary **Hayes**, an undivided moiety in store known as Jas. H. **Young** and Co., disputed claim to negroes belonged formerly to Jennette **Nelson** of Tennessee, purchased by her from William **Glenn** of Tennessee, land whereon Mrs. Elizabeth **Melton** lives formerly laid off as her dower.

237- Aug. 6, 1844- Joseph H. **Gooch** appointed sheriff of County.

240- thru 242- Jan. 11, 1842- proved May court 1845
James **Wyche**- - - - wills to wife Pamela, negroes, stock, furniture, tools and all kept together for children that are with her and the charges for board and give them credit for work on farm or other services rendered with wife Pamela in complete control and she may give to the children as she wish of negroes and other personal property; In two years when ¾ths of my children will be over 18 yrs. old the land on Tarr river may be sold and 1/3rd of proceeds kept for my wife for her lifetime, or she may buy another place in this State or elsewhere. At her death to be sold and divided among the children; To Excrs. in trust for my son William and wife Sally, during their natural lives, land I bought of Lewis **Reavis** adjoining town of Henderson, N. C. containing 10 or 11 acres and at their death to Sally's survivors; That of personal estate that my wife can spare and my lots and houses in Henderson, and my interest in tobacco ware house, my shares in Raleigh and Gaston railroad, to be sold and all debts collected and my bills paid. The residue of estate to children deducting from share of sons John, William and George $1000.00 and from share of son Peter and son Ira, $300.00; The estate of D. L. **Evans** is complicated and no other person can explain it and the guardianship of his children. The arrangements made by Lewis **Reavis** Esq., Mary J. **Evans** and John B. **Manier** relative to that and other matters, I have settled and owe none of them anything except Mary **Manier** dower money deposited in my hands by order of court and my estate is not to pay them anything by lawsuit or otherwise.- - -
Exrs: son Parry **Wyche** and Ira T. **Wyche**.

Wts: John **White**, William E. **Wyche**, David **Speed**, Hugh **Waddell**.
243- Oct. 23, 1844- proved May court 1845.
Mitchel **Satterwhite**- - - - wills to brother Elijah, my gold watch, $225.00 and one acceptance on Robert A. **Smiley** for $100.00 which has been protested in bank of Va. at Richmond; to brother Stephen, all my interest and stock of goods in firm of M. and S. **Satterwhite** amounting to $300.00, also all book accts and bonds, my leather trunk and its contents excepting money and papers; after debts paid, to Susan **Burroughs**, ½ of estate including money and bonds and other half to Sally Ann **Borroughs** and if either die then the property to the other or heirs of them and if neither have heirs to go to E. and S. **Satterwhite**.
Exrs; Stephen and Howel **Satterwhite**.
Wts: Charles **Barker**, William **Satterwhite**.

401
244- Jan. 26, 1845- proved May court 1845.
Zachariah **Allen**- - - - wills to wife 280 acres whereon I live, negroes furniture, tools stock etc for her lifetime or widowhood, then sold and divided among my children, but Elizabeth **Pruit's** part to remain in trust with excr. for her and her children, and also 30 acres of land she lives on, furniture, stock etc on that tract of land and at her death sold and divided among her children; Each child to have a horse, bed and furniture, hogs etc.
Exrs: Thomas B. and James **Allen**.
Wts: Tinsley J. **Walker**, Lemuel **Mitchel**.

245- Nov. 11, 1844- May court 1845.
Nuncupative will of William **Montague**, deceased, proven on oaths of Dr. Z. M. **Paschall** and Archibald **Powell** before Donaldson P. **Paschall**, J. P. willed to daughter Polly Ann, a negro and a horse; to son Alexander a negro and he to remain on land with his mother; to wife Barbary land whereon I live and all personal property not disposed of and at her death equally divided among my children; my son Thomas is now ill and I think he will not live, but of he does he is to get his share to be equal to daughter Polly Ann and son Alexander.
Exrs: brother John **Montague** and Latney **Montague**.

246- 247- Apr. 10, 1845- proved May court 1845.
William **Veazey**- - - wills to wife Nancy, the 121 acres known as the *Fielding tract* whereon I live, for her lifetime or widowhood, 2 negroes and their increase, all furniture, 4 horses and all stock, a road wagon, all crop and provisions; When any one of my four children who are living with me come of age or marry my wife to give them enough to make them equal with that given the other children; those living with me now are Rebecca, Elizabeth, Isham and William; To son Isham, a horse and to equal that given son William; My sons Isham and William to have the 114 acres to cultivate by paying $20.00 a year rent; At death of wife the personal estate sold and daughter Rebecca given $100.00, and rest divided equally between all my children; Son Fielding owes me money as does my son Joseph for which they are not to pay interest.
Exrs: son Alfred M. **Veasey**.

Wts: Elijah **Hester**, Elisha **Umsted**.

247- thru 253- Inv. and sale of perishable estate of and money of Capt. John **Royster**, deceased, by Clark **Royster**, excr, Jan. 4, 1845 and sold Mar. 14, 1845- among buyers were M. D. **Royster**, William **Royster** Jr., Wiley and Banester **Royster**, James **Royster**, S. B. **Royster** and others.

254- thru 256- Estate of Lemual **Goodwin**, deceased, by Samuel W. **Smith** admstr. Inv. and sale Mar, 24, 1845.

256- thru 261- Inv. and sale of estate of George **Floyd**, deceased, by executor Samuel **Fuller**- - - excr. including that left widow and two deaf and dumb daughters and that left William **Floyd**. Sold Dec. 9, 1844.

261- thru- 263- Anthony **Sale** died without a will, leaving widow, Margaret M. **Sale** and children; Mary T. **Epes**, Allen H. **Higgs** and Eliza G, his wife, Thomas A. **Sale**, Theophilus A **Sale**- We agree May 5, 1845 to separate the estate between us, that is certain negroes divided and to widow certain personal estate also and at her death to go to Thomas A. **Sale** who is admstr. of estate and Thomas A **Sale** is also to take into his possession the share belonging to the heirs of Washington A. **Sale**, and that not divided to be sold.
Wts: Moses A. **Neal**.

264- Other estate of George **Floyd**, deceased, found by excr. Samuel **Fuller** which says in one part that Lewis **Floyd** son of George **Floyd** made note payable to William **Floyd** Sr. excr. of William **Floyd** Sr. given Feb. 16, 1828 and no doubt the father settled it with his son and we are told Lewis is not good for anything.

264- 265, 266- Inv. and sale of estate of Wyatt **Currin**, deceased, by Fleming **Beasley** admstr. Feb. 1845- and sale made Mar. 1, 1845. Buyers include Ansel, Mrs. **Currain**.

402

267- thru 269- Inv. and sale of estate of Thomas **Critcher**, deceased, Feb. 28, 1845 by William **Fleming**, admstr. - Among buyers were Elizabeth **Critcher**, John **Critcher**, Minty Ann **Critcher**, Anderson **Critcher**, Mary **Critcher**- also gives widow a years support.

270- 271- Inv. of estate of Mitchel **Satterwhite**, deceased, by Stephen **Satterwhite**, admstr. May court 1845.

271- thru 273- Inv. of property of estate of Isaac **Duncan**, deceased, May court 1845- by Affa **Duncan**, excrx.

274- thru 276- Acct. with Wardens of the Poor of County May Ct. 1845.

Estate Records of Granville Co, NC Volume 13-16   119

276- Mar. 13, 1845- Sale of estate of Benjamin **Wilson**, deceased, by Letha **Wilson**, special admstr.

277- List of property sold by Burgess **Adcock**, admstr of estate of Stephen **Adcock**, deceased, Nov. 27, 1844-

278- Years support laid off for widow of George **Floyd** Sr., deceased Dec. 9, 1844.

278- Inv. of estate of Charles **Wilkerson**, deceased, Feb. 12, 1845 and Inv. of estate of Martha **Wilkerson**, deceased, by J. H. **Young**. admstr.

278- Inv. of estate of Margarett **Daniel**, deceased by J. H. **Young**, admstr Feb. 12, 1845

279- Estate of Mary **Baily**, deceased by Peleg S. **Rogers** May 7, 1845.

279- thru 282- Nov. term 1842- Petition of Edward **Steed** and wife Lucy, and of Mary, Harriet, Sally, Damsel, La Fayette, William and Frank children of Frank and Sally **McCraw**, minors, by their guardian Lucy **Coghill** and Robert **Hughes** trustee- - Stating that Thomas **Coghill** (**Cogwill**) died leaving will in which he devises certain negroes and other personal estate as well as land in trust with Robert **Hughes** for the support and maintenance of his daughter Sally **McCraw** and her children for the life of his daughter and then the estate to be divided among her children and that the estate remaining is to be divided (after Sally's part taken out) to the other children (and his wife Lucy); children are Damsel **Debnam**, Lucy **Hughes**, Mary **Reavis**, and daughter Sally **McCraw**, in trust with Robert **Hughes**. Sally **McGraw** died before her father Thomas **Coghill** and Edward **Steed** has married Lucy the daughter of Sally **McGraw**, deceased. They ask division of estate left children of Sally **McGraw**, deceased in eight equal parts- Division and allotment made Nov. court 1842- - -

283- 284- Feb. term 1843- Petition of Nancy **Walker** - widow of John **Walker**, and children and heirs of John **Walker**, namely: Alexander, Anderson, Joseph, Thomas, William, Tensly, Bemis, Rebecca, Catherine, and Amarilis **Walker**- state that John **Walker** died in Oct. 1842, possessed of 200 acres adjoining lands of Lewis **Heflin**, Zachariah **Allen**, Thomas **Thomason**, Dr. **Dorsey**, Richard **Stroud**, Berry **Pretty** and others and that Anderson, Alexander, Joseph and Thomas reside outside the State- Nancy **Walker**, the widow, asks her dower right in land. She received 56 acres May 27, 1843.

284 thru 286- Aug. term 1842- Petition of William W. **White** and wife Mariah L., Mary **Southall**, Martha S. **Staunton**, minor, by guardian Mary **Southall**, William H. **Staunton**, minor, by guardian Mary **Southall**- - - - State that Henry J. **Staunton** died some years ago possessed of certain negroes of which two were sold by N. N. and Mary **Southall** (Mary being the widow of Henry **Staunton**, and married after

his death said **Southall**) for $750.00 and one of the children namely, Mary **Staunton**, has married James **Southall**, brother of N. N. **Southall** and both consented to sale of said negroes. James **Southall** and wife Mary are both now dead leaving N. N. **Southall**, sd. James **Southall**'s only brother, and that he too is now dead. The heirs ask petition of all negroes. The negroes were divided into 3 parts and allotted to William W. and Mariah **White**, Martha S. **Staunton**, and William H. D. **Staunton** Oct. 25, 1842.

287- 288- Nov. term 1843- Petition of Rowan **Blalock** States that Thomas **Blalock** died Oct. 1843 and that she is widow- that he owned 1164 acres of land. That Thomas **Blalock** left surviving him Rebecca and Millington

403
Blalock, minors; Widow asks dower in land- allotted to her Nov. 28, 1843.

289- 290- Nov. term 1843- Petition of Rebecca **Roberts** widow of James **Roberts**, deceased, who died Aug. 1843 possessed of lands in Orange and Granville Co., N. C. adjoining lands of Wm. H. **Jones**, William **Hampton**, America **Wheeler**, Thomas and Mark **Roberts** containing 980 acres on Nap of Reeds creek whereon James **Roberts** lived and died and also a tract adjoining Wm. **Ferebeau**, Abner **Jones**, Edward **Jones** and Henry **Gates** containing 380 acres of which a part was given to Presley **Roberts** son of James, dec'd. The widow asks that her dower be laid off in those lands lying in the county of Granville, N. C. - The following are the heirs of said James **Roberts** deceased: Sylvia married to Mark **Roberts**, Lively married to Thomas **Roberts**, Prestly **Roberts**, Simeon W. **Roberts**, Alcy **Roberts**, Walter A. **Roberts**, Willie P. **Roberts**, Nathaniel **Roberts**, Rebecca **Roberts** and Martha **Roberts** of whom the last are under age. Rebecca **Roberts** was given 396 acres of which 82 lies in Orange Co., N. C. Feb. 2, 1844.

291- 292- Petition of Elizabeth **Butler**, widow of John P. **Butler**, deceased who died Sept. 1843 leaving the widow Elizabeth and children: Virginia, Annis and Rebecca. He was possessed of 200 acres on Fox creek and widow asks her dower in same. She was allotted 66 2/3rds acres Dec. 4, 1843.

292- 293, 294, 295, 296- Nov. term 1843- Petition of Samuel **Hunt**, admstr. of Alfred **Hester**, deceased, Lewis **Parham** admstr of William **Hester**, dec'd, Henry **Hobgood** admstr. of Mary **Hayes** deceased, Wm. **Gordon** and wife Nancy by D. J. **Young** their agent, David J. **Young** assignee of Garland **Hester**, Solomon **Hayes** and wife Milly and Francis **Hester** Jr. and also as assignee of the late Robert **Hester** deceased- -
State that Benjamin **Hester**, who died in 1830 left a will in which he devises certain things to the children of his brother Francis **Hester** deceased, of personal property. They state that there are 42 negroes not divided and ask division to them the legatees. They also state that David J. **Young** has purchased the portions of Garland **Hester**, Robert, Francis **Hester**, Solomon **Hayes** and wife Milly, and a half the share of William **Gordon** and wife Nancy and also the division hereafter to be

Estate Records of Granville Co, NC Volume 13-16   121

made in estate of Mary **Hayes** among her heirs at law; Archibald **Hayes**, Francis **Hayes** and ½ the share of Stephen **Hayes** and also share of Samuel **Clark** in right of his wife Sally in division of share divided by Lewis **Parham** admstr. among heirs of William **Hester** deceased. The negroes were divided into 8 lots and distributed Dec. 28, 1843.

296- thru 303- Nov. term 1843- Petition of Samuel **Hunt** and wife Sarah, Gardner **O'Briant** and wife Ann Eliza, Parthena **O'Briant** a minor by her guardian Gardner **O'Briant**, Francis G., William P. and Emily R. **Hester**, minors by their guardian James **Ellis**, all heirs of Alfred **Hester**, deceased. And of John H. **Tippett** and wife Mary, Henry **Hobgood** and wife Milley, James **Hayes** and Elizabeth **Hayes** minor heirs of Alfred **Hayes** by their guardian Thomas **Hobgood**, Stephen **Hayes**, Archibald **Hayes** and Francis **Hayes** heirs of Mary **Hayes**, deceased, and Francis K., and Thomas G. **Hester**, Samuel **Clark** and wife Sally, Solomon **Clark** and wife Rebecca, and Harriet, James and William **Hester** minors by their guardian heirs of William **Hester** deceased. William **Gorden** and wife Nancy, Francis **Hester**, Solomon **Hayes** and wife Milley, Garland **Hester**, Daniel T. **Gooch** and wife (who is only heir of Robert **Hester**, deceased), and Daniel J. **Young** assignee of late Robert **Hester** and of Garland and Francis **Hester**, Solomon **Hayes** and wife Milley, Wm. **Gorden** and wife Nancy, Stephen, Archibald and Francis **Hayes**- - - - State that Benjamin **Hester** died in 1830 after willing certain land containing 2500 acres to William, Alfred, Francis and Robert **Hester** and we being children and heirs at law wish our allotted part of said land divided to us; that is 1/8th part of land to each of following; heirs of Alfred **Hester**, William **Hester**, Mary **Hayes**, Robert **Hayes**, Solomon **Hayes** and wife Milly, William **Gordon** and wife Nancy, Francis **Hester**, Garland **Hester**, each 1/8th part David J. **Young** purchased the shares of most of them- The land was divided and allotted Jan. 20, 1844- - = see plat on next page.

404
Benjamin Hester Land see p. 299 Bk 16, page 313 for other part of plat herein.

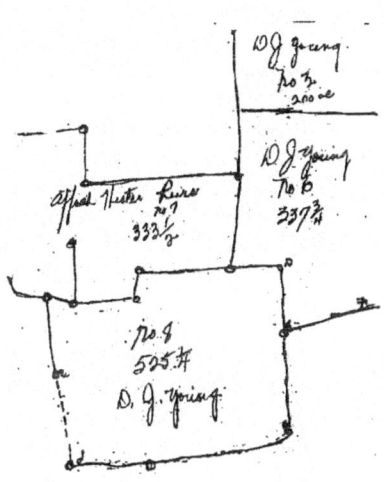

405
Benjamin Hester land p. 299 Vol 16

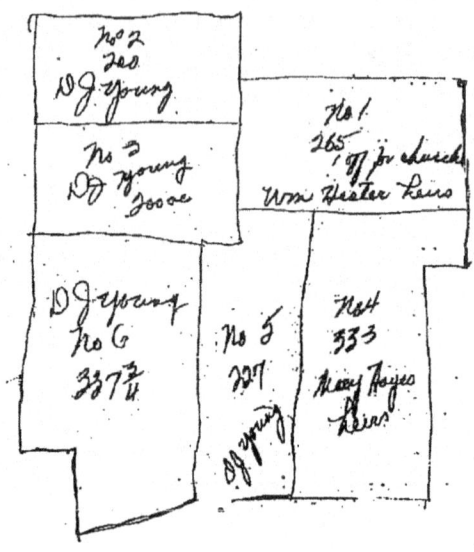

406
304- 305- Feb. term 1844- Petition of George T. **Cook** and Mary B. **Cook**, Narcissa, Elizabeth, Henry and Lucy **Cook** (**Cooke**) - stating that they were devised under the will of their grandfather Thomas **Blacknall**, deceased, certain property of which there are 8 negroes; They ask a division of negroes. They are all minors represented by their guardian Augustine **Harris**. The negroes were divided and allotted Mar. 16, 1844.

305- thru 308- Feb. term 1844- Petition of Wm. **Hester** and Rowan **Hester** by their guardian James **Ellis**, Francis G. **Hester**, Gardner **O'Briant** and wife Ann Eliza, Parthenia **O'Briant** by their guardian Gardner **O'Briant** and James **Ellis** and wife Mary, Samuel **Hunt** and wife Sarah- Mary **Ellis** is widow of Alfred **Hester** deceased, now wife of James **Ellis**- - state in petition that they wish negroes of estate of Alfred **Hester** deceased, divided among them as widow and children and nearest of kin of sd. Alfred **Hester**. Parthenia **O'Briant** in right of her mother, now deceased. They ask 7 equal shares and each allotted his rightful share. Allotted to James **Ellis** in right of wife Mary, William **Hester**, Rowan (Roan) **Hester**, Gardner **O'Briant** in right of wife Ann Eliza, Parthenia **O'Briant**, Samuel **Hunt** in right of wife Sarah, Francis G. **Hester**.

308- thru 310- Feb. term 1844- Petition of Sarah **Husketh**, widow of William **Husketh** who died in 1842, leaving widow and the following heirs at law, namely: Archibald **Husketh**, Eliza wife of Charles **Quarles** (**Qualls**) Wm. D. **Husketh**, Charles H. **Husketh**, Lucy Ann **Husketh**, Emeline **Husketh**, and Eliza **Husketh**, the last two minors. That William **Husketh**, deceased, was possessed of 120 acres of land adjoining that of Rose **Blackwell**, Stephen **Johnson**, Robert **Jones**, Henry **Williams** and others and another of 68 acres adjoining John **Davis**, Israel F. **Dilliard** and others and an undivided 1/10th part of 60 acres formerly belonging to Thomas **Husketh** The widow asks her dower in the lands. She was given 65 acres Apr. 3, 1844.

310- thru 312- An amended petition of James **Ellis** and wife Mary, state that Alfred **Hester** late husband of Mary, now wife of James **Ellis**, died leaving the widow and following children: Sarah wife of Samuel **Hunt**, Ann Eliza wife of Gardner **O'Briant**, Francis G. **Hester**, Parthenia **O'Briant**, a minor, by her guardian Gardner **O'Briant**, William and Rowan **Hester** minors by their guardian James **Ellis**- State that Alfred **Hester** died possessed of 1012 ½ acres of land and that Mary, widow of Alfred **Hester**, now married to James **Ellis** is entitled to dower right in land, and therefore asks for same. She received 332 ½ acres Feb. 1844.

313- thru 316 - Feb. term 1844- Petition of Samuel **Hunt** and wife Sarah, Francis G. **Hester**, Ann Eliza and husband Gardner **O'Briant**, Parthenia **O'Briant**, minor by guardian Gardner **O'Briant** and William **Hester** and Rowan **Hester** minors, by their guardian James **Ellis**- state that as heirs of Alfred **Hester** they are entitled to 1012 ½ acres of land he died possessed of subject to dower of Mary **Ellis**, formerly widow of Alfred **Hester**, dec'd. They ask division of land- It was divided into 6 lots, No. 1 contained 120 acres, 2=109 acres, 3= 103 acres, 4=131 acres, 5=117 ½ acres, 6=89 acres. Gardner **O'Briant** No. 1- Lot No. 2 to Samuel **Hunt**, Lot no. 3 to Francis G. **Hester**, No. 4- to Rowan **Hester**, lot No. 5 to William **Hester**, lot 6- to Parthenia **O'Briant** she being infant daughter of Jane **O'Brient**, dec'd late wife of Gardner **O'Briant**- Feb. 17, 1844.
See plat on following page- - Page No. of Vol. 15 Wills- - 314

316- thru 318- Lewis **Reavis** died in Nov. intestate, leaving widow Sarah **Reavis** and children: Peter S., George J., John J. **Reavis** and Elizabeth J., wife of Lewis **Kettle**, Mary W. wife of Alexander **Butler**, Sarah T. wife of William E. **Wyche**. He sd. Lewis **Reavis** had a tract of land containing 800 acres, one of 200 acres, 175 acres, and 50 acres in Warren county. Asks dower right and is allotted same June 11, 1844.

407
Land of Alfred **Hester**, deceased, divided to his widow, her dower and children–page 314 - Vol 16.

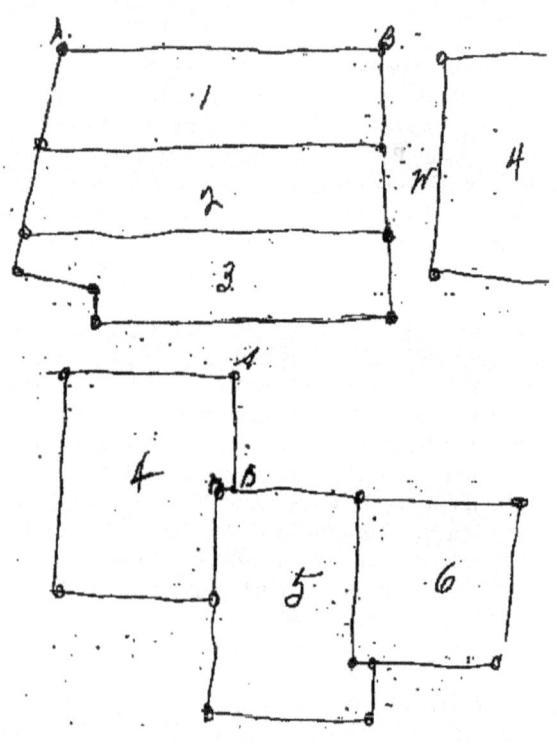

408
319- thru 320- May term 1844- Charles **Eastwood** died March 1844, leaving a widow, Sarah and the following children: Elizabeth, Lucy, Henderson, Nancy wife of James **O'Briant**, Willie, Izabel and Robert **Eastwood** of which Izabel and Robert are minors, and Willie **Eastwood** lives outside the State. State that Charles **Eastwood** was possessed of 280 acres being land whereon he lived and died. The widow, Sarah **Eastwood**, asks dower in land. She was allotted 81 acres Oct. 31, 1844.

321- Nov. term 1844- John **Washington** died leaving a will probated Nov. term 1844 and the widow Nancy **Washington** not satisfied with the provision made for her, entered her dissent thereof. She state that he owned 75 acres in the county and asks her dower in same. John **Washington** died in Oct. 1844- She was given 25 acres Jan. 15, 1845.

Estate Records of Granville Co, NC Volume 13-16

322, 323, 324- Nov. term 1844- Joseph and Benjamin **Kittrell** by their guardian Thomas J. **Hicks** and Louisa **Kittrell** and Melissa wife of Robert B **Gilliam**, and Robert B. **Gilliam** as executor of estate of Eliza T. **Kittrell** deceased, as children of the late Benjamin **Kittrell**, are heirs to certain negroes. They ask division of negroes to them, each their share. The negroes were divided and allotted thus: to Louisa **Kittrell**, to R. B. **Gilliam**, to heirs of Eliza **Kittrell** deceased, to Benjamin **Kittrell** and Joseph **Kittrell** - Nov. 16, 1844.

324- thru 326- Nov. term 1844- Benjamin **Williams** died in 1844, and was survived by his widow, Henrietta and the following children: Robert A., William S., Julia A., Plummer H. **Williams** minors. He was possessed of a tract of 162 acres and one of 103 acres and a lot in Oxford, N. C. The widow asks her dower right in lands. She was allotted 88 2/3rds acres Jan. 31, 1845.

327- thru- 328- Nov. - term 1844- Littlebury **Tucker** Sr. died leaving surviving him a widow, Elizabeth **Tucker** and son Littlebury **Tucker**, his son and four grandchildren: Susan, Green, William and Robert **Tucker**. He died in August 1844- possessed of 210 acres of land and widow Elizabeth asks dower allotted her. She received 71 acres Dec. 23, 1844.

328- 329, 330- Wyatt **Currin** died leaving survivors: wife Elizabeth and children; James, Wyatt Jr., Betsy, Thomas, Ansel and Susan **Currin**. He was possessed of 500 acres of land and widow Elizabeth **Currin** asks dower right in land. She was allotted 136 acres Apr. 2, 1845.

330- thru 332- Feb. term 1845- John A. **Norwood** died July 1842 leaving his widow Penny G. **Norwood**. She asks her dower in lands he possessed. She was allotted 67 acres Apr. 15, 1845.

332- thru 334- James **Levister** died in 1841, leaving widow Anna **Levister** and the following children: George, William and Patsy **Levister** and Beckey who married John **Loyd**. The widow Anna **Levister** asks her dower in 135 acres of land. She is allotted 42¼ acres Mar. 28, 1845.

334, 335- Nov. 14, 1839- proved Aug. court 1845.
Darling **Bass**- - - wills to wife Roday, all my property as long as is widow but if marries only that law allows her; After her death to her son she had by Jesse **Charves** before I married her called Henry **Anderson** and he is to take care of his mother and when he dies to leave the property to his children. Henry **Anderson** executor.
Wts: John, Eliza J. Mary T. **Mallory**.
John **Mallory** appointed admstr.

335- 336- Jan. 28, 1838- proved Aug. court 1845.
Philip **White** - - - wills to wife Ann a bed and furniture, chest, bible. To daughter Holley **Mitchell**, negro slaves; to son William R. **White**, negroes; To daughter

Jaccey **Sims**, negroes and land whereon I now live and he to take care of his mother and all else sold and divided to my three children and my wife.
Exrs: son William R and friend Pleasant **Floyd**.
Wts: E. J. **White**, Jordan D. **Moss**.

336, 337- June 11, 1845- proved Aug. 1845.
William **Barnett**- - - - wills to have as much of estate as necessary sold

409
to pay his debts and that left to be kept together for support of his family and my wife Emerly to hold all as long as is my widow, and if re-marries then divided to all my children.
Exrs: George E. **Norwood**.
Wts: Banester and Willis A. **Royster**.

337- thru 342- Inv. of estate of James **Wyche** deceased, May 1845 mentions a library of more than 200 volumes and maps, etc, Aug. 1845.

343- thru 346- Property of William W. **Searcey** deceased, sold by James **Jenkins**, excr Apr. 21, 1845.

346- May 24, 1845- Inv. of personal estate of William **Veazey** deceased by A. M. **Veazey**, excr.

347- July 21, 1845- Inv. of property of Zachariah **Allen**, deceased, by Thomas B and James **Allen** including an inv. of that left to Elizabeth **Pruit** and her heirs which included 30 acres of land.

348- thru 349- Estate of Mitchell **Satterwhite**, Inv. of personal property by Stephen **Satterwhite**, excr. and sale which listed among buyers Elijah **Satterwhite**, William, Howell, J. P. **Satterwhite**.

350- Sale of negro belonging to estate of William **Husketh**, dec'd, by order of court by John **White** admstr., Feb. 19, 1845.

350- Sale of property of James **Roberts** deceased, by Presly **Roberts**, admstr. Aug. court 1845.

351- Inv. of hire of negroes of estate of Thomas **Blalock**, deceased, Dec. 26 by John **Sherman** admstr.

351- 352- Bonds, judgements etc of estate of Charles **Eastwood**, deceased, as guardian of Izabbella **Eastwood**, by J. H. **Gooch**, admstr and sale of estate June 14, 1845.

352- Aug, 4, 1845- Estate of John **Walker**, deceased, by Bunice **Walker**, admstr. mentions sale of Mar. 22, 1843- and amt. to widow Nancy **Walker**.

353- thru 356- Estate of Lewis **Amis**, deceased, by William **Amis** from Aug. 1843 to Aug. court term 1845.

356- thru 358- Estate of Sarah **Smith**, deceased, by John **Lewis** admstr. from Dec. 1842 to Aug. court 1845.

359- 360- Acct. of Sheriff Joseph H. **Gooch** in acct with Granville Co. Aug. 1845 -

360- 361- Debts of estate of Mary **Chambliss** deceased, Aug. court 1845.

361, 362- Assets received of estate of Benjamin **Bullock**, deceased, by D. C. **Parrish** from 1841- mentions Cash received from Edwd **Bullock** excr. of Micajah **Bullock** deceased, - returned to Aug. court 1845.

363- Joseph W. **Gooch** appointed Sheriff of county Aug. 5, 1845.

365- Acct of estate of James **Roberts** deceased, by Presly **Roberts** admstr. Nov. court 1845.

366- thru 370- Estate of Alfred **Hester**, deceased, by Samuel **Hunt** admstr. Oct. 28, 1845 returned to Nov. court 1845.

370- thru 375- Estate of Warren **Amis**, by William **Amis** admstr. from Oct. 1844- returned to Nov. court 1845.

375- Estate of Joseph **Amis**, deceased, by Lewis and E. **Amis**, excrs. from Aug. 1840 to Nov. court 1845.

381- thru 383- Estate of Thomas **Blalock** deceased, by John **Sherman** admstr mentions sale of Dec. 1, 1843 to Nov. court 1845.

384- 385- Estate of Mary **Hayes** deceased, by Henry **Hobgood** admstr. mentions amt. received from B. **Hester** estate, and admstr of A. **Hester** rendered to Nov. court 1845.

385- 386- Estate of James **Smith** Sr. deceased, by Jno. P. and Wm. F. **Smith** excrs. from Jan. 1844- to Nov. 1845.

387- 388- Estate of James **Roberts**, acct. of by administrator, Presly **Robards** mentions years support to Rebecca **Robards**, widow. Nov. court 1845.

388- Nov. court 1845- Estate of Charles **Wilkerson**, deceased, by James H. **Young** admstr. from Feb. 1845 and also acct. of estate of Martha **Wilkerson**.

410

389- 390- Estate of Isaac **Huskett**, deceased, by John **White**, executors from Nov. 6, 1843- to Nov. term 1845.

390- thru 394- Inv. of estate of William **Meadows**, deceased, and debts due Aug. 11, 1845 list amt. to Mrs. **Meadows**- Sale of property of Wm. **Meadows**, deceased Sept. 20, 1845 and Oct. 24, 1845- by Elijah **Meadows** admstr.

395- thru 400- Inv. of property of George **Bullock**, deceased, with ages and names of negroes by Joshua A. **Bullock**, admstr. also sale made Sept. 29, 1845 of estate of George **Bullock** Sr., deceased. mentions Sarah and Nancy, the widow, D. C. **Bullock**, George **Bullock** as buyers at sale List of sale of Oct. 29, 1845 also.

401- 402- Inv. of estate of Jonson M. **Hancock** deceased, by Sarah Ann **Hancock**, excrx. Feb. 25, 1845 (also spelled Johnson M. **Hancock**) and sale Feb. 28, 1845- by Sarah Ann **Hancock** admstr.-

403- 404- Estate of D. J. **Young**- sale Feb. 27, 1845- mentions sale of Fan Mill and manufactured tobacco.

404- thru 406- Sale of books belonging to estate of Thomas H. **Spruill** by Wm. **Eaton** Jr. admstr., at Oxford Sept, 6, 1845 lists sale in Warren Co. Oct. 29, 1845 of gold watch to Louisa **Spruill** (this is a legal library) and also Inv. of that not sold.

407- thru 410- Sale of estate of Philip **White** deceased, by William R. **White**, excr. Oct. 8, 1845 mentions that estate willed to legatees has been delivered by Nov. 1845.

411- Inv. and sale of estate of Mary A. O. **Hillyard**, deceased, by Dennis J. **Paschall** admstr- Nov. court 1845- sold Sept. 12, 1845- and mentions Elizabeth **Hillyard** as buying French bedstead and bureau.

412- Inv. and Acct of sale of Sally S. **Davis**, sold Oct. 27, 1845 by Lewis J. **Davis** Admstr.

413- Inv. of property of Warren **Amis**, deceased, by Wm. **Amis** admstr. Oct. 3, 1845- sale of same.

414- Inv. of estate of Alfred **Hester**, deceased, by Samuel **Hunt**, admstr Nov. court 1845.

414- 415- Apr. 10, 1845- proved Nov. court 1845.
Simpson **Mangum** - - - - wills to wife Nancy, land whereon I live, all furniture and everything else for her lifetime; to son Peighton G. **Mangum** and family to move into one of my houses and stay there until my wife's death and he is to sell any negro disobedient to my wife and give her the money; To Lucy, wife of my son

Peighton G. **Mangum** shall not ride my horses except to preaching and then not a greater distance then 10 miles unless urging necessity; To nephew Simpson **Estes** 22 acres known as the *Sam Jones Tract*; At my wife's death all else to be divided to son Leighton and his children.
Exrs: James M. **Mangum**, my friend.
Wts: D. S. **Cannady**, Thomas **Hicks**.

416- June 1, 1839- proved Nov. court 1845.
Frances **Henderson**- - - - wills to son John L. **Henderson**, all I own and he to be executor.
Wts: Thomas **Newton**, Jeremy **Hilliard**.

417 thru 422- Estate of Francis **Hester** deceased, by Thomas **Hester** admstr. Inv. and sale thereof Nov. 27, 1845- mentions as buyers Francis **Hester**, among many others.

422- thru 426- Inv. and sale of property of William **Barnett**, dec'd Nov. 25, 1845 by G. W. **Norwood**, excr. and sale Nov. 25, 1845 mentions among buyers Robert S., Mrs. Emily, Thomas B., Joseph W., James P. **Barnett**.

426- thru 428- Inv. and sale of property of James **Allen** deceased, by Wm. J. **Mallory**, admstr- Nov. 22, 1845 sold Dec. 19, 1845- mentions among buyers - Dosea **Allen**, William P. **Allen**.

429- thru 433- Inv. and sale of property of James **Hicks**, deceased, by James A. **Hicks** admstr. Dec. 2, 1845- mentions among buyers Fabian, Nancy, Alfred B. **Hicks**.

411
434- The legatees of estate of Thomas **Coley** Sr., deceased, namely; James **Coley**, Richard **Coley**, Thomas **Coley**, William G. **Coley**, William **Coley**, Willis B. **Robertson**, Silas F. **Robertson**, Joshua **Bullock**, Thomas **Moore**, Miss Polly **Colley**- - Dec. 21, 1844- - - have agreed to divide the negroes of the estate agreeably between them and ask certain commissioners to make division for them which division they will stand by without dissent. Therefore the division was made in 10 lots to the legatees Dec. 21, 1844.

436- 437- Inv. and sale of estate of Simpson **Mangum**, deceased, by James M. **Mangum** excr. - sold Nov. 26 1845 and among buyers were Peighton G. **Willia**, James T. **Mangum** - and land sold to John **Byrd**.

438- thru 445- Estate of B. G. **Long** deceased, by Stanford **Long**, admstr mentions that paid over for funeral expense of Rebecca **Long** and funeral sermon of B. G. **Long**. Also asks to be given guardianship of ward as is best than caring for ward as admstr. Feb. 3, 1846.

445- 446- Inv. and sale of estate of Littlebury **Tucker**, deceased, by Thomas B. **Lewis** agent for Elizabeth **Tucker**, admstr of sd. **Tucker** Dec. 24, 1844- almost all furniture bought by John R. **Hicks**, John **Tucker** and Littlebury **Tucker** Jr. recorded Feb. court 1846.

447- 448- Estate of Joseph **Lewis** deceased, by Thomas B. **Lewis**, excr. Dec. 2, 1844 and sale thereof -

448, 449- Sale of Elizabeth **Tucker** by Manson **Breedlove** Feb. 1846.

450- Jan. 1, 1846- George **Floyd** estate by Samuel **Fuller**, excrs. lists hire of negroes of estate for benefit of Susan **Cordain (Cardain)**.

450- 451- Rent of mills, dwelling house, plantation of estate of B. G. **Long** deceased, by Stanford **Long**, admstr. Sept. 13, 1845 mentions P. T. **Long**.

451- Estate of Darling **Bass** deceased, by John **Mallory**, admstr Feb. court 1846 taken Jan. 23, 1846.

454- Nov. court 1843 Estate of William G. **Elexson**, deceased, by Stephen **Beasly** Jr., admstr to Jan. 29, 1846.

456- 457- Estate of Kennan **Parham** Sr. deceased, by Kennon **Parham** Jr. excr. mentions sale of Dec 4, 1843- to Jan. 31, 1846.

458- Estate of William **Kittrell**, deceased; by John W. **Young** excr. mentions sale of Dec. 6, 1843 to Jan. 9, 1846.

459- Estate of Susan **Willis**, deceased, by Edward **Royster** excr. from June 1844 to Jan. 3, 1846.

460- Estate of Samuel **Cottrell**, deceased, by James A. **Crews** excr. from Feb. 1844 to Feb. 5, 1846.

462- 463- Sept. 21, 1842- proved Feb. court 1846-
Samuel **Blanks**- - - - in his will states that he is taking a long journey and not knowing that he may ever return wills that all he has of personal property be sold and also the land he has in Person and Granville Co., that part of estate he will have - from his father's when his mother is dead, also that of same estate I bought of my brother Richard in May 1833, also all that part in Person Co. and any other he may be entitled to after Mothers death and I wish all, after debts paid, to be divided into three parts and given to my sister Sarah R. wife of James R. **Watson** and her children, one third to sister Jane, wife of Thomas **Stokes** and her children; the other part to all my brothers and sisters and my mother if she outlives me.
Excrs: John T. **Wilkerson** and if does not outlive me or if my mother die, I wish David S. **Wilkerson** to be executor.

Wts: James, Warren **Amis** and Gabriel **Jones**.

463, 464- Sept. 4, 1838- proved Feb. court 1846.
Sarah **Gooch**- - - wills to her daughters Betsey **Gooch** and Prudence **Terry** the $120.00 already given them; to daughter Martha **Smith** and son John **Gooch** $120.00; To daughter Elizabeth **Gooch** ¼ part of my estate, to daughter Prudence **Terry** ¼ part of my estate; to son John **Gooch** a feather bed and furniture and ¼ part of estate; To daughter Martha **Smith**, I loan for her life ¼ part of my estate then at her death to her children.
Exrs: son John **Gooch**.
Wts: Jno. R. **Hicks**.

412
464, thru 476- Sale. and Inv. of estate of Richard **Blanks**, deceased, by John T. **Wilkerson**, excr. Feb. 24, 1846 and among buyers were Miss Mary **Blanks**.

477- Inv. and sale of estate of Samuel **Blanks**, deceased, by John G. **Wilkerson**, excr. Feb. 24, 1846- May court 1846.

478- Inv. of estate of Joseph **Amis**, deceased, by Lewis **Amis** excr. Jan. 8, 1846- sold Jan. 8, 9, 10, 1846 mentions Miss. Railroad Co. and negro hire at Natchez, Miss, and money in hands of A. **Burwell** of Vicksburg, Miss. and suit in Miss. courts.

481- Acct. of sale of estate of Joseph **Amis**, deceased, by Lewis **Amis** surviving excr. Jan. 8, 9, 10 1846- - - - covers pages 481 thru 495-

496- thru 500- Inv. of estate of and sale of estate of William **Weaver** deceased, by John W. **Weaver**, admstr. Feb. 23, 1846- mentions as buyers William G. **Weaver**, Rebecca **Weaver**, Charles **Wynn**, says there is a negro in his mothers possession which she claims as her own and not part of his fathers estate. - - May court 1846.

500- thru 507- Estate of John **Brame**, deceased by James W. **Brame** and Geo. W. **Wilkerson**, admstrs. mentions allowance to widow, and sales acct. given for Mar 6, 1846 listing among buyers; John, Nancy, Sally **Brame**, John R. **Brame**, Thomas R. **Brame**, widow **Brame**, William **Brame**, William L. **Brame**- Apr. 1846.

507, 508- Sale of estate of Sarah **Gooch**, deceased, by John **Gooch**, excr May court 1846.

508- Estate of Mrs. Elizabeth **Hillyard** by D. T. **Paschall** guardian- May court 1846- mentions distributive share in estate of Mary A. Q. **Hillyards** estate.

509- 510- Inv. of estate of Mary A. Q. **Hillyard**, deceased, by D. T. **Paschal** admstr. and sale of same Sept. 12, 1845 and May 1846.

510- 511, 512- Oct. 24, 1845- proved May court 1846.
Samuel **McGehee**- - - wills to wife Susanah, for life or widowhood, 150 acres of land, 3 negroes, 2 beds and furniture, clock, chest, table, all chairs, tools, cattle, horses, wagon, hogs and sheep etc and at her death to my sons John T and William R. **McGehee** and all else when son William R. is 21 years old.
Exrs: son John T. **McGehee**.
Wts: Jno. **White**, William A. **Bobbitt**.

512- 513- July 9, 1836- proved May court 1846.
William **Lasiter** (**Lassiter**)- - - - wills to wife Elizabeth 3 negroes, a horse, saddle and bridle, a bed. and furniture and lend her, 17 other negroes, all tools, blacksmiths tools, furniture, Hatters tools and all else excepting that herein bequeathed; to son Robert W., a horse, bridle and saddle, furniture, watch capped and jeweled and after wife's death, all I have lent her; To daughter Sarah T. **Thornton** all I have given, her; to daughter Elizabeth P. **Royster**, 5 negroes and at her death to her children. Also to daughter Elizabeth all I have given her that is in possession of her husband Fabian A. **Royster**.
Exrs: wife Elizabeth and son Robert W. **Lasiter**.
Wts: L. and R. B. **Gilliam**.
Codicil Dec 23, 1844- He wills to wife all stock for life then to his son Robert W. **Lassiter**.
Wts: Jas. A. **Pattillo**, Wm. H. **Webb**.

514- 515- Oct. 17, 1833- proved May court 1846.
Sally **Royster** - - - wills to son Willis A. **Royster** all I own and he excr.
Wts: Lewis **Amis**, Jas. A. **Mealer**.

515, 516, 517, 518- - Thomas R. **Brame**, Jesse J. **Kelly**, John R. **Brame**, Saml **Brame**, Nancy J. **Brame**, Sally **Brame**, Elizabeth **Brame**, James W. **Brame**, George W. **Wilkerson**, Nancy **Brame**, widow of John **Brame**, deceased- - agree to have negroes of estate of John **Brame** deceased of whom they are all children and widow Nancy, divided without dissent, and also other property. Feb. 23, 1846.

413
518- May 7, 1846- Inv. of estate of hire of negroes of heirs of Thomas **Blalock**, deceased, for 1846, by John **Sherman** admstr.

519- Sale of part of estate of Rowland **Bryand**, deceased, by Jas. H. **Bryant** at Staunton, Dec. 7, 1844- recorded May court 1846.

519, 520- May court 1846- Inv. of personal estate of Littlebury **Tucker** deceased, by Horace H. **Rowland** admstr. -

520- 521- Estate of James **Boswell**, deceased, by Jos. D. **Hobgood** admstr Apr. 13, 1846.

Estate Records of Granville Co, NC Volume 13-16

522- Estate of James **Lyon**, deceased, by John **White** admstr. beginning Jan. 1844- to May 1846.

523- Sale and debts of estate of William **Husketh**, deceased, from Dec. 1844 to May court 1846- by admstr.

524- thru 526- Acct. of the Wardens of the Poor of Granville Co., N. C. May court 1846.

527- Mar. 13, 1845- proved Aug. court 1846-
Joe **Jackson** - - - - wills to wife Priscillah, 196 acres and 4 negroes, furniture and live stock, tools, crop; To son Ransom **Jackson**, tools; to daughter Fanny and Nancy and all my lawful children or their representatives.
Exrs: wife and son Ranson.
Wts: H **Crenshaw**, Jno. M. **Crenshaw**.

527- 528- Aug. 26, 1843- proved Aug. court 1846
John **Mangum** - - - - wills to wife Sarah, furniture which she owned at time of our marriage and lend her the land whereon I live and other articles of furniture, horse, and other things; to daughter Jane **Johnson** a bed and furniture; to Rebecca **Kemp**, Hawkins **Ray**, John **Kemp**, Miles **Kemp**, children of my daughter Sarah **Kemp**, deceased, $300.00; All negroes not given away divided into 6 parts and given to: my four sons James M., Samuel, Wilie and Wyatt; to grandson Thomas R. **Robertson** and if he die without heirs then $100.00 to his father John **Robertson** and the rest of negroes or their worth to children of daughter Rebecca **Ferrell**, dec'd that are six in number.
Exrs: son Wyatt **Mangum**, Duncan S. **Cannaday**.
Wts: D. **Cannady**, John **Nevill**.

529- Nov. 17, 1845- proved Aug. court 1846.
Nancy **Chapman**- - - - wills to all she owns to her sister Elizabeth **Chapman** and her brother Robert **Chapman** to be executor.
Wts: J. W. **Hargrove**, John **Clardy** Sr.

529- Dec. 25, 1822- proved Aug. court 1846.
Peter **Hutchinson (Hutcherson)**- - - to wife Liddy all left after debts paid for her life or widowhood and at her death to my daughter Julian **Young** and at her death to her children if any living and if not to her husband.
Exr: son- in- law David J. **Young**.
Wts: Alexander **Elixson**, Henry **Humphries**.

530- Oct. 3, 1841- proved Aug. court 1846.
Martha **Vaughn**- - - - wills to son John, a negro I bought at sale of my late husbands estate, that is Vincent **Vaughn's** estate; grdau. Martha Vincent **Edwards**; to dau. Fanny **Edwards**; to son Vincent; to daughter Martha **Edwards**; to daughter Nancy **Moss**.

Exrs: John S. **Eaton**.
Wts: Robert **Freear**, Robt. W. **Eaton**, Jas. B. **Ellington**, John **O'Brien** Jr.
Codicil- daughter Patsy **Edwards**, granddaughter Elizabeth D. **Edwards**, to grandchildren; Sarah, Lumega, Arisa, Rebecca, and Angelina **Edwards** children of my daughter Fanny **Edwards**; to sons John and Vincent- codicil added 1846-

530- July 5, 1346- James H. **Young** said in presence of Dr. William **Thorp** and Dr. John R. **Hicks** that if he died he wished his mother Mrs. Julia **Young** and his grandmother Mrs. Lydia **Hutchinson** should have all his estate and after their death to his brothers and sisters. Richard **Young** excr. - - proved Aug. court 1846.

414
    531- Joseph H. **Gooch** appointed Sheriff of Co. Aug. 5, 1846.

    532- Inv. and sale of estate of John **Bailey**, deceased, May 28, 1846 mentions John **Henly** buying furniture at sale, Ephriam, Peleg, John A. and William P. **Bailey** buyers also- Aug. court 1846.

    533- Estate of N. H. **Hill** by Walter A. **Bullock**, admstr- July 11, 1846

    534- 535- Estate of William B. **Parham**, deceased. Inv. and sale Aug. 4, 1846- by Williamson **Parham** admstr. mentions N. C., Lewis M., Asa and Collins **Parham** as buyers at sale.

    535- 536- Sale of property of Simpson **Mangum**, deceased, by Jas. M. **Mangum**. excr. Aug. court 1846.

    536 - Hire of negro of estate of Wm. G. **Elixson**, deceased, by S. **Beasley** Jr., admstr. May 5, 1846.

    536- thru 538- sale of estate of Sally **Husketh**, deceased, by Jno **White** admstr- from Feb. 28, 1846 mentions Archeby, William D. **Husketh**, John **Hendley** as buyers and mentions that paid legatees and that coming from estate of William **Husketh** deceased, for two children he is guardian for. Aug. court 1846.

    538- Acct. of J. H. **Gooch**, Sheriff of Co. - Aug. court 1846.

    539- Estate of Rowland **Bryant** Sr. in acct. with Jas. H. **Bryant**, excr. Aug. court 1846 mentions beef for Mrs. **Bryant**-

End Book 16

Abbet
  Betsey Luceean, 62
  Lucy Butler, 62
  Mary Ann, 62
  Salley Weaver, 62
Abbett
  Bennet, 62
  Bennett, 62
  Sally, 62
Abbott
  William, 92
Adams
  John Pinkney, 22
  Isaac, 23, 25
  Wilmouth, 22, 23
Adcock
  Abner, 98, 101, 103
  Ann, 101
  Burgess, 53, 119
  David Y, 98, 101
  Eady, 9, 10, 88
  John C., 99, 101
  Katey, 53
  Mary W, 101
  Rachel, 98, 101, 103
  Rowlen, 98
  Stephen, 119
  Susan, 101
  Susannah, 98
  Thomas H, 98
  Wm., 99
Addcock
  Eady, 9
Akin
  John, 64
  Polly, Mrs, 64
  William, 64
Alderman
  Tazwell S., 60
Allen
  Archibald, 99
  Dosea, 129
  Elizabeth, 117
  James, 99, 117, 126, 129
  Jo, 19
  Judith J, 99
  Mary B, 99
  Permela W, 99
  Susannah P., 99
  Thomas, 34
  Thomas B., 117, 126
  William, 99, 113

William D., 49, 61, 75, 92
William P, 129
Zachariah, 8, 117, 119, 126
Allison
  Elizabeth, 23, 36, 37
  Wm. D, 29
Alves
  James, 29
Amis
  Alex, 107
  Alexander, 112, 116
  Ann, Miss, 116
  Betsey, 69
  E, 127
  Elizabeth, 69, 72, 76, 101, 116
  James, 69, 107, 113, 116, 131
  John, 60, 69
  John, Jr, 116
  Joseph, 69, 72, 101, 116, 127, 131
  Joseph, Col, 57
  Lewis, 60, 69, 76, 101, 106, 107, 116, 127, 131, 132
  Lewis, Dr, 116
  Lewis, Sr, 72
  Martha, 4
  Susan, 112
  Thomas, 4, 17, 19, 107, 116
  Warren, 107, 113, 116, 127, 128, 131
  William, 4, 17, 19, 107, 113, 116, 127
  Wm., 55, 106, 128
  Wm. D., 97
Anderson
  Elizabeth, 14
  Henry, 125
  James, 14
  Martha, 5, 7, 26
  Mary, 5
  Mary W., 5
  Nathan D., 19
  Patience, 109
  R, 97
  Robert, 97
  Thomas P, 5

Arnold
  Ira E, 1
  Salley, 100
Ascue
  Molly, 50
Ashley
  William, 45
Askew
  Matilda, 27
  Matildy, 27
Avey
  Elizabeth, 27
Avrets
  Sally, 106
Badgett
  William, 12
Bagley
  John, 98
Bailey
  Allen, 51
  Anderson, 6, 9, 81, 87, 89
  Angram, 77
  Cairy, 11
  Cynthia G., 89
  Cynthia J., 81
  Elizabeth, 73
  Ephriam, 10, 14, 134
  Flavius J, 87
  Flavius Josephus, 81
  Glaffry, 73
  Glaphrey, 11
  Glaphry, 11
  Henderson, 51
  Israel, 6, 10, 14, 55
  Israel, Sr, 51
  Isreal, 9
  Jeremiah, 6, 9, 10
  John, 6, 9, 14, 73, 76, 134
  John A., 134
  John W., 51
  Jones, 51
  Louisa, 77
  Lucretia, 10, 11, 14, 31
  Martha, 6. 9
  Mary, 10
  Nancy, 10, 11
  Nancy G., 87
  Nancy H., 81
  Peleg, 134
  Penelope, 73

Polly, 73
Prudence, 77
Samuel, 10, 14, 73
Solomon, 51, 52, 55, 77
William, 9, 10, 11, 14, 31, 73, 76
William P., 51, 134
William T., 14
William Y., 14
Wm., 6
Baily
  Mary, 119
Baley
  Anderson, 55
  Cyntha G., Mrs, 55
Ball
  Alexander, 62
  Elizabeth, 62
  Hinton Hall, 62
  James, 62
  John, 62
  Joseph, 62, 65, 72
  Martha, 62
  Osborn, 16
  Temperance, 62
  Vinam, 62, 65, 72
Ballard
  Martha E., 112
Baptist Society, 110
Barclay
  James, 18
Barker
  Ambrose, 64, 97, 101, 102
  Charles, 64, 67, 92, 117
  Davy, 64
  James, 64
  Jemima, 97, 101, 102
  John, 64, 67, 92
  John G., 64, 92
  Martha, 64
  Polly, 64
  Sarah, 64
  Thomas R., 64
  Washington, 64
  William, 64
  Wilson, 64
Barnes
  Milley, 49
Barnett
  Benjamin, 41
  Benjm, 44

Elijah, 33, 62, 65, 95, 104
Elizabeth, 61
Elizabeth Ann, 17
Emerly, 126
J. W., 617
James, 17, 24, 44, 62
James P, 129
Jane, 61
Jesse, 41, 44
Jesse F., 44
John, 26, 41, 44
Jos, Jr, 5
Jos, Sr, 5
Joseph, 18, 24, 33, 65, 110
Joseph W., 17, 129
Joseph, Sr, 17, 23, 61
L. B., 63
Margaret, 63
Martha, 17, 61
Mary, 17, 61
Mary, Mrs, 24
Matilda, 62, 65, 104
Mrs. Emily, 129
Polley, 63
Polly, 63
Robert, 61
Robert S, 17, 33, 129
Samuel, 41, 44
T. B., 24, 61, 70, 110
Thomas B, 23, 33, 104, 112, 113, 129
Thomas D., 62
Thomas G, 41
Thos. B., 5, 17, 18, 63
Thos. G., 44
Widow, 61
William, 24, 44, 92, 126, 129
Barns
  George, 71
Bass
  Amey, 56
  Chesley, 52, 56
  Darling, 125, 130
  Diza, 38
  Hilliard, 56
  Honon, 38
  Iliza, 38
  Jesse, 38
  Maria, 56

Martha, 37, 38, 44
Mason, 52, 56
Moses, 52, 56
Nathan, 37, 44, 66
Patsy, 44
Roday, 125
Sally, 38
Warner, 38
Warnes, 44
William, 44
Woodson, 56
Wouton, 52
Bat
  John, 110
Bates
  Ann Eliza, 54
  Candis, 54
  Elizabeth, 54
  John, 54
  Susan, 54
  William, 54
Bayley
  William, 98
Baynham
  Caroline, 84
  W. J. G, 84
Beardan
  Elizabeth, 89
Beasley
  Flemeng, 87
  Fleming, 33, 74, 95, 98, 105, 106, 115, 118
  James, 22, 74
  Robert, 8
  S., 108
  S, Jr, 134
  Stephen, 13, 74
Beasleys, 29
Beasly
  Stephen, Jr, 130
Beck
  William, 60
  Wm., 77
Bennett
  Betsey, 61
  L., 88
Best
  Benjamin, 91
Blackley
  James, 16
  Jas, 62
Blackly

Estate Records of Granville Co, NC Volume 13-16   137

James, 73
Blacknall
  Carolina, 52
  Caroline, 50, 64
  Caroline G., 79
  Charles, 37, 79
  Elizabeth, 62
  Elizabeth, Mrs, 14
  George, 37, 79
  Henry, 79
  John, 37, 44, 57
  Jonathan, 37
  Jonothan, 37
  Lucy, 37
  Nancy, 37
  Thomas, 37, 41, 52, 79, 122
  Thomas, Jr, 66
  Thomas, Sr, 50
  William, 37
  Wm., 14, 37, 55, 64
Blackwell
  E, Mrs, 7
  Elizabeth, 62, 87, 94, 106
  Fanny A., 94
  James, 66, 72, 109
  John, 72
  John P, 87, 94
  Rebecca, 100
  Rebeckah, 72
  Rose, 123
  Rosey, 66, 67
  Sarah, 66, 67
  St, 66
  Stephen, 62, 72
  Temperance, 66
  William, 94
  William M., 87, 106
  William N., 79
Blackwood
  Tabitha, 89
Blalock
  Etna, 55, 79, 115
  John P., 44, 79, 108
  John S., 54
  Lucetta, 44
  Lucretta, 54
  Luetta, 79
  M., 68
  Martha, 55, 79
  Millington, 43, 44, 55, 61, 66, 79, 80, 115,
120
  Milly, 79
  Nancy, 79
  Rebecca, 44, 79, 115, 120
  Rebecca, Mrs., 66
  Robert, 55, 79, 114
  Rowan, 108, 120
  Sally, 79
  Thomas, 44, 53, 54, 66, 68, 79, 100, 108, 114, 120, 126, 127, 132
  Thos, 61
  William, 55, 79, 108, 115
Blaney
  Jonothan, 100
Blanks
  Elizabeth, 82, 59
  Jane, 82, 130
  Joseph, 59, 82
  Mary A, 82
  Mary, Miss, 131
  Nancy, 82
  Richard, 59, 60, 82, 130, 131
  Samuel, 59, 82, 130, 131
  Sarah, 82
  Sarah R., 130
  Susan, 82
Bledsoe
  Caroline, 3
  Elizabeth, 3
  Frances, Mrs, 42
  Francis, 3
  Jechoniah, 3
  Lewis, 3, 5, 42
  Meekins, 42
  Mekins, 81
  Polly, 89
Blockley
  Halyard, 14, 28
  Obeda, 14
Bobbitt
  John, 77
  Peggy, 34
  William A, 106, 132
Bodenhammer
  Wm., 54
Bodenhammers, 54
Bolby
  Prudence, 56
Boles

Molley, 29
Booth
  Joseph, 24
Boothe
  Abner, 73, 75
  Eliza, 73
Boswell
  Edward, 54, 79
  James, 99, 107, 108, 132
  Lueta, 99
  Luetta, 108
  Luetty, 107
  Milley, 54
  Milly, 79
  Rebeccah, 99
Bowdon
  John, 43, 51
  Nancy, 22
Boyd
  Amy, 4
  George, 17
  George M., 19
  George W., 4, 15
  John, 4, 15, 17, 19
  Martha, 4
  Sarah, 4
  Sylvania, 4
Bradford
  Benjamin, 75
  Davis, 75
  Hardy, 75
  Hickly, 49
  Jacob, 75
  John, 31, 75, 92
  Judith, 75, 92
  Nancy, 31
  William, 38, 75
Bragg
  Beckey, 9
  Betsey, 9
  Cisbey, 9
  David, 9
  Fanny, 9
  Hugh, 9
  James, 9
  Massey, 9
  Patsey, 9
  Peggy, 9
  Robert, 9
  Stephen, 30
  Suaney, 9
  Thomas, 9

Brain
  Thomas, 90
Bramblett
  Lonsford M, 12
Brame
  Elizabeth, 132
  George W., 132
  James W., 131, 132
  John, 131, 132
  John R., 131, 132a
  Nancy, 114, 131, 132
  Nancy J., 132
  Sally, 131, 132
  Saml, 132
  Thomas R., 131, 132
  Widow, 131
  William, 131
  William L., 131
Branstetter
  Daniel, 2
Brasfield
  Caleb, 36, 38
Breedlove
  Manson, 130
Briant
  Samuel, 110
Briggs
  Henry, 92
  Howel, 92
  Lucy, 92
Brigs
  Howel, 7
Brinkley
  Henry A, 8, 9,
  Jane, 7
Brodie
  Sally H., 111
Brogden
  James, 64
Brogdon
  David, 100
  James, 100
Brooks
  Willie, 49
Brummett
  Samuel, 75
Brummit
  Mary, Mrs, 56
  Samuel, 56
Bryan
  Joseph, 3
  Mary, Mrs, 24
  Samuel, 24
  Thomas, 24
Bryand
  Rowland, 132
Bryant
  Edward, 3, 103
  Edward T, 8
  James, 103
  James A., 104
  James H, 30
  Jas. H., 132, 134
  John, 70, 103
  John F, 40
  John F, Jr, 40
  Mary, 103
  Mrs., 134
  Nancy, 40
  Robertson, 103
  Rowland, 103
  Rowland, Sr, 103, 134
Btockley, 14
  Halyard, 14
  James, 14
  Obeda, 14
  Sally, 14
Buchannon
  Elizabeth, 99
  Hillyard, 25, 47
  Hinton, 48
  James A., 25, 47
  John R, 47
  Mary, 25, 47, 61
  Priscilla, 25, 47
  Rosa, 25, 47
Buchanon
  Agnes, 31
  Hilliard, 31
  Hinton, 31
  Hixey, 31
  James A, 31, 33
  John Ruffin, 49
  Mary, 31, 49
  Patsey, 31
  Priscilla, 31
  Prudence, 31
  Rosa, 31
  Ruffin, 31
Buckhanan
  Mary, 49
Buckhannon
  John, 11
Bugg
  Jno. L., 9
Bullock
  Adeline, 81
  Agnes, 41, 53, 80, 83
  Alexander H, 83
  Amey, 18
  Ann, 83
  Ann A, 83
  B, 19, 26
  B. F., 63
  Benjamin, 3, 18, 59, 83, 127
  Benjamin F, 41, 86
  Benjamin T., 41
  Benjamin, Dr, 101
  Catherine, 83
  Charles, 85, 86
  Christian, 53, 83
  D. C., 128
  Edward, 41, 53, 63, 77, 80, 81, 83
  Edwd, 127
  Eliza, 83
  Erasmus D, 83
  Fanny Ann, 96
  Frances, 81, 83
  Francis C, 80
  George, 86, 88, 128
  George, Sr, 128
  James, 85, 86, 96, 102
  James M., 73, 81, 82, 86, 96, 101
  James, Capt, 88
  Jane, 83
  Jas, 41
  Jerimiah, 85
  Jno. 86
  John, 2, 7, 15, 19, 43, 78, 90, 96, 97, 101
  John B., 50
  John D, 41, 55, 56
  John H., 105
  Joshua, 85, 129
  Joshua A., 128
  Joshua B., 88
  Leonard, 41, 53, 67, 80, 81, 83, 87
  Leonard H, 41
  Lucy, 96
  Lucy, Mrs, 97
  Maria, 83
  Martha, 81, 88

Mary, 85
Mary H, 105
Mary L., 53, 80, 83
Micajah, 63, 77, 81, 83, 127
Mildred, 53, 83
Mildred A, 80
Millington, 53
Minerva, 88
Nancy, 10, 85, 128
Pamela, 41, 53
Pamelia, 80, 83
Philip P., 67, 80
Phillip P., 41, 53, 83
Rebecca, 53
Richard, 3, 5, 8, 26, 28, 34, 42, 88
Richard H., 41, 63, 81, 86
Sally, 53
Sara 80
Sarah, 41, 80, 81, 83, 128
Sophia, 55, 56
Susan, 53, 80, 83, 85
Thomas J, 81
Walter A., 83, 113, 134
Weldon E., 53, 80, 83
William, 97
William H., 96
Wm., 15
Burchett
  James A, 23
  James A. J, 23
  Robert H., 3
Burchitt
  Robert A., 16
Burns
  George, 57, 105
Burroughs
  Sally Ann, 117
  Susan, 117
Burton
  Agatha, 14
  Alfred M, 14
  Augustus, 14
  Edward, 86
  Elizabeth, 14
  Fanny H, 14
  Horace A, 14
  James M, 14
  Robert H, 14

Robert M, 35
Burwell
  A, 131
  Blair, 105
  Jno. A., 69
  John A., 3, 7
  Spottswood, 3, 79
  business
  Bank of N. C., 68
  Bank of VA., 57, 117
  Bryanville Gold mine, 91
  Fan Mill, 128
  Farmers Bank of VA., 57
  Farmers Bank Stock of VA., 57
  Gaston and Raleigh railroad, 111
  Jas. H. Young and Co., 116
  Jenkins and Morris, 30
  Miss. Railroad Co., 131
  Newbern Bank, 68
  Railroad, 47
  Raleigh and Gaston Railroad, 46-48, 53, 116
  Roanoke Navigation Co., 56
  State Bank of N. C., 68
  U.S. Bank, 57
  Western & Atlantic Rail road of Georgia, 88
Butler
  Alexander, 123
  Annis, 120
  B, 6
  Elizabeth, 91, 120
  James P., 45
  John P., 107, 120
  Leonidas, 48
  Linsey, 91
  Lucy, 62
  Margaret, 110
  Mary W., 123
  Nancy, 91
  Rebecca, 120
  Virginia, 120
Byrd
  John, 129
Callet
  Cisbey, 9
Campbell

Peter, 12
Robert, 57
Canaday
  Dorris, 87, 89
  Wyatt, 82
Cannaday
  D, 133
  Duncan, 87
  Duncan S., 133
  N. E., 2
  Nancy, 2
  Nathaniel E., 2
  Wyatt, 2, 51, 56, 57, 60, 75
Cannady
  D. S., 129
Cannon
  Newton, 33
Cardain
  Susan, 130
Cardin
  Susanna, 113
Cardwell
  Anna, 62
Carmick
  Solo, 100
Carnal
  Elizabeth, 92, 93
  James, 7
  John, 92, 93
  Lucy, 30
  Margaret, 7, 24, 32, 33, 47, 92, 93
  Margret, 11
  Morris, 16
  Moses, 7, 25, 32, 33, 36, 42, 92, 93
  Moses C., 47
  Sally, 29
Carne
  Woodson, 67
Carrington
  C. H., 10
Carroll
  William, 12
Carter
  Edwd H, 2, 49
  Frederick Jones, 104
  Frederick S., 49
  Louisa A., 104
Cash
  Anderson, 81

Barsheba, 22, 23
James, 81
Jennet C, 22
Jennett, 22, 23
Nancy, 10
Prudence, 10
William, 22
Cattlett
  George, 100
Cattrell
  Thomas, 1
Cawthorn
  Archibald, 44
  James, 74
  James H., 44
  Phebe, 74
Chambliss
  Mary, 127
Champion
  Elizabeth, 112
  John, 45, 65
  Joseph, 112
  William, 112
  Wm., 14, 45
Chandler
  Daniel, 51
  David, 51, 76
  David, Sr 55
  Littleberry, 51, 52, 55, 76
  Mary Ann, 51
  McVey, 95
  Nancy, 51
  Panthia, 114
  Phoebe, 51
  Rebecca, 51
  Thomas, 51, 52, 55, 76
  William, 51
Chapman
  Elizabeth, 133
  Nancy, 133
  R. M., 92
  Robert, 133
Charves
  Jesse, 125
Chatam
  Edward, 6
Chavass
  Anderson, 109
  John, 109
Cheatham
  Eliza, 60
  Isaac, 58, 60

Isaack, 35
Isham, 35, 58, 60
James, 35, 58, 60
James, Jr, 58
James, Sr., 35
Mary, 60
Prudence, 58, 60
Sally, 35
Thomas, 60
Clardy
  John, Sr, 133
Clark
  Archibald, 4
  Cearn, 90
  Francis, 64
  John, 64
  Nancy, 64
  Rebecca, 121
  Sally, 120, 121
  Samuel, 120, 121
  Sarah, 64
  Solomon, 121
Clay
  Archer W, 2
  Charles, 2
  Charles W, 2
  Fanny, 2
  Permele T., 2
  Sophan H, 2
Clement
  Jane, 39
  Nancy, 49
  Samuel, 10
  Simon J., 49
  William, 10, 25, 28, 88, 95
  Wm., 32, 86, 89, 105
Clements
  William, 64
Clopton
  Benjamin, 13
  Sarah, 66, 67
Coaly
  David F, 8
Cobb
  Elizabeth, 43
  Jesse, 14
  Jesse H, 17
  John, 43
Cogbill
  Thomas, 90
Coghill

Damsel, 90, 119
Lucy, 88, 90, 94, 111, 119
Mary, 90, 119
Sally, 90, 119
Thomas, 88, 90, 94, 111, 119
Cogwill
  Thomas, 119
Cole
  Thomas, 30
Coley
  James, 129
  John, 114
  Mary, 114
  R. H., 114
  Richard, 106, 129
  Richard H., 114
  Thomas B., 114
  Thomas, Sr, 114, 129
  W. J. G, 114
  William, 114, 129
  William G., 129
  Willis B., 129
  Wm., Sr, 114
Colley
  Miss Polly, 129
Cook
  C. H, 9
  Elizabeth, 122
  George T., 122
  Harry, 37
  Henry, 122
  Lucy, 122
  Mary B., 122
  Narcissa, 122
  Stephen, 8
Cooke
  Benjn C., 87
  C. H., 65
  Claborn H., 51, 71
  Elizabeth, 37
  Howel, 28
  John W, 33
  Lucy, 122
  Shem, 44
  Thomans Y, 14
  Thomas B, 41
  Thomas T., 35, 73
  Thomas Y., 14, 77, 106
  Thos. Y., 65
Cooper

James, 91
James C., 105, 107, 113
Jas., 54
Cordain
　Susan, 130
Cordle
　C, 6
Cosby
　Lewis, 4
　Mary, 4
Cothron
　Archibald, 47
　Celia, 47
　Charlotte, 47
　Elizabeth, 47
　James, 47
　John, 47
　Lemuel, 47
　William, 47
Cottrell
　Amey, 105
　David, 105
　James, 105
　Mathew, 105
　Samuel, 105, 107, 130
　Solomon, 105
Cowan
　Joseph, 29
Cozard
　William, 52
Cozart
　Allen, 25, 50, 51, 59, 88
　Gemima, 50
　Hubbard, 25, 28, 32, 88
　James, 32
　James C, 25, 30, 36, 50, 52, 71
　James W., 23
　Mary, 50, 88
　Mary Ann, 50
　Mary, Mrs, 25
　Pinckney, 50
　Robert, 25
　Simeon, 25, 50, 51, 59, 88
　William, 25, 30, 32, 36, 71
Cozarts, 49
Craft
　Amey, 66
　William W., 89
Crenshaw

H, 133
Jno. M., 133
Crews
　Ashley, 1
　Gideon, 8, 31
　James A., 105, 107, 130
　Kitty B, 1
　Mary, 91
　Meredith, 96
　Meredith, Capt, 91
　Temperance, 1, 8
　William B., 96
Critcher
　Anderson, 118
　Elizabeth, 118
　John, 118
　Mary, 67, 118
　Minty Ann, 118
　Thomas, 118
Crocker
　Thomas, 110
Crook
　Rutha, 23, 41
　Ruthy, 36
Crudup
　Josiah, 46
Currain
　Mrs., 118
Curren
　Betsey, 109
　Davis, 109
　Elijah, 109
　Elizabeth, 109
　James, 109
　Lemuel, 109
　Lemuel, Sr, 109
　Lucy Ann, 109
　Mary, 109
Currien
　Lemuel, 109
Currin
　Abner, 72, 100, 115
　Ansel, 118, 125
　Ansil, 115
　Benjam, 110
　Betsy, 125
　Elizabeth, 112, 114, 125
　Elizabeth, Mrs 115
　James, 114, 125
　Lemuel, 114
　Lemuel, Sr, 112
　Stephen, 64

Susan, 125
Thomas, 125
Wyatt, 114, 115, 118, 125
Wyatt, Jr, 125
Dallahite
　Robert, 115
Dance
　Sarah, 7
　Sarah D. B., 7
　Stephen, 6
Daniel
　Arena, 48
　Arrena, 50
　Argen, 83
　Beverly, 109
　Cephas, 48
　Cephos, 11
　Chesley, 58, 80
　Chesley B, 80
　Eliza, 50
　Elizabeth, 106
　Elizabeth M, 80
　Henry M., 58, 77, 80
　James, Sr 109
　Jas. B., 63
　John, 48, 50
　John G, 109
　John J, 80
　John Sondser, 50
　Lethe, 48
　Lucy, 50
　Madison, 83
　Margaret, Mrs, 86
　Margarett, 119
　Mary, 58, 77
　N, Mrs 66
　N. S., 58
　Nancy, 77
　Nancy S., 58, 80
　Nancy, Mrs, 58
　Nathl, 7
　Nelly, 50, 51
　P. S., 58
　Priscilla S, 80
　Stephen R., 80
　Thomas, 58, 75, 86
　Thos, 50
　William N, 80
Daniels
　Artethy, 11
Davie

Ambrose, 32
Kendal, 32
Davis
  Archibald, 48
  Jacob, 33
  James B., 12, 13
  James W., 66
  John, 51, 73, 77, 82, 123
  Jonathan, 6, 26, 66, 67
  Lewis J., 128
  Martha, 12, 13
  Mary, 5
  Sally S., 128
  Sarah S., 66
  William, 63
Deadman
  Amanda, 67
  Hanry, 74
  Mrs., 67
Dean
  Daniel, 61
  Elizabeth, 7, 92, 93
  Francis, 61, 67, 72
  J., 61
  Jesse, 36, 47, 56, 60, 61, 92, 104
  Jesse C., 47, 56, 70, 82, 86, 92, 93
  Jesse Colin, 93
  Jinsey, 82
  Joseph R., 47, 92, 93
  Margaret, 47, 92, 93
  Sarah, 7, 36, 47, 56, 61, 86, 93, 104
  William, 47, 56, 70, 92, 93
  Wm. Joseph, 82
Dear
  Daniel, 27
Debnam
  Damsel, 119
  John B., 104
Debriana
  John B., 83
Dedman
  H. H., 74, 108
  Henry H, 67
Deekins
  Fanny, 15
  Fanny H., 14
  Samuel, 14
Dement

Howard, 8
Dent
  John B, 36
Dew
  Penelope, 26
  Thomas, 26
Dewey
  Julian, 96
Dickerson
  Thomas, 26
Dillard
  Cairy, 11
  Israel F., 73, 123
Diment
  Charlotte, 47
  John, 8
  Mathew, 47
  William, 38
  Willis, 8
Dixon
  John W., 78
Dodson
  Polly, 84
  Stephen, 77, 84
Dolbey
  Micajah B, 8
Dolby
  Ann, 83
  Anna, 55, 56
  Dick H., 8, 53, 55, 56, 99
  Edward, 55, 56
  James, 55, 56
  John A., 55, 56
  Penelope, 55, 56
  Prudence, 55, 56, 99
  Sophia, 56
Dorsey
  Dr, 119
Dortch
  Ann P., 14, 17
  William E., 7, 19
Douglas
  A. H., 8
  Alfred H., 9
Downey
  Izabella, 52
  Jane Smith, 57
  John, 52
  John A, 65
  Margaret, 52
  Mary Ann, 52
  Rebecca, 51

S. S., 19, 69
Saml S, 65
Samuel S., 57, 65
Samuel Smith, 57
Susan Ann, 52
Driscoll
  Timothy, 34
Drumgold
  E, 92
Due
  Thomas, 11, 73
Duncan
  Affa, 114, 118
  Anderson J., 89, 109
  Aphia, 54
  Elizabeth, 89
  George, 89
  Isaac, 54, 114, 118
  John B., 89
  Sterling H., 89
  Sterling W., 7
Dunkin
  Affa, 114
  Alfred, 70
  Anderson, 70, 78
  Elizabeth, 69, 78
  Franky, 70
Duty
  Samuel, 16, 39, 44, 76
Eastes
  Mary, 10
Eastwood
  Abraham, 32, 44
  Charles, 32, 39, 44, 124, 126
  Elijah H, 32
  Elizabeth, 32, 44, 124
  Henderson, 44, 124
  Isabella, 32
  Izabbella, 126
  Izabel, 124
  John, 31, 39, 44, 52, 63
  Lucy, 32, 124
  Mary, 31, 32, 39, 44
  Nancy, 32, 124
  Robert, 32, 124
  Sarh, 124
  Wiley, 32
  Willie, 124
Eaton
  Geo., 64
  George C., 51, 57

John L., 3, 4
John S., 19, 55, 90, 92, 95, 134
Robt. W., 134
Susan, 90
Susan, Mrs, 58, 98
Thomas R, 90, 98
William, Jr, 90
Wm, Jr 128
Edwards
  Angelina, 134
  Ann, 78
  Arisa, 134
  Betsey, 92
  Betsy, 92
  Dilly, 92
  Elizabeth, 96
  Elizabeth D., 134
  Fanny, 133, 134
  Judith, Miss 74
  Lumega, 134
  Martha Vincent, 133
  Mary, Mrs 74
  Patsy, 134
  Pomphret, 96
  Pompret, 92
  Pumphrey, 43
  Rebecca, 134
  Saml L., 66
  Samuel, 19, 111
  Sarah, 134
  Susan, 74
  Washington, 78
Elexson
  William G., 130
Elixson
  Alexander, 133
  William, 115
  Wm. G., 134
Eliza
  D, 24
Ellington
  Arrenia, 35
  Gran, 20
  Jas. B., 134
Elliott
  Alexander, 48
  Elizabeth, 48
  Frances, 48
  Nancy, 48
  Polly Ann, 48
  Robert, 48

Samuel, 48
Stephen, 48
Ellis, 111
  Elizabeth, 3
  Fanny, 110, 111
  James, 121-123
  Jno, 110
  John, 111
  Leaven, 3
  Mary, 122, 123
  Rheany, 3
  Squire, 3
  Stephen, 3
  William, 3
Ellixon
  William, 53
Ellixson
  Sally, Mrs, 108
  Sarah, 53
  William, 53
  William G., 45, 108
Emery
  Henry, 59, 74
  John, 59
  Polly, 59
Emry
  Elizabeth, 100
Epes
  Mary T., 118
Eppes
  Isham, 7
  Mary, 7, 38
Epps
  Isham, 11, 24, 38
Erwin
  William, 60
Espy
  Robt, 12
Estes
  Elizabeth, 94
  Israel, 89
  James M., 96
  Jeremiah, 89, 96
  Lucy, 13
  Simpson, 129
  Triplett, 94
Evans
  D. L., 116
  David, 2
  David L., 2, 14
  Elizabeth, 2
  Elizabeth J., 14

  George, 2
  George W, 14
  Mary J., 116
  Thomas, 2
  Thomas J. W, 14
  William, 2
  William Henry, 14
Everitt
  Joseph, 3
Falconer
  John Ingles, 68
Fane
  Jacob, 43, 50
  James, 43
  Sally, 43, 50
Farrarr
  Martha, 4
  Thomas J, 4
Farrow
  Absalom, 91
  Almire, 50
  Cicero, 91
  Elizabeth, 91
  Emily, 91
  Fanny, 91
  James, 83
  Lucy, 50, 83
  Martha, 91
  Matilda, 91
  Mildred, 91
Female Humane Society of Richmond, VA., 57
Ferebeau
  Wm., 120
Ferrand
  Em. P., 100
Ferrell
  Rebecca, 133
Flemeing
  William F., 67
Fleming
  William, 8, 32, 41, 56, 70, 73, 75, 87, 98, 118
Flemming
  Frances, 83
  William, 83
Fletcher
  Joseph, 71, 82
  Leanah, 78
  Mary, 82
  William, 78
  William L., 71

Floyd
  Ann Mariah, 29
  Buck, 76
  Charles, 11, 39, 44, 76, 113
  Delila, 39
  Delilah, 39
  Elizabeth, 11, 113
  Geo.., 71
  George, 11, 39, 44, 76, 118
  130
  George, Jr, 11
  George, Sr, 113, 119
  Henry, 28, 29, 36, 113
  James, 28, 29
  Joshua, 39
  Juda, 113
  Judy, 113
  Lewis, 113, 118
  Mariah, 28
  Martha, 76, 113
  Nelly, 113
  Obedience, 39
  Pleasant, 39, 44, 76, 99, 126
  Polly, 113
  Presley, 39
  Rachel, 76
  Rosey, 113
  Salley, 28, 29
  Sally, 11
  Samuel, 39
  Stephen, 28, 29, 39, 44, 76
  Susan, 29
  Susanna, 113
  William, 11, 27, 39, 44, 76, 113, 118
  William, Jr, 27
  William, Sr, 118
  Wm., 71
  Wm., Jr, 11
Floyde
  William, 11
Ford
  Sally, 89
  William, 57
Forkner
  Dilly, 92
  Littleton, 92
Forrest
  William P., 73
  Wm. P., 70
Forsythe
  Christian, 26
  James, 6
  L. P., 61
  Mary, 85
  Saml P., 38, 56
  Samuel P, 25, 52
  William, 56
Fosters, 29
Fowler
  Daniel, 73
  Moody, 65
  Patsy, 73
Fraizer
  Elizabeth, 62
  Ephraim, 62, 66
  Ransom, 62
  William, 62
Freear
  Betsy, 53
  Elizabeth, 53
  Elizabeth B., 95
  John, 53
  John E., 95
  Margaret, 53
  Margaret H, 95
  Mary, 53
  Mary S., 95
  Robert, 1
Freeman
  Lucy, 30
  Penny, 99
Fruar
  E. J., 3
Fuller
  Crofford, 13
  Daniel, 13
  Green, 74
  James, 70, 113
  Jas., 115
  John, 78
  Jonathan, 111
  Lucy, 13
  Mary, 13
  Nancy, 40, 74
  Ozborn, 13
  Ruffin, 105
  Saml, 5
  Samuel, 40, 113, 118, 130
  William S., 12
Furguson
  Mary G., 70
Gales
  Joseph, Sr, 68
Gardner
  Jno. A, 36
Garner
  Margret P., 70
Garrard
  William W, 39
Gates
  Henry, 120
Gay
  Abner U., 49
George
  Susan, 29
Gill
  A. E, 100
  Benjamin, 81
  Francis, 81
  Gideon, 81, 87
  Gideon E., 51, 60
  James, 81
  John M., 60
  Joseph, 81
  Mary, 81
  Polly, 51, 87
  Robert, 81
  Samuel, 81
  Widow, 60
  William, 81
  William A., 51, 60
  Wm. A., 86, 99, 103
Giiliam
  John, 24
  L., 19, 43, 49, 112, 132
  Leslie, 35, 51, 61, 62, 71, 77, 103
  Melissa, 125
  R. B., 125, 132
  Robert B, 35, 105, 125
  Robert G, 9, 50
  Robt. B., 69
  Wm. H., Capt, 50
Gilloom
  Robert G., 50
Glandening
  Wm., 11
Glendening
  Sarah, 11
Glenn

Chargls, 12
William, 116
Glover
  Absalom, 2, 23
  Charles, 2, 30, 46
  Charles P, 2, 68
  Daniel, 2, 46, 59
  David, 33
  David K., 46, 52, 59
  Elisabeth, 33, 46
  Joseph P., 2, 52
  Mary, 30, 46, 68
  Phebe, 33, 46
  Polly, 33, 46
  William, 33
  William B., 46
Gooch, 29
  Ailey, 78
  Amos, 39, 44, 64, 84, 85
  Betsey, 131
  D. F., 77
  Daniel, 17, 39, 44, 64
  Daniel T, 39, 44, 64, 84, 100, 112, 121
  Danl T., 109
  Dudley S, 39, 44, 64
  Elizabeth, 131
  Hannah, 39, 44, 64
  J. H., 126, 134
  James, 17, 39, 44, 64, 75, 96
  Jane, 39
  John, 131
  Joseph, 39, 44, 64
  Joseph H., 67, 72, 95, 105, 116, 127, 134
  Joseph W., 127
  Martha, 131
  Nancy, 39, 64
  Prudence, 131
  Rachel, 39
  Radford, 56
  Rowlin, 53
  Samuel, 39, 64
  Sarah, 131
  Thomas, 32, 39, 44, 52, 64
  Thos., 63
  William, 39, 44, 64, 78
Goock
  Hannah, 39
  Nancy, 39
Goodloe
  David S., 49
Goodman
  Francis, 110
Goodwin
  Lemuel, 53, 109, 118
Gorden
  Calvin, 54
  Elizabeth, 54
  James, 54
  John, 54
  Lawson N., 54
  Mary, 54
  Mary Jane, 54
  Samuel, 54
  Sarah, 54
  William, 54, 121
  Wm., 121
Gordon
  John, 8
  Nancy, 120, 121
  William, 120, 121
Graham
  Saml. L., 57
  Wm. A., 6
Gramer
  Margret P., 70
Gran
  Rachel, 10
Graves
  Betsey B, 15
  Betsy, 7
  Betsy C, 4
  Betsy, Mrs 7
  E. C., 7
  Elijah, 4, 7
  Elijah C., 4, 15
  Elijah Calvin, 15
  Elizabeth, 15
  Elizabeth C., 4
  Henry, 7
  Henry L., 4, 15
  James L., 7
  Jesse, 7
  Jesse D., 4
  Jessee D., 7
  Jesse Deekins, 15
  Ralph, 7, 15
  Ralph H, 15
  Ralph H.[enry], 4
  Ralph Henry, 4, 15
  Salina, 7
  Selina, 7
  Selina F., 4
Green
  Ann L., 70, 74
  Elizabeth, 2, 22, 32
  Elizabeth, Mrs, 25
  George W, 2, 22
  Isaac, 2, 22, 32, 42
  John, 1, 2
  John B, 2, 22
  Joseph, 2, 22, 25
  Lewis, 70, 74
  Martha, 40
  Mary, 10, 22
  Mary A, 2, 22, 25
  Nancy, 2, 22
  Nathaniel M., 58
  Rachel, 32
  William, 2, 22, 25, 74
Gregory
  J. R., 60
  William O, 33
Griffin
  Phebe, 33, 46
  Weldon, 33, 46
  William, 33, 46
Grisham
  E. Grissom, 44
  H. J., 44
  Hilliard J., 44
  Nancy, 44
  Polly, 113
  Salley, 44
  Willie, 44, 65
Guarner
  John, 100, 104
  Nancy, 100
Halliburton
  Lethy, 55
  Letty, 55
Hamilton
  Alexander, 16, 28
  Charles E., 97
  P., 28, 76, 114
  Patrick, 16
  William A., 76, 114
Hamme
  Elizabeth, 67
  Henry, 67
Hampton
  Wilborn L., 49
  William, 120

Hancock
  Johnson M., 128
  Jonson M., 128
  Sarah Ann, 128
Handley
  Thomas, Sr, 66
Haraway
  John T, 39
Hare
  J. M., 111
  Agnes, 68
  Dr., 6
  Dr. Len. H, 18
  H, 18
  L. H., 25, 66
  Len. H., 45, 111
  Leonard, 50
  Leonard H., 51
Hargrove
  Charles M, 17, 27
  Charles W., 20
  Hartwell W, 20, 79
  Israel, 20, 27
  Israel W, 20, 95, 98
  Isreal, 17, 20
  Isreal W, 20
  Isreal, Sr, 20
  J. W., 133
  Mary, 20
  Mary A., 95, 98, 106
  Nancy J., 95
  W, 106
  William, 17
  William R., 20
  Wm. R, 20
Harnett
  Martha, 105
  Thomas, 105
  Wially, 105
Harper
  William, Dr, 78
Harris
  Arena, 48
  Augustin, 22
  Benj F., 107
  Benjm F., 87
  Catherine, 83
  Charles, 9
  Elizabeth, 11, 73, 82
  Hanson, 81
  Hardy, 22
  Harvey, 82
  J. W., 11
  James, 73
  John, 9, 11
  John, Sr, 16
  Lethe, 48
  Mrs., 11
  Rebeckar, 100
  Robbin H., 31
  Robert, 83, 87
  Robert H., 11
  Robin Hood, 28
  Rowland, 11, 48
  S. J., 107
  Samuel J., 87
  Thomas, 28, 31, 73, 76
  Thomas H., 11
  Thos., 97
  William, 9, 11
  Willis, 20
Harrison
  Robert, 28, 36
Hart
  Amy, 63, 94, 95
  Ann, 70, 94
  Edward, 70
  Elisha B., 41
  Elizabeth, 63
  James, 63, 65
  James A., 94
  James, Jr, 65
  James, Sr, 16, 63, 104
  John, 94, 95
  John G, 5, 63, 65, 70, 82, 94
  John G., Col, 70, 112
  Joseph, 70
  M. S., 65
  Maurice, 112
  Maurice S., 63, 65, 70, 94, 95, 104
  Nancy, 63, 65, 112
  Pleasant, 63, 65, 70
  Polley, 63
  Polly, 63
  Rebecca, 63, 65, 70, 94, 95
  Susan, 50, 82, 94
  Susan G., 94, 95
  W. S., 5
Haskins
  Aaron, 10
  Ann, 10, 32
  Anney, 32
  Aron, 16, 32, 59
  Elizabeth, 10, 32
  Geo, 59
  George, 10, 16, 32
  Isaac, 10
  Isaack, 32
  James, 10, 16, 32, 59
  John, 10, 32
  Mary, 10
  Pirsely, 10
  Polley, 32
  Prissey, 32
  Rachel, 10, 32
  Thomas, 32
Haswell
  Julia Adaline, 73
  N, 77
  Nancy, 73
  Nathan, 73
  Sabilia Hawkins, 73
Hawkins
  Alexander B., 97
  George W., 97
  Henry A., 2
  James M., 52
  Joseph W, 22
  Joseph W., Dr, 57
  Madison, 50
  Thomas P, 2
  William J., 92
Hayes
  A., 59
  Alfred, 71, 74, 121
  Archibald, 120, 121
  Elizabeth, 121
  Francis, 120, 121
  Francis K., 121
  James, 121
  Mary, 76, 108, 116, 120, 121, 127
  Milley, 121
  Milly, 120, 121
  Nancy, 37, 121
  Peter, 31, 48
  Robert, 121
  Simon G, 55
  Solomon, 120, 121
  Stephen, 76, 120, 121
  Thomas G., 121
Haylander
  Julian, 96

Haywood, 90
Haze
  Alfred, 110
Hedgepeth
  Carter, 67
  Richard B., 67
  Sally, 82
  Sarah, 67, 70
Heflin
  Ava, 74
  Buckhorn William, 74
  Cary, 74
  Charles, 8, 74
  Elizabeth, 8, 74
  Lewis, 49, 74, 119
  Mary, 74
  Nancy, 74
  Phebe, 74
  R. T., 75
  Susan, 74
  William, 74
Hegee
  Jas. W., 2
Heggie
  James M., 59, 74
Helfin
  Rufus T., 74
Henderson
  A., 6
  A. E., 6, 65, 70
  Archibald, 28, 48, 50
  Archibald E., 50
  Frances, 129
  John L., 6, 12, 24, 25, 129
  L., 15, 25
  Leonard, 6, 12, 24
  Wm. F, 111
Hendley
  Hudson, 44
  John, 134
  William, 13
Henley
  John, 9
  Patsey, 9
Henly
  John, 134
Hennings, 29
Herndon
  Rhodes W, 8
  Rodes N., 50
Hester

A, 127
Alfred, 67, 71, 76, 89, 98, 109, 110 120-124, 127, 128
Alphia, 54
Ann Eliza, 121-123
Aphia, 54
B, 77, 127
Banja, 110
Benj, 43
Benjamin, 49, 50, 54, 74, 76, 108-110, 120, 121
Benjamin B., 70
Benjamin, Capt, 64, 65, 89, 97
Bennet, 91
Bennett, 64, 65, 74, 89, 97
Drucilla, 44, 54
Druciller, 54
E, 45, 52
Edmund, 97
Elijah, 5, 7, 8, 14, 23, 24, 38, 55, 61, 64, 69, 95, 105, 117
Elizabeth, 54
Elizabeth Ann, 7
Emily R., 121
Faith, 54
Francis, 49, 110, 120, 121, 129
Francis G., 44, 77, 89, 121-123
Francis, Jr, 120
Garland, 120, 121,
H., 91
Hamilton, 16, 26, 27, 41, 44, 54, 72, 73, 86, 89, 92, 104
Harriet, 121
Hiram G., 44, 54
Huggins, 110
Isaac, 49
Isham E., 7
James, 24, 121
Jane, 123
Jeremiah, 54, 110
John, 54, 110
Joseph, 6, 7, 8, 10, 11, 24
Mary, 24, 54, 89, 91, 96, 121-123
Mary D., 91

Mary Dyer, 110
Mary J., 24
Mary W, 7
Mary, Mrs., 64
Milley, 49, 121
Milly, 120, 121
Nancy, 49, 54, 77, 84, 121
Polly, 22
Rebecca, 49, 121
Roan, 122
Robert, 77, 84, 100, 109, 110, 112, 120, 121
Rowan, 122, 123
Sally, 120, 121
Samuel, 110
Sarah, 121-123
Solomon, 121
Thomas, 129
Thomas T., 49, 111, 115
Thos. T., 49, 52
William, 15, 50, 110, 120, 121-123
William P., 121
Wm., 116, 122
Zachariah, 41, 44, 54, 72, 73
Hicks
  Abner, 61
  Alfred B., 129
  Benjamin, 1
  Fabian, 129
  James, 129
  James A., 129
  Jno. R., 63, 64, 69, 131
  John, 1
  John R, 1, 54, 91, 130
  John R, Dr, 113, 134
  John W., Jr., 78
  Lucy, 37
  Mary, 60
  Nancy, 129
  Polly T, 1
  Thomas, 22, 73, 129
  Thomas J., 1, 5, 12, 19, 114, 125
  William, 78
  William R., 113
Higgs
  Alfred, 20, 21, 27, 28, 36
  Allen, 6, 15, 21
  Allen H., 15, 20, 21, 118

Ann, 28
Calvin, 15, 20, 21
Cassey, 21
Eliza, 21
Eliza G., 118
Elizabeth, 9, 21, 23, 28, 40, 45
Ella, 20, 21, 28
Ellen er, 38
Elly, 70
Francis M, 28
Jackson, 21
John, 20, 21, 28, 38, 48, 113
John, Jr., 21
John, Sr, 20, 21
Kenchen, 15
Kenelin, 48
Kesiah, 21
Kinchen, 21, 25
Kinchen H, 20, 21
Kinchen, Sr., 21
Kinchn, 15
Leonard, 20, 21, 48
Mary, 5, 21, 28, 36, 38
Nancy, 21, 27, 36
Nelly, 21
Polly, 21
Rebecca, 21
Rebecca, Mrs., 6
Sebert J., 20, 21
Sibert J., 15
Sothern, 40
Sothorn, 38, 40
Southan (Southern), 6, 8, 9
Southan J., 6
Southen, 28
Southern, 5, 13, 15, 20, 21, 23, 25, 27, 30, 36, 38, 45, 48
Southey J., 20, 21
Susan, 15, 21
Susan A., 15, 20, 21
Thomas H, 20
Willia, 21
William, 20, 21, 27, 28, 36
Willis, 21
Willis H, 20, 21
Willis L., 38
Woodson, 15, 20, 21

Hight
  Harbira H., 107
Hill
  N H, 134
  N. L., 113
Hilliard
  Jeremy, 57, 129
Hillyard
  Banjamin, 54
  Benja F., 54
  Benjamin, 54
  Benjamin F, 54
  Betsy, 54
  Elizabeth, 16, 54, 128
  Elizabeth, Mrs 131
  Harriet, 54
  J. W., 54
  Joseph W., 54
  Martha, 54
  Mary, 54
  Mary A. O., 128, 131
  Sally, 54
Hobgood
  Barnett, 35
  Fowler, 86
  Henry, 76, 86, 108, 120, 121, 127
  Hezekiah, 86, 94, 98, 106
  James B., 86, 98, 106
  James H., 106
  James P., 33
  Jas. D., 100
  John, Jr ., 35
  Jos. D., 132
  Joseph D., 54, 79, 107
  Mary, 106
  Milley, 121
  Nancy, 54, 79
  Sarah, 86, 94
  Sterling, 33
  Thomas, 86, 121
  William, 86
Hockaday
  William, 88
Hodge
  Frances A, 28
  William H, 28
Hodges, 91
Hogan
  William G., 5
Holmes
  Wm., 111

Hope
  Benjamin, 1, 6, 18, 19
  Eliza Elizabeth, 6
  Elizabeth, 1, 18, 19
  Mariah, 18
  Mary, 18
  Nancy, 18
Hopkins
  Nancy, 21
Hough
  Cornelius, 18
House
  Joseph, 39
Howard
  Allen, 17, 20, 24, 52
  Anderson, 17, 24
  Elizabeth, 17
  Joseph, 17, 20, 24, 31, 40, 46, 52, 91, 96
  Mary, 31, 40, 46, 91
  Phebe, 17
  Rachel, 39, 64
  Solomon, 17, 24
  Thomas, 17, 24, 39, 64
  William, 17, 23
Howell
  Elizabeth, 111
Howerton
  Ann C., 6
  Mariah, 6
  Thomas, 6, 38
Howze
  James, 30, 42, 45
Hubbard
  Elizabeth, 16
Hubble
  Ransoms, 9
Huddeston
  L., 67
Huddlestone
  Nancy, 110
Hudson
  Nancy, 74
  Susan, 74
Hudspeth
  Sally, 71
Huggins
  S. B., 100
Hughes
  Lucy, 90, 119
  Robert, 90, 119
  Robert P., 88, 94, 101,

111
Robt, 90
Humphries
 Henry, 133
Hunt
 Absalom, 64
 Alfred, 109
 Amy, 78
 Ann M, 16, 26, 27
 Edward, Jr., 109
 Elizabeth Taylor, 78
 Fanny Ann, 96
 J.T, 109
 James, 78
 John, 15
 John T., 96, 104
 Mary S., 78
 Mary T., 78
 Memucan, 3, 31
 Sally Anderson, 78
 Samuel, 71, 76, 109, 121-123, 127, 128
 Samuel, Jr, 67, 89, 98
 Sarah, 121-123
 Thomas P., 78
 Thomas T, Maj, 3
 William, 3, 34
 William, Col, 31
 Wm., 34, 97
Husketh
 Ann, 59, 79
 Archeby, 134
 Archibald, 122
 Archiby, 59
 Charles H., 122
 Eliza, 122
 Emeline, 122
 Isaac, 109
 John, 32
 Lucy Ann, 122
 Sally, 134
 Sarah, 122
 Thomas, 59, 79, 99, 123
 William, 122, 123, 126, 133, 134
 William D., 134
 William Jr., 59
 Wm. D., 122
Huskett
 Archeby, 110
 Isaac, 128
 Sally, 110

William, 110
William R., 110
Huskey
 Ann, Mrs., 68
 Archeley, 106
 Elizabeth, 106
 Isaac, 106
 Isham, 106
 James, 106
 John, 106
 Mary, 106
 Thomas, 68
 Wm., 65
Husted
 Hiram W, 6
Hutcherson
 Agnes, 31
 Asa, 16
 James M, 16
 John, 5, 16, 40
 Joshua, 16
 Lewis M., 5
 Peter, 133
 William C., 5
 Willis, 16, 31, 48
 Willis B., 53
Hutchinson
 John, 23
 Julia, 134
 Julian, 133
 Mrs., 113
 Lydia, Mrs, 134
 Peter, 133
Hutchinsons
 Joshua, 38
Hutson
 Cephos, 65
 Elizabeth, 63
Inge
 William B., 96
Ingles
 Courtney, 68
 John, Col, 68
Jackson
 Fanny, 133
 Joe, 133
 Nancy, 133
 Priscillah, 133
 Ransom, 133
James
 Solomon, 27
Jeffrets

Sarah, 5
Jeffreys
 Betsey, 102
 Betsy, 102
 Dorcas, 102, 104
 Elizabeth, 6
 Robert, 100
 Sally, 102
 Sarah, 6
 Sidney, 102
 William, 102, 103
Jeffries
 Betsey, 102
 Sally, 102
 Sidney, 102
Jeffrys
 Littleton Washington, 27
 Sarah, 27
 William, 27
Jenkin
 James, 82
Jenkins
 Haskey Ann Nelson, 37
 James, 126
 John, 73
 John W., 104
 Mansfield D, 30
 Nancy, 22, 23
 Robert A., 95, 98, 109, 113
 Walter, 22
 William, Jr, 58
Jiggers
 Lewis M., 114
Jiggetts
 Susan, 96
Jiles
 John, 22
 Sally, 22
Jinkins
 Haskey Ann Nelson, 37
 Elizabeth, 10
 James, 71
 John, 10, 18
 Mansfield D, 36, 45
 Margaret, 58, 72
 Mary, 26
 Robert, 42
 William, 72
 William, Jr, 58
 William, Sr, 58
Johnson

Alfred, 21
Anderson, 40
Aveyrilla, 40
Betsy, 21
Celestia R., 103
Clary, 89
Daniel, 20, 21, 23, 40
Drusilla T., 103
Eleanor, 40
Eliza, 20, 21
Elizabeth, 23, 25, 40, 45, 48
Ellen er, 38
Elly, 21
Hugh B., 115
Jane, 133
John, 21
Kasandra, 40
Lucinda, 103
Martha, 53
Martha J., 103
Mary, 20, 28, 36, 103
Mary W., 21
Nelly, 21, 48
Permela W., 99
Polly, 21
Sarah, 36
Sarah A., 103
Southern H., 40
Stephen, 14, 36, 103, 123
Stephen, Jr, 36
Virginia P., 99
White, 21
Willey, 21
William, 21, 23, 25, 40, 45, 53
William A., 99
Willia[m], 28
Willis, 20, 21, 33, 36
Willis H, 21
Wm. A., 113
Wm. H, 36, 38
Zachariah, 40
Jones
  A., 36
  Abner, 32, 41, 43, 78, 120
  Abner N. M., 86
  Ailey, 78
  Alfred, 28, 41, 59, 78, 86
  Alfred N., 78
  Alfred, Capt, 25, 26

Allen, 78, 86
Amos, 43
Amos P, 43
Amos T., 84, 85
Amos T. T., 88
Amy, 78
Ann A., 111, 114
Ann Alston, 71
Ann H., 111
Betsey Ann, 13
Daniel, 68
David, 26, 31
David P., 88
Dicey, 32
Duffy, 43, 84, 85, 88
Eady, 26
Edward, 86, 87, 101, 120
Edward, Jr, 41, 78, 86
Elizabeth, 1, 12, 94
Elstada, 78
Everad S., 104
Gabriel, 24, 48, 49, 101, 106, 131
Gabriel, Sr., 17
H. W., 61
Hannah, 78
Henry W., 43, 44, 86, 88
Henry, Jr, 44
Horon, 38
Indianna, 12, 94
Jane, 41, 45, 75
Jinsey, 42
John, 101, 115
John K, 37
Jonathan, 26, 31
Leanah, 78
Lewelen, 71
Lewellen, 111
Littleton Y, 86
Lotan, 42
Loton, 43
Lotus, 88
Louisa A., 104
Lucy, 49, 104
Marion, 78
Martha, 9
Mary, 78, 92
Mary Ann, 81, 97
Mary F., 92
Nancy, 9, 10, 68, 88
Nash, 103
Nicolas, 9, 10

Nicholas G., 88
P. E., 86
P. E. A., 92
P. E. A., Col, 92
Polly, 9, 34, 77, 78
Portheus A, 12
Protheus E. A., 96, 19
Ralph, 78
Rebecca 10, 78
Reuben, 7
Riffin, 88
Robert, 37, 78, 111, 123
Robert A., 67, 81
Robert B., 97
Ruffin, 43, 84, 85
Ruffin T, 84
Sally, 9, 10
Saly, 9
Sary, 88
Solomon W., 88
Thomas, 41-45, 59, 65, 75, 84-86, 88
Thomas L., 4
Thomas W., 44
Wiley, 34
Wiley E., 77
William, 1, 12, 44, 78, 86, 94
William D., 4
William H., 88
William, Capt, 33
Willie, 101, 115
Wm., 49
Wm. H., 120
Jordan
  John, 68
Jordon
  John, 52
Juliner
  Tamazer, 109
Junel
  Amy, 4
  John, 4, 19
Junior
  John, 17
Kay
  Cynthia J., 81
Kearney
  Kinchen, 100
Kearny
  Joseph, 57
Kemp

Hawkins Ray, 133
John, 133
Miles, 133
Rebecca, 133
Sarah, 133
Kendall
　Eli, 5
Kennon
　Lewis, 43
　Mildred, 43
Kettle
　Elizabeth J., 123
　Lewis, 123
Kimball
　B., Col, 68
　Bart, 3, 16
　Bartholomew, 33
　Edward, 32
　W. P., 68
　Winifred P, 33
King
　Edwin, 92, 96
　Henry N, 18
　John, 48
　Long, 38, 48, 61
　Mary Ann, 48
　Sally, 48
　Susan, 48
　Thomas, 39
　Thomas L., 47, 61
　Thos. L, 37, 64, 70, 104
Kingsbury
　R. H., 57
Kittrell
　Abagail, 55, 59
　Benj, 8
　Benja, 8, 38
　Benjamin, 27, 30, 42, 82, 125
　Benjm, 27
　Eaton H., 111, 114
　Eaton S., 111
　Egbert, 105
　Eliza, 82
　Eliza T., 125
　Elizabeth, 106
　Eugenia, 105
　Eugenia E, 105
　Eugenia Elizabeth, 105
　Fielding, 55, 59
　Geo., 66, 70
　George, 30, 42, 47, 50, 104
　J. H., 114
　John William, 105
　Joseph, 82, 125
　Loretta, 105
　Loretta Y, 105
　Louisa, 125
　Louise, 82
　Lucy Frances, 105
　Maria, 105
　Maria Jane, 105
　Martha, 105
　Martha B., 105, 107
　Mary, 105
　Melissa, 82, 125
　Rebecca, 105
　S. L., 114
　Tabitha, 105
　Tabitha Ann, 105
　William, 37, 105, 107, 115, 130
Kivon
　Virginia, 13
Knight
　Alfred, 105
Knott
　Caleb, 36
　David, 97, 101, 102
　David W., 74
　Elizabeth, 36
　Erasmus, 36
　George, 36
　Jas, 6
　John, 36
　Lundy, 97, 101, 102
　Milly, 36
　Risdon, 36
Landers
　Clark, 3
Landis
　Augst, 49
　Augustin, 67
　Elizabeth, 22
　John, 22
Lanear
　Robert, 25
Lanier
　Benja A, 23
　Benjamin, 22
　Elizabeth, 22, 23
　John, 22
　Mary, 45
　Nancy, 22
　Polly, 22, 23
　Robert, 22-24, 45
　Sally, 22
　W. H., 1
　Wilmouth, 22
Lasiter
　Elizabeth, 132
　Elizabeth P., 132
　Robert W., 132
　Sarah T, 132
　William, 132
Lassiter
　Robert W., 132
　William, 132
Lawrence
　A., 75
　Abraham, 37, 62, 75
　Anna, 62
　E. O., 75
　Elizabeth, 70
　Henry B., 70
　John P, 13, 62, 75
　Leanah, 70
　Leannah, 62, 98
　Leanner, 75, 98
　Lemuel J., 70
　Lydia, 75
　Margret P., 70
　Mary G., 70
　Robert, 70
　Turner, 75
　William, 62, 70, 98
　William T., 13
　William, Sr, 73
Laws
　Jonathan, 85
　Louisa, 85
　Susan, 85
Leamon
　Temperance, 8
Lears
　Jane, 77
　William, 77
Ledbetter
　Richard, 13
Lee
　Jane, 83
　Robert, 83
Lemay
　Ann, 30
　Easter, 68

Jno. P., 67
Joel, 1
John, 1, 5, 8, 31
John C., 5, 97, 101
John J, 75
John P, 13, 24, 30, 75
John T., 30
Kitty B, 1
Lewis, 1, 31
Lucy, 24, 75
Lucy A, 30
Margret, 75
Milderd, 101
Mildred, 97, 101
Polly T, 1
Richard, 5
Richard W., 1, 31
Robert M., 5
Samuel, 1, 5, 8, 26, 31
Susa, 5
Susan, 1, 8
Susanna F., 75
Temperance, 1, 8
Lemon
  Judith, 34
  Judy, 87
Levister, 102
  Ann, 114
  Anna, 125
  Beckey, 125
  George, 114, 125
  James, 114, 125
  Patsy, 125
  William, 125
Lewis
  Ann, 112
  Charles, 112
  Edward A., 82
  Eliza, 112
  Elizabeth, 43
  Emily, 112
  Fanny A, 96
  Henrietta, 112
  James, 69, 82, 86, 112
  James, Sr., 73
  Jno, Jr., 11
  John, 86, 112, 127
  John, Col, 88
  Joseph, 112, 130
  Lucy, 96
  Martha, 112
  Mary A., 82

Mary Eliza, 88
Nancy, 68, 69, 112
Polly, 112
Sally, 112
Sally Ann, 112
Susan, 112
Thomas, 112
Thomas B., 43, 54, 112, 130
Willis, 43
Wm. H., 50
Ligon
  Alexander, 55
  Rebecca, 55
  William P., 48, 55, 106
Lile
  Benjamin, 99
  Catherine, 99
  Thomas, 11
Littlejohn
  J. A., 97
  James T., 97
  Jas. B., 97
  Thomas B., 15, 41, 54, 56
Logan
  James, 12
  William P., 49
Long
  B. G, 115, 129, 130
  B. H., 100
  Benja G., 100, 114
  Benjamin G., 100, 108
  P. T., 130
  Pharimono T., 108
  Rebecca, 129
  Stanford, 100, 108, 114, 115, 129, 130
  William P., 100, 108
Longmire
  Robert, 22, 86, 89
Loyd
  Beckey, 125
  John, 125
  Pomfret, 1
  Rebecca, 39
Lumpkin
  Fleming, 19, 25
  Frances, 74
  John, 25
  Joseph, 74, 104, 108
  Martha, 74

Mrs., 25
Nancy, 74
Lumpkins
  Fleming, 17
  Polly, 17
Lunsford
  Alexander, 50
  Elizabeth, 17
Lyne
  George, 29
Lyon
  C, 56
  C. B, 28
  C. Clement, 56
  Clement B., 64
  E, 56
  Elk, 28
  Elkanah, 28, 56
  Gemima, 50
  James, 28, 108, 133
  John, 22, 28, 56
  John W, 28
  Lydia, 28, 56
  William H., 95
  Zachariah, 22
Maben
  J Robert, 26
Mabry
  David, 115
Macey
  Ann, 76
Maclin
  John C, 15
  John D, 29
  William M., 15
  William W, 29
  Wm. W., 29
Macon
  Gideon H, 37
Maconily
  Elizabeth, 76
Maddox
  R. G., 49
Madison
  James, 25
  Levin, Salley, 30 25
  Mary Ann, 25, 48
  Peyton, 25
  William, 25
Madison
  Peyton, 56
  William, 52, 56

Estate Records of Granville Co, NC Volume 13-16   153

Magehee
  Susan, 36
Malconily
  Elizabeth, 76
Mallory
  Agathy M, 22
  Aggy, 95
  Betsey, 95
  Charles, 21
  Eliza J, 125
  James, 21, 22, 95
  John, 21, 22, 95, 96, 125, 130
  Lucy, 21
  Mary, 22
  Mary Ann, 95
  Mary T., 125
  Nancy, 21
  Pleasant, 21
  Polly, 95
  William, 21, 95
  Wm. J., 129
Mangum
  Eliza, 83
  James M., 129, 133
  James T., 129
  Jane, 133
  Jas. M., 134
  John, 53, 133
  Leighton, 129
  Lucy, 128
  Nancy, 128
  Peighton G, 128, 129
  Polly, 26
  Rebecca, 133
  Samuel, 133
  Sarah, 53, 133
  Simpson, 128, 129, 134
  Solomon, 53
  Walter, 83
  Wilie, 133
  Willia, 129
  Willie, 10, 43
  Wyatt, 133
Manier
  John B., 116
  Mary, 116
Mann
  Abagail, 39
  Delila, 39
  James, 74
  Martha, 39
  Mary, 74
  Nancy, 111
  Thomas, 71
  Thos., 39
  William B., 43, 111
Marrett
  Joel, 71
Marror
  Alexander F., 46
Marrow
  Alexander, 46, 52, 69
  Alexander F., 2, 33, 46
  Daniel, 68
  Daniel, Sr., 33
  Drury, 69
  Drury S., 33
  Easter, 68
  Elizabeth, 68, 69
  James, 7, 15
  Jesse D., 15
  Nancy, 68, 69
  Parthena E. J. W., 111
  Polly, 33, 46
  Selina, 15
  Solomon L, 111
  Thomas, 69
  Thomas F., 46, 69, 111
Martin
  Henry L., 67
Masery
  Ann, 76
May
  Temperance, 13
Mayes
  E. R., 81
  Francis E, 81
  Jno. B, 81
  Lucretia, 81
  Martha N, 81
  Mary Ann, 81
  Virginia C., 81
  William, 81
  William W., 81
Mayhoe
  Joyes, 109
  Varnal W., 109
  William, 109
Mays
  Eliza, 67, 86, 113
  Eliza R., 97
  Frances, 113
  Francis, 67, 86
  Francis E, 97
  John, 67, 115
  John B., 67, 86, 97, 113
  Lucrecia, 67, 86
  Lucretia, 97
  Margaret, 67
  Martha, 86
  Martha N., 97
  Mary Ann, 97
  Robert, 86
  Virginia, 86, 113
  Virginia C, 97
  William, 67, 86, 97, 113
  William W., 97
McClanahan
  W. S., 99
McCram
  Sally, 101
McCraw
  Frank, 119
  Harriet, 119
  La Fayette, 119
  Mary, 119
  Sally, 119
  William, 119
McDaniel
  Stephen, 7
McFarland
  M, 8
McFarlin
  Wm, 26
McGehee, 102
  John T., 132
  Lemuel, 66, 87
  Samuel, 132
  Susan, 23, 37
  Susanah, 132
  William R., 132
McGraw
  Frank, 94
  Lafayette, 90
  Lucy, 119
  Sally, 90, 119
McKinney
  Joseph, 100
McLemore
  John W., Hon, 115
McIver
  Roderick, 23
Meadows
  Elijah, 128
  Mrs., 128

William, 128
Mealer
  Jas. A., 132
Medows
  Elijah, 62
Melton
  Elizabeth, 55, 106
  Elizabeth, Mrs, 116
  Stephen, 106
  William, 106
Merritt
  Abagail W., 71
  Amy H., 71
  Benjamin, 8, 71
  Celia, 71
  Jane, 71
  Joel, 71
  John, 71
  John G., 71
Middleton
  Sally, 34
Miller
  Alexa, 100
  Thomas, 90, 91
Mine
  David, 58
  Henrietta, 58
  Henry, 58
  John, 58
  Mary F., 58
  Sally, 58
Miner
  Ann, 60
  David, 60
  Henrietta, 60
  Henry, 60
  Joseph, 60
  Lucy, 21
  Mary Frances, 60
  Rachel, 60
  Randole, 58
  Sally, 60
Mingay
  Dudley, 19, 33
  Dudly, 16
Minis
  James, 103
  Mary, 103
Minor
  Annie, 89
  Clary, 89
  David, 86

Elizabeth, 89
Francis, 89
Henry, 86, 89
Jinsey, 89
Jo, 86
John, 86, 89
Joseph, 86
Lazerus, 89
Marshal, 89
Massa, Mrs, 86
Massey, 89
Polly, 89
Randal, 89
Randol, 60
Tabitha, 89
Mitchel
  Lemuel, 117
Mitchell
  Booker A., 106
  David, 7, 18
  Holley, 125
  Hooker A., 66
  Hutchins B., 6
  James Coffield, 12, 13
  Patsy, 48
  Susan, 80, 83
  William A., 62
  Willis, 80
  Willis B., 67, 83
  Williss, 80
Montague
  Alexander, 117
  Barbary, 117
  Elizabeth, 26
  Hixey, 31
  James P, 76
  John, 117
  Latney, 69, 76, 117
  Lewis, 31, 48, 76
  Polly Ann, 117
  Thomas, 117
  William, 117
  Young, 26
Moody
  Ann, 1
  Arthur, 1
  Benjamin, 1
  Edward, 1
  Frances A, 1
  James M., 18
  Mary, 1, 114
  William, 1

Wm. A., 1, 18
Moore
  Hester, 10
  Jeremiah, 7
  John B., 75, 96
  Julia, 114
  Lucretia, 10
  Nancy, 69
  Patsy, 26
  Porteus, 3
  Portius, 35, 78
  Thomas, 129
  Thomas B, 106
  Thomas R, 10
  Wesly, 1
  Wm. P., 100
Moreman
  Lewis, 18
Morgan
  Piety, 99
Morris
  Asa, 73
  Phebe, 73, 75, 89
  Stephen, 44, 73, 75, 89
  Stephen, Jr, 73
  Thomas G., 73
Moss
  Benjamin, 66, 111
  Charity, 99
  Elizabeth, 110, 111
  Fanny, 111
  Franklin, 22
  Jordan D., 126
  Nancy, 133
  Samuel, 115
  Sarah, 111
Murphey
  Elizabeth, 8
  William, 8
Nance
  John, Jr, 113
Neal
  Alexander G., 4
  Harriet, 4
  Martha, 4
  Moses A., 118
  Mrs., 33
  Peggy, 4
  Sarah, 4
  Thomas, 33, 52
  William H, 4
Negro

Jesse, 95
Nelson
  Dr., 57
  Jennette, 116
Netherland
  George W., 3
Nevill
  John, 133
Newbold
  Jas, 100
Newton
  Elizabeth, 62
  Thomas, 129
Norman
  E, Mrs, 16
  Elizabeth, 33
  Elizabeth, Mrs, 5, 16
  George, 5, 19, 33
  John, 15
  Sarah, 5, 94
  Sarah, Mrs., 94
  Thomas D, 12
  Thomas W., 12, 94
Norwood
  Arabella, 95
  Benjamin, 43
  Benjamin, Jr, 59, 65, 95, 98
  Catherine, 95
  E. W., 17, 42
  Edward W., 38
  Elizabeth, 33, 46
  G. W., 129
  George, 38
  George E., 126
  Harriett, 95
  Harriette, 98
  John, 38, 98
  John A., 95, 109, 113, 125
  John M., 98
  Jos. A., 60
  Joseph A., 1, 4, 11, 112
  Letty, 4
  Mary, 95
  Mrs., 98
  Nathaniel M., 38
  Nathaniel W., 62
  Parthena, 95
  Penelope, 95
  Penny G 125
  Pheby, 95
  Philip H 20
  Rebecca, 38
  Thomas, 38
  William, 20
  William A., 92
Nowlin
  Mary, 13
Nunn
  James, 4, 7
  Joshua, 20
Nuttall
  Alexander H., 57
  Charles, 37
  Frances, 37
  George A, 30
  Jas, 43
  John, 14, 30, 57
  Mary, 71
  Sally, 30
O'Briant
  Ann Eliza, 121-123
  Gardner, 121-123
  Jane, 123
  Parthena, 121
  Parthenia, 122, 123
O'Brien
  John, Jr, 19, 134
O'Brient
  Elizabeth, 54
  Faith, 54
  Patrick, 54
  Thomas, 54
Oakley
  Caty, 30
  Elijah, 10
  Elsbey, 10
  Francis, 10
  Hannah, 10
  Haywood, 10
  James, 10, 14
  James W, 10
  Joannah, 29
  John, 10
  Lucrecia, 10
  Martha, 10
  Nancy, 10
  Patsey, 30
  Prudence, 10
  Rebecca, 10
  Thomas, 30
  William, 30
  William Y., 10
  Yancey, 30, 85
Obriant
  Patrick, 110
OBrien
  Courtney Ingles, 68
  Dennis, 68
  Fanny, 68
OBrient
  Elizabeth, 54
  Thomas, 54
OBryan
  Courtney Ingles, 68
  Dennis, 68
Oliver
  Baren, 4
  Berrin, 4
  Mary, 4
  Olivers, 29
Olmstead
  Ready, 26
Overby
  David, 114
  Elizabeth, 114
  Mary Ann, 51
  Nancy, 51
Overton
  Benjamin, 115
  Harriet, 115
  James, 71
  Jane, 71
Owen
  Edward, 6
  James, 18
  John W, 18
  Thomas, 18
  Thomas G, 18
  Thomas, Esq, 18
  William L., 8, 48
Parham
  Arseneth, 39
  Asa, 20, 40, 134
  Canaan, 105
  Canann, Sr., 105
  Cannon, 115
  Cannon, Jr, 115
  Cannon, Sr., 105
  Collins, 134
  Elizabeth, 20, 31, 46, 105, 110
  Elvira, 105
  Emily, 39
  James, 105

Kannon, 108
Kenan, Jr, 108
Kennan, Sr., 130
Kennon, Jr., 130
Lewis, 9, 16, 20, 33, 36, 40, 46, 67, 70, 91, 105, 120
Lewis M., 134
Lewis R., 20, 31, 40, 46
Lewis, Col, 27, 38, 40
Lewis, Jr 40
Lewis, Sr, 40, 50, 109
Lucindy, 105
Lucy, 39, 40, 44
Martha, 40, 105
Mary, 31, 40, 46
Mary W, 20
N. C, 134
Nancy, 40
Robert, 91
Robert B, 31
Robert E., 40, 46
Saml R, 31
Samuel, 40, 46
Samuel R., 16, 29, 31, 46, 91
Tabitha, 105
Thomason, 105
Thompson, 105
Warner, 20, 21
William B., 134
Williamson, 20, 39, 40, 45, 46, 105, 134
Willie J., 20
Parkam
  Samuel R., 16
Parker
  Ann, 30
  Chloe, 9
  D., 101
  Daniel, 92
  David, 9, 14, 56, 77, 101
  Lucy, 30
  Priscilla, 30
Parrish
  Agathy M, 22
  C, 36
  Christian, 26
  Claborn, 25, 28, 59
  D. C., 101, 127
  Eady, 26
  Eliza, 60

Elizabeth, 66
H. J., 116
Nancy, 26
Patsy, 26
Polly, 26, 78
Ready, 26
Reamy, 26
Rheaney, 26
Rheany, 26
S., 116
Shadrack, 87
Sibon, 26
Thomas, 88
William, 26, 78, 87, 101
William B, 60
Wm., 52
Wm. B., 60
Paschal
  A, 16
  D. T., 131
Paschall
  Anderson, 5, 6, 8, 9, 13, 15, 20, 21, 27, 31, 36, 48, 61, 63
  Betsey, 61
  D. A., 38, 63, 115
  D. T., 131
  Daniel, 61
  Daniel A, 28, 40, 77, 84, 111
  Dennis, 61
  Dennis J., 128
  Dennis T., 21, 26, 54, 67, 70
  Donaldson, 16
  Donaldson P., 117
  Donaldson Potter, 61
  Donaldson S., 54
  Edwin, 54, 61
  Harriet, 54
  Isaiah, 61
  Isaiah Mitchell, 61
  John, 61
  Judah, 40
  L. A., 59, 76, 113, 115
  Lucy, 61
  Lumsford, 61
  Lumsford A, 105
  Lunsford, 61
  Lunsford A, 41, 43, 44, 57, 67, 86, 97
  Mary, 61

Mildred, 61
Potter, 61
Sally, 54
Wesley W, 24
William, 40
William H., 109
William Henry, 61
Z. M., Dr, 117
Zebulon, 61
Zebulon Montgomery, 61
Patrick
  J. C., 100
Patterson
  Elizabeth, 33
  Hardy, 6, 51
  J. R., 33
  James R, 33
  Robert, 6
Pattillo
  Jas. A., 132
Patton
  William C, 27, 38
  Wm. C., 5, 6
Peace
  Anderson, 47
  Ann, 76
  Catherine, 76
  Celia, 47
  Charlot, 76
  Charlotty, 76
  Elizabeth, 47, 57, 76
  Francis, 47
  H. W, 5, 104
  John, 76
  Joseph, 47, 76
  Josiah, 17
  Lemuel, 17, 38
  Margaret, 76
  Mary, 76
  Willie, 47
Peddyford
  Sidney Turner, 27
Perdue
  Rowland, 62
Perkins
  Jacob, 23
Perkinson
  Mary, 50, 65, 70
Perry
  Elizabeth, 100
  John, 100
  Nancy, 100

Peter, 100
Polly, 100
Rebeckar, 100
Rodey, 100
Rody, 104
Salley, 100
Sollomon, 100
Sollomon, Sr, 104
Solomon, 100
Thomas, 100
Petiford
  Diza, 38
  Iliza, 38
  Lewis, 38
Pettiford
  Sidney Turner, 27
Peyton
  Ann C., 15
  Bailee, 15
Phillips
  Susan, 62
Philops
  Benj, 64
Philpott
  Emily, 16
  James, 16, 32, 38, 50
  Jas, 32
  Lindon, 16
  Lyndon S., 95, 105
  Martha, 55, 79, 87, 108
  Mary Ann, 16
  Milley, 54
  Milly, 55, 79
  Milly A F., 79
  Saml, 54
  Samuel, 16, 54, 79, 87, 95, 105, 108
  Simeon, 16, 38, 87
  Simon, 32
  Solomon, 16, 53, 67, 110
  Thomas, 32
  W. A., 67, 87
  William, 16
  William A., 110
  Wm., 32
Pittard
  Anne, 65
  Anne S, 64
  Dolly, 1
  Elizabeth, 1, 69
  H. G., 57
  Howell G., 1, 30, 49, 69,
97
John, 35
John, Jr, 1
Letty, 1, 64, 65
Nancy, 1, 69
Rebecca, 64, 65
Place
  Alabama, 47
    Lauderdale county, 39
  Alexandria, 78
  Ark
    Pulaski Co., 12
  Arkansas Little Rock, 12
  Bevil Tract, 12
  Bryanville Gold mine, 91
  Connecticut, 97
  Dickersons Bridge, 102
  Edgecombe, 100
  Edwards Place, 91
  Franklin City, 97
  Franklin Co, 107
  Georgia, 88
    Washinton Co, 83
  gold mine, 91
  Halifax County, 92
  Hard Bargain, 91
  Horseshoe, 91
  James River and Kanawaha, 90
  Jonathan Creek, 29
  Kentucky
    Breckenridge Co., 18, 19
    Graves Co., 40
    Henderson Co., 29
  Louisiana
    Avovyelles Parish, 41
  Maryland, 78
    Port Tobacco, 78
  Mattamuskeet Lake, 91
  Mecklenburg Co,, 116
  Mississippi, 41, 69, 76, 97
    Natchez, 131
    Vicksburg, Miss, 131
    Yalabooshe Co., 115
    Yalabusha Co., 114
  Missouri
    New Madrid, 66
  Moores Mine, 91
  Nap of Reeds, 120
  Newbern, 68
N. C
  Beaufort, 100
  Caswell Co., 49
  Craven Co., N. C, 100
  Franklin Co., 42, 100
  Green Co., 100
  Henderson, N. C., 92, 116
  Hillsborough, 7
  Lenoir Co., N. C, 100
  Newbern, 100
  Northampton Co., 56, 92
  Orange Co., 7, 12, 13, 24, 25, 120
  Person Co., 10, 18, 33, 35, 130
  Raleigh, 11
  Swansboro, 100
  Wake Co, 82
  Warren Co., 46, 66, 68, 110, 128
  Williamsborough, 28, 91
  N. C. Bank, 68
Ohio, 57
Obslow Co, 100
Peach Grove, 29
Person City, 97
Raleigh, 68
Robards Castle, 91
Ruin Creek, 94
South Carolina, 48
Tennessee, 21, 37, 47, 54-57, 76, 79, 105, 115, 116
  Carroll Co., 69
  Fayette County, 43
  Henderson Co., 63, 66
  Henry County, 5, 115
  Madison County, 23
  Maury county, 12, 60
  Roberson, 23
  Roberson county, 23, 40
  Robertson County, 40
  Rutherford Co., 12, 13
  Shelby County, 2
  Sullivan County, 2
  Sumner Co., 8, 9, 15, 40

Weakley County, 27, 33, 36, 38
Wilson County, 35
The South Mountain Speculation, 91
Tract
  Fielding tract, 117
  Harrisburg Tract, 15
  The Hedgrith Tract, 12
  Indian Grave tract, 69
  LaGrange tract, 90
  mill tract on Littel Nut Bush, 91
  The Old Tract, 9
  Sam Jones Tract, 129
U.S. court Raleigh, 45
Virginia
  Charlotte Co, 80
  Clarksville, Va., 97, 116
  Greenville Co., 15
  Halifax county, 15
  Halifax, Va., 97
  Harrison Co., 57
  Mecklenburg Co., 29
  Mecklenburg Va., 116
  Monongahala Co., 57
  Richmond, 57
  Wake Co., 82
  Warren City, 97
  Warren Co., 57, 68
Plummer
  H. L., 34
Pomfret
  Amy, 59
  Robert, 59
Pomfrett
  John, 17
Pool
  Alexander, 106
  Alexander Petty, 106
  Anna, 20, 48
  Charles W. P, 20
  Claborn P, 42
  Clabourn P, 20
  Clarborn, 18
  Dosha, 106
  Elizabeth, 106
  Logustin P, 82
  Margaret, 20
  Meredith, 22
  Patsey T, 106
  Patsey Tailor Petty, 106
  Philip P, 42
  Phillip, 18
  Phillip P., 20
  Sally, 106
  Samuel, 115
  Seth, 106
  Seth Petty, 106, 107
  Thomas, 106
  William, 48
  William P., 49
Porter
  Thomas K., 5
  William, 5
Powell
  Amy H., 71
  Archibald, 117
  Charity, 47
  Elizabeth, 105
  Elvira, 105
  Harriet, 64
  Harriot, 67, 70, 76
  Honor, 67
  James, 39, 64, 67, 70, 76
  Mary Ann, 64
  Robert, 105
  William 64, 67
Pretty
  Berry, 119
Prewitt
  Elisha, 65
  Nancy, 12, 13
  Susannah, 65
  William, 12, 13
Price
  Jno. F, Dr, 78
Priddy
  Betsey Ann, 13
  Harriot Amanda, 13
  Joseph, 13
  Mary, 13
  Virginia Kivon, 13
Proctor
  Joseph, 104
  Nancy, 104
Pruett
  Elizabeth, 35
  Parker, 35
  Robert, 35
  William, 35
Pruit
  Elizabeth, 117, 126
Purkinson
  Elizabeth, 105
  Permealey, 105
  Seth, 105
  Whitfiel, 105
Puryear
  Aplin, 4, 17
  Daniel, 55
  Elizabeth, 4, 55
  Harmon, 19
  John, 4, 17, 19
  John, Jr, 4, 13, 15
  John, Sr, 4, 15, 17
  Lethy, 55
  Letty, 55
  Martha, 4
  Peggy, 4
  Peyton, 15, 55, 58, 75
  Polly, 55
  Randal, 55, 58, 75
  Rebecca, 55
  Sarah T., 13, 17
  Semore, 55
  Simon, 15, 19
  Sylvania, 4, 19
  William, 55, 58, 75
Qualls
  Charles, 122
  William, 81
Quarles
  Charles, 122
  Eliza, 122
Ragsdale
  John H., 1
Rainey
  James G., 49
Ramsey
  Elizabeth, 82
  Isaac, 100
  James L., 59, 82
Rand
  Parker, 11
Rasmus
  Martha, 62
Rawlings
  Mary A., 78
Ray
  Hawkins, 133
  Henry C., 81, 87
Rayburn
  D. M., 115
  Davidson M., 115

Read
  C., Dr, 15
  Charles L., 43, 80
  Elizabeth M, 80
  Howel L., 69
  Howel L., Esq, 43
  Howel S., 69
  John, 40, 43, 65
  Nancy J., 3
  Thomas H., Dr, 3
  Thomas, Dr, 15
  Wm, 15
Reaves
  Saml J, 11
Reavis, 45
  A, 112
  Elizabeth, 22
  Elizabeth J., 123
  George J., 112, 123
  John J., 123
  Lewis, 45, 62, 90, 94, 112, 116, 123
  Lewis, Jr, 62
  Lucy, 39
  Mary, 90, 119
  Mary W., 123
  Mrs., 112
  Peter L., 112
  Peter S., 123
  Samuel J., 62
  Samuel T, 40
  Sarah, 123
  Sarah T, 123
  Thos, 112
  William, 3
Redmon
  Saml, 56
Reed
  Mary Ann, 111
Reeks
  Thomas, 89
Rice
  Betsey, Mrs, 56
  Fleming, 56, 68
  John, 56, 68
  Thomas, 56
Richards
  Richard H., 74, 92
Richmond
  Caleb H., 49
Ridley
  Col, 110

Elizabeth, 34
Howel L., 30
Howell L., 53
James, 33
James, Dr, 34
Jas., 33
John C., 44
Jos. James, 52
Joseph J., 35
Mary R, 34
Thomas D., 19, 34
Robards
  George W., 91
  H. J. 92
  Henry J., 90
  Henry James, 91
  Horace, 91
  Horace L., 90, 91, 96, 105
  James, 78
  Jane, 90, 91
  Nathaniel, 4, 91
  Presly, 127
  Rebecca, 78, 127
  William, 90, 96
  William H., Jr, 91
  William, Col, 91
  Wm., 68, 111
Roberds
  Horace L, 90
Roberson
  John, 15
  Martha, 13
Robert
  Dorcas, 41
Roberts
  Alcy, 120
  Alsey, 108
  Christian, 59
  Eldred G, 41
  James, 120, 126, 127
  James R., 108
  James T., 108
  Lively, 120
  Mark, 26, 108, 120
  Mark, Sr, 108
  Martha, 120
  Nathaniel, 120
  Presly, 108, 120
  Prestly, 120
  Rebecca, 108, 120
  Rebecca, Mrs, 108

  Simeon W., 120
  Sylvia, 120
  Thomas, 108, 120
  Walter A., 120
  William, 59
  Willie P., 120
Robertson, 4
  Adnah, 82
  Charles, 29
  George, 29
  J, 100
  John, 133
  John H, 100
  Leonard, 29
  Martha, 29
  N, 4
  Nathaniel, 4, 28, 29
  Nathl, 4
  Sally, 29
  Sarah, 29
  Silas F., 129
  Thomas R., 133
  Willis B., 129
Rockhold
  Thomas, 3
Roffe
  Sarah, 75, 96
Rogers
  Benjamin, 31
  George, 38
  Jubilee, 31
  Mary Ann, 50
  Peleg, 31
  Peleg S., 119
  Samuel, 39
  Thomas, Jr, 8
Rowland
  Horace H., 132
  Pleasant, 97
Royster
  Ann, 94, 95
  Banester, 4, 11, 118, 126
  Banister, 91
  Clark, 114, 118
  D, 108
  E, Mrs, 4
  Edward, 109, 112, 130
  Elizabeth, 4, 91, 114
  Elizabeth P., 132
  Emily, 4
  Emily E., 11
  Fabian A, 4, 132

Francis, 4, 11
H. T., 92
H. T., Dr, 19
Horace T., 6, 12, 94
Horace T., Jr, 94
Indiana E. W., 94
Indianna, 94
Indianna E., 94
James, 8, 118
Jane, 90, 91
John, 114
John, Capt, 118
Julia, 114
Letty, 4
M. D., 67, 91, 92, 104, 108, 118
Marcus D., 4, 11, 52, 74
Martha, 4, 91
Mary, 4, 114
Mary Ann, 52
Nancy, 114
Panthia, 114
Robert, 4
S. B., 118
Sally, 132
Stephen S., 90
Stephen Sampson, 91
Susan, 109
W. D., 108
Wiley, 118
William, 4, 11, 94, 95
William J., 94
William James, 94
William, Jr, 14, 52, 118
William, Sr., 14
Willie, 4
Willis, 49
Willis A., 91, 126, 132
Rud
  Elizabeth, 113
  Mary Ann, 111
Rudd
  Daniel, 111
  John, 88, 111
  Thomas, 111
  William, 111
Rufuf
  Martha, Mrs, 48
Russ
  Averilla, 77
Russell
  James A., 103

James A., Dr, 43
James, Dr, 99
Jas. A, 39, 101
Timothy, 12
William, 88
Rust
  Averillah G, 34
  Jeremiah, 27
  Susan, 34
Sale
  Anthony, 115, 118
  Eliza G, 118
  Margaret M., 118
  Mary T., 118
  Theophilus A, 118
  Thomas A., 115, 118
  Washington A., 118
Sandford
  John Y., 17, 24, 88, 101
  Mary, 87
  Robert, 87
  Tomas S., 60
  Thomas J., 77
Satterwhite
  David, 32, 42
  Dr, 91
  E, 117
  Elijah, 117, 126
  Frankey, 45
  Howel, 3, 27, 45, 97, 117
  Howell, 126
  J. M., 92
  J. P., 126
  James, 3, 27, 32, 42, 45, 97, 105
  James M., 115
  M. and S., 117
  Mitchel, 117, 118
  Mitchell, 126
  S, 117
  Solomon, 3, 45, 92
  Stephen, 117, 118, 126
  William, 32, 42, 117, 126
Saunders
  Eugenia, 6
Seal
  W, 23
Searcey
  Dorcas, 71, 82, 103
  Hargrove, 82, 103
  Mary, 82
  Sally, 82

William H., 71
William W., 126
Sears
  Amey, 105
Seegroves
  Feabay, 8
servant
  Edward, 78
  Jenny, 78
Shannon
  Aveyrilla, 40
  Samuel, 40
Shearman
  Hannah, 78
  John, 10, 14, 36, 48, 56, 60, 61, 77, 78
Sheriff of Granville Co., 95, 105
Sherman
  John, 87, 92, 100, 101, 108, 114, 126, 127, 132
Sherrin
  Elizah Adaline, 100
  John M., 100
  Polly, 100
Shoer
  William, 110
Short
  Vines, 6
Shotwell
  James, 94, 95
  Rebecca, 94, 95
Shurman
  George W, 12
  John, 12, 13
  Martha, 12, 13
  Mary F., 12
  Nancy, 12, 13
  Parsons, 12
  Parsons M, 12
  Squire, 12, 13
Sikes
  Henry, 62
Simms
  Allen, 11
Simons
  Judy, 77
Sims
  Charles, 44
  Guilford D., 23
  Jaccey, 126

Estate Records of Granville Co, NC Volume 13-16   161

Joseph, 46, 102
William D., 44
Slater
  William, 78
Slaughter
  Abraham, 3, 69, 72, 78
  Abraham S., 69
  Ailsey G., 70
  Charity, 70
  Elizabeth, 69
  Franky, 70
  Isaac, 61
  Jacob, 2
  Jacob G., 69, 70
  Jacob L., 70
  Jacob, Jr, 2
  Jacob, Sr, 3
  James H., 69
  Madison, 2
  Sally P., 70
  Susanna, 70
  Thomas, 69
  William P. B., 70, 72, 69
  slave
    Mack, 27
    Ritty, 50
Smiley
  Robert A., 117
Smith
  Alexander, 18, 31, 57, 84
  Allen R., 19
  Amey, 18, 53
  Amy, 6, 13, 46, 79
  Amy W, 25, 45
  Amy W., Mrs, 29, 45
  Amy, Mrs, 25
  Ann, 57, 65
  Ann A., Mrs, 57
  Ann R., 29
  Ann Rebecca, 46, 53, 79
  Ann, Mrs, 57
  Ava, 74
  Bennett, 77
  Bennitt, 84
  Caroline, 84
  Catherine, 84
  Charles, 71, 74
  Elizabeth, 8, 18, 31, 84
  Frances, 57
  Francis S, 25, 29, 46, 53, 79
  G. W, 12

Guy, 18, 31
Harriot W., 3
Henry, 17, 18
Henry T., 84
J. H., 6
James, 3, 6, 17, 18, 31
James A., 45, 45, 53, 79
James W., 29, 57
James, Jr, 7
James, Sr, 6, 127
Jno, 18
Jno. P., 127
Joel, 77, 84
Joel R., 84
John, 18, 31
John B., 19, 29, 46, 53, 57, 79
John G., 57
John P., 6, 17
John P., Jr, 7
John, Jr, 31
Joseph M. W., 87
Kasandra, 40
Lemuel, 55
Leroy, 31
Lucy, 18
M. A., 99
Man B., 53
Mann R., 46
Martha, 131
Martha P., 6
Mary A. G, 29
Mary G, 46, 53, 79
Maurice, 17, 19, 45, 46, 53, 57, 79
Maurice, Col, 25
Men R., 29, 79
Mrs., 88
Nancy, 18, 31, 84
Polly, 84
Reuben, 77, 84
Richard I., 29
Richard J, 19, 29, 45, 46, 53, 57, 58, 79
Richd. J., 25
Sally, 78, 88
Sally P., 57
Saml Henry, 25
Saml W., 46
Samuel, 57
Samuel Henry, 6
Samuel G., 57

Samuel N., 53
Samuel W., 15, 19, 79, 95, 109, 118
Sarah, 86, 127
Smith, 29
Sudy, 18
Thomas J., 18, 74
Thomas M, 29, 45, 46, 53, 79
William, 25, 29
William F., 7
William H., 6
William K., 40
William P., 59
Wm. F., 127
Sneed
  Albert, 83
  Elizabeth, 52
  George W., 39
  John R., 52, 55, 61
  Lemuel, 52
  Maria, 83
  Richard, 19, 50
  Stephen, 34
  Stephen K, 19, 54
  William, 94
  William M., 12, 19, 33, 49, 115
  Wm. M., 19, 49
  Wm. N, 8
Solomon
  Luke, 111
Somerhill
  Horace, 39
Somerville
  Robert P., 58
  George, 60
  George C., 58
  James, 34, 51, 58
  John, 58
  Joseph B., 58
  Joseph J., 58
  Mary, 51, 55, 58, 71, 90
  Mary, Mrs, 58
  Richard, 58
  Susan, 58, 90
  Thomas S., 58
  William A., 51, 58, 71
  William B., 60
  Willis L., 58
  Wm., 58
  Wm. A., 55

Southall
  James, 119, 120
  Mary, 89, 119
  Mrs., 89
  N. N., 89, 119, 120
Speed
  David, 116
  Emily, 112
  James, 112
  John J., 96
Spruill
  Louisa, 128
  Thomas H., 128
Stafford
  Dorcas, 41
  Elouisa A., 41
Stanly, 29
Stanton
  Green, 5, 20, 21, 48
  Mary, 5, 20, 21, 48
Stark
  Elizabeth, 111
  James T., 111
  Jas. T., 110, 111
  Jno. T., 111
  Julia, 97, 101, 102
  Kysar J., 97, 101, 102
  Sarah, 110, 111
Starke
  James T, 97, 115
Staunton
  Henry J., 119
  Mariah, 120
  Martha S., 119, 120
  Mary, 119
  William H., 119
  William H. D., 120
Stedman
  John B., 94
Steed
  Edward, 119
  Lucy, 119
Stephens
  Robert, 18
Stiths, 29
Stockley
  James, 14
  Joseph, 14
  Mary, 14
  Obeda, 14
Stokes
  Jane, 82, 130

Thomas, 82, 130
Stone
  Averilla, 77
  Claiborn, 34, 77
  Delphia, 34
  J. M., 62, 77
  Jonathan, 34, 41
  Jonathan M, 34, 41, 77
  Jonothan, 77
  Judith, 34
  Nancy, 77
  Peggy, 34
  Polly, 34, 77
  Sarah, 34
  Susan, 34
Stotts
  John W, 18
Stovall
  Elizabeth, 33
  Hester, 33
  John W,, 33
  Thos., 52
Straton
  Mary, 66
Strom
  Pleasant, 63
  Rebecca, 63
Strother
  Margret, 75
Stroud
  Richard, 119
Strum
  Rebecca, Mrs, 65
  William, 109
Strums
  Bartholomew, 34
Stuart
  James, 19
  Thomas A, 19
Sturdivant
  Charles, 95
  Dilley R., 111
Suit
  Harriet, 64
  John, 64, 68, 87
  Mary, 64
  Nancy, 64
  Sarah, 64
  Susannah, 64
  William, 64, 68, 69, 87
Summerhill
  Elizabeth, 103

Swinney
  Joel, 18
Tailer
  Drury R, 111
  Elizabeth, 111
Taimer
  Drury R., 111
Tally
  Reuben, 91
  Robert, 91
Tamer
  Drury R., 111
Tanner
  Daniel, 68
  Thomas, 68
  Warner, 38
Tapp
  Jane, 4
  Lewis, 4
Tayloe
  Mills, 73
Tayloes
  Wills, 70
Taylor
  Agnes B, 84
  Agness, 34
  Agness B, 34
  Ann S., Mrs, 38
  Charles H. K., 97
  Edward, 88
  Edward T., 78
  Elizabeth, 34
  Francis O., 60
  George, 58
  James A., 88, 78
  James H., 34, 84
  Jeese, 66
  Jno. C., 34
  Jno. O., 97
  John, 11
  John C, 17, 34, 40, 84
  John H., 78, 88
  John Y., 60
  John, Capt, 88
  John, Sr, 34, 84
  Mercer, 60
  Mildred, 43
  Mrs., 88
  Nancy, 34
  Robert, 43
  Sally, 88
  Sally T., 78

Samuel, 88
Samuel T., 78
William, 88
William A, 7, 78., 88
William B., 56
William P., 78
William R., 88
William V., 12
William, Major, 88
Wm. V., Dr, 6
Terry
  Edward, 15
  George, 7
  James, Jr, 70
  Prudence, 131
  S., 70
  Stephen, 7, 27, 85
  Susanna, 70
  William, 7, 11, 25, 27, 33, 36, 85
  Wm., 7, 16, 32, 42, 60
Thomas
  Henrietta, 112
  John A., 54
  Thomas G., 58
  W. G., 86
  Was. H., 112
  Wash, 24
  Washington H, 24, 58, 110
  William G, 112
  William P., 75
Thomason
  Ann, 28
  Anne, 12
  Benjamin, 91
  Elizabeth, 12, 26
  Garland, 26
  George, 12, 26, 30, 98
  George P., 20, 21
  George, Sr, 28, 87
  James, 12, 26, 28, 30, 98
  Jas, 87
  John, 12
  L. R., 39
  Lucetta R., 39
  Lydia, 12
  Mally, 12
  Martha, 26
  Martha, Mrs, 98
  Mary, 91
  Nancy, 20, 21, 27, 34, 36, 110
  Nathaniel, 12
  Nelson, 12
  Richard, 39
  Southern, 39
  Thomas, 12, 119
  William, 26
Thompson
  Allen, 106
  James, 78
  J. C., 86
  John C., 78, 86
  Nancy, 77
Thornton
  Sarah T., 132
Thorp
  William, Dr, 134
Tiner
  Warner, 38
Tippett
  John H., 106, 121
  John, Jr, 9
  John, Sr, 9
  Jonathan, 106
  Mary, 121
  Thomas, 34
  William L., 61
Tippitt
  Betsy, 86
  Eli, 86
  John, 86
  John H., 86
  Jonathan, 86
  Mary, 86
  Thomas, 86
Toles
  Thos, 29
Towns
  Edmund, 3
Tuck
  Lucy P., 77
  Phaltick, 115
Tucker
  Charles D, 18
  Elizabeth, 125, 130
  George W., 4, 17, 19
  Green, 125
  Harriet, 4
  John, 130
  Littlebury, 125, 130, 132
  Littlebury, Jr., 130
  Littlebury, Sr, 125
  Robert, 125
  Susan, 125
  William, 125
  William C., 417, 19
Tucks
  Edward, 101
Turk
  Phaltial, 101
Turner
  Drury, 111
  Drury R., 110
  Elizabeth, 111
  Izabellah, 111
  Martha, 113
  Puss, 111
  Seaton H, 8
  Stephen H, 8
  Thomas, 91
Umsted
  Elisha, 117
Upstead
  Nathaniel Harris, 12
Usery
  Temperance, 97, 101
Ussery
  Joel, 8
  Susan, 8
Valentine
  Lemuel, 38
Vaughn
  Ann, 38
  Ann, Mrs, 41
  Anne C., 6
  Fanny, 133, 134
  James, Col, 41
  John, 51, 66, 133, 134
  Jonathan G., 66
  Martha, 43, 51, 66, 133
  Martha, Mrs, 51
  Nancy, 133
  Patsy, 134
  Sarah Matilda, 15, 41
  Vincent, 43, 51, 66, 133, 134
  Vinson, 66
  William, Dr, 15, 41
  William T., 90
  Woodson, 66
  Woodward, 66
Veazey
  A. M., 126
  Abner, 23

Alfred M., 117
Anderson, 16
Andrew J., 23
Elijah, 16, 24
Elizabeth, 117
Ezekiel, 23
Fielding, 52, 117
Francis, 49
Isham, 117
James L, 23
Jesse, 16, 24
John C., 16, 23, 52
John R., 16
Joseph, 23
Joseph H, 16
Mark, 23, 42
Mary, 16
Nancy, 7, 117
Rebecca, 117
William, 7, 23, 42, 117, 126
Venable
  A. W., 113
  Abraham W., 43
Vincent
  Amey, 66
  Ann, 66
  Anna, 75
  Elizabeth, 66
  Henry H., 66
  Jacob, 66, 71, 75, 89
  John M., 66
  John W., 66
  Mary, 23, 36, 37, 66
  William, 66
Volentine
  Dilley R, 111
  Elizabeth, 111
  John W., 111
  Mary Ann, 111
  Nancy, 111
  Rigdon, 111
Voss
  W. W., 89
  William V., 43
Waddell
  Hugh, 116
Wagstaff
  John, 55
  Polly, 55
Wales
  Fred, 78

Walker
  A. H., 38
  Alexander, 119
  Amarilis, 119
  Anderson, 119
  Anderson H., 37, 44, 65, 66
  Bemis, 119
  Bunice, 126
  Burnis, 100
  C. W, 100
  Catherine, 119
  James, 64
  John, 74, 100, 119, 126
  Joseph, 74, 119
  Mary, 64
  Nancy, 100, 119, 127
  R. D, 100
  Rebecca, 119
  T. J., 100
  Tensly, 119
  Thomas, 119
  Tinsley J., 117
  William, 119
  William M., 79, 96
  Wm., 100
Waller
  Calvin, 113
  Carter, 95, 113
Walton
  John Taylor, 34
Wardens of the Poor, 5, 16, 35, 51, 61, 70, 76, 90, 101, 112, 118, 133
Wardlaw
  William A, 15
Wartman
  John H., 8
  Rebecca, 8
  Tabitha, 8
Washington
  Alsey, 93
  Barbary, 27, 31
  Barbery, 53
  Celestia, 93
  Delphia, 34, 77
  Demaris, 93
  Elizabeth, 27, 69, 93
  Emant, 93
  Ephraim, 69, 93
  George, 69, 93
  John, 93, 112, 124

Mary Ann, 93
Matilda, 27
Matildy, 27
Nancy, 112, 113, 124
Roan, 93
Roane, 93
Sally, 54, 79
William, 27, 31, 53, 69, 72, 93, 113
Woodson, 27, 54, 69, 72, 79, 93
Watkins
  Joel T., 109
  Thos. L, 12
Watson
  Catharine, 7
  James, 82
  James R., 130
  Lot, 67
  Lot G., 49
  Loton L., 54
  Martha, 54
  Sarah, 82
  Sarah R., 130
Weartress
  Betsey, 9
Weatherman
  Peggy Bragg, 9
Weathers
  Catherine, 99
  Charity, 99
  Edward, 99
  Elizabeth, 99
  Gilly, 99
  James, 99, 106
  John P., 99
  Mary, 99
  Penny, 99
  Piety, 99
  Priscilla, 30
  Prudence, 99
  William, 99
Weaver
  John W., 131
  Mary, 65
  Rebecca, 131
  Salley, 62
  William, 58, 131
  William G., 131
Webb
  A. L, 16
  A.S, 32

Ann H., 6
Elizabeth, 18
Isaac, 18
James, 6, 7
John, 6, 17, 18, 30, 36
John P., 13, 35
John, Jr, 18
Lewis, 57
Martha P., 6, 7
Martha P. Smith, 6
Thomas, 18, 30, 36
Thomas, Jr, 7
William, 16, 57
William H., 58
William H, Jr, 18
Wm. H., 77, 89, 109, 132
Welch
  Sarah, 34
West
  Anne, 53
  James R., 98
  John, 53
  Joseph, 87
  Peter, 74, 87, 98, 106
  Susan, 74, 87, 98
  Thomas, 87
Westray
  Samuel, 92
Wheelas
  Mary, 106
Wheeler
  America, 120
Wheson
  William H., 56
White
  Cary, 74
  Casey, 21
  Cassander, 15
  Cassandra, 8, 48
  Cassy, 20
  Ceily Coleman, 37
  Celia, 23, 42
  Celia C, 23
  Coleman R, 23, 36, 41, 45
  E. J., 126
  Eaton J, 99
  Edward, 74
  Elizabeth, 9, 20, 28, 36, 37
  Frances, 42
  Frances Lany Jane, 37
  Frances Shelia, 23
  Francis, 23
  Francis L. L, 23
  G. W, 23
  Haskey Ann Nelson, 37
  Hester Coleman, 37
  Holley, 125
  Jaccey, 126
  James, 55, 104
  Jno, 66, 110, 132, 134
  John, 23, 36, 37, 59, 68, 71, 75, 87, 89, 106, 108, 109, 116, 126, 128, 133
  Joshua A., 48
  Kenchen H, 20
  Kenelin(Kenchen?) F., 9
  Kinchen, 28
  Kinchen H, 21
  Larkin, 29
  Mariah, 120
  Mariah L., 119
  Mary, 36, 37
  Phillip, 23, 125, 128
  Polly, 37
  Prudence, 31
  Rebecca, 105
  Ruthy, 36
  Susan, 36, 37
  Thomas, 8, 15, 20, 21
  Thomas O, 23
  Thomas P, 23
  Thomas Person, 37
  Thomas V., 45
  William G. V, 42
  William George Vaughn, 37
  William R, 37, 51, 125, 126, 128
  William W, 119, 120
  Wm. G. V., 23
Whitfield
  John C., 24
  John W, 24
  William, 35
  Wm., 24
Wiggins
  Argen, 83
  Benjamin, 49
  Edney, 49
  Elizabeth, 22
  Fred, 25
  Frederick, 22, 45
  Gulielmus, 22
  Gulielmus C., 1
  Harold, 22
  Howel, 25
  Hundley, 22
  James H, 83
  James M. T., 72
  Jaqueline, 22
  John, 22, 25, 52, 68
  Julia, 49
  Lucy, 83
  Nancy, 22, 25
  Thomas, 22
  Theophilus H, 83, 104
  Thomas Hundley, 49
Wilkerson
  Alexander, 53
  Anne, 53
  Charles, 119, 127
  Charles I., 87
  David C., 4
  David S., 17, 130
  David W, 19
  David, Jr, 11
  Geo. W., 131
  George, 53
  James, 53
  John, 53
  John G., 131
  John T., 130, 131
  Katey, 53
  Letty, 55
  Martha, 4, 30, 119, 127
  Sarah, 53
  Woodson, 45, 53
Wilkins
  Allen, 23
  Clement, 2, 5, 7, 23, 25, 26, 32, 42. 70, 74, 83, 100, 103, 104
  Clemeny, 59
  Francis, 89
  John, 70
Williams
  Benjamin, 49, 111, 115, 125
  Bennett, 58
  Elizabeth, 75, 82, 96
  Henrietta, 125
  Henry, 123
  John S, 115

Jinsey, 89
Julia A., 125
Leonard, 77
Mrs., 115
Nancy, 89
Nathaniel, Sr, 45
Person, 115
Phebe, 82
Plummer H., 125
Robert A., 125
Thomas L., 43, 101
Thomas Lorton, 4
Thos, 41, 52
Thos. L., 2
W. D., 52
William B., 49, 75, 82, 96
William S., 125
Williamson
  Jane Smith, 57
  Thomas J., Dr, 57
Willie
  D. T., 42
  Lewis K., 43
  Thomas H, 1, 15, 19, 25, 27, 42, 43, 58
  Thos. H., 19
Willis
  Susan, 109, 112, 130
Wilson
  Benj, 98
  Benjamin, 97, 101, 118
  Henry, 59, 74, 79
  J. P., 98
  Jemima, 97, 101, 102
  John A., 115
  Julia, 97, 101, 102
  Letha, 118
  Lethe, 97, 101
  Lundy, 97, 101, 102
  Martha, 64
  Mary, 50
  Masa, 74
  Mason, 59
  Massey, 79
  Mildred, 97, 101
  Mrs., 98
  Priscilla, 111
  Rebecca, 49, 92, 97, 101
  Richard, 50
  Ritter, 92, 97, 101
  Robert, 92, 97, 98, 101, 102, 110
  Robt, 50
  Saml, 101
  Samuel, 64, 97, 102
  Samuel P., 92, 110
  Solomon, 97, 101, 102, 111
  Solomon G., 92, 98, 110
  Stephen, 97, 98, 101
  Susan, 97, 101, 102
  Temperance, 97, 101
  Thomas, 19, 40, 50
  William, 97
Winfree
  Charles, 101
  Collin, 115
  Collins, 101
  James, 82
  Nancy, 82
Winston
  David, 36
  Elijah, 106
  George, 9
  Gilly, 99
  Mary, 99
  Moses, 103
  Obadiah, 81, 83
  Obediah, 53, 67, 80
  Pamela, 53
  Pamelia, 80, 83
  Thomas, 99
Wirrel
  William B., 110
Wood
  A. S, 85
  Annie, 89
  Anthony, 30
  Ezekiel, 30
  George, 85, 96
  John, 32, 33, 35
  Mary A. E, 85
  Nancy, 85
  Peyton, 1
  Richard, 87
  Richard S, 85
  William C, 85, 96
Woodlief
  Martha, 104
Woods
  Anthony, 29, 30
  Caty, 30
  Joannah, 29
  John, 29
  Lucy, 30
  Molley, 29
  Nancy, 30
  Patsey, 30
  Sally, 29
Woodson
  Judah, 40
Woodsworth
  Henry, 28
Woodwirth
  H, 7
Woodworth
  Benjamin, 79
  Clarissa, 79
  Clarissa B., 79
  Henry, 13, 4043, 59, 65, 79
  Mary E, 79
  Samuel, 79
Worsham
  Nancy, 26
Wortham
  Fanny, 68
  Fanny A., 94
  James L., 46, 53
  Thomas, 68
  William, 94
Wright
  John H., 111
  Martha, 105
Wyche
  George, 116
  Ira, 116
  Ira T., 116
  James, 2, 25, 30, 33, 35-37, 41, 45, 88, 99, 104, 106, 116, 126
  John, 116
  Pamela, 116
  Parry, 116
  Peter, 116
  Sally, 116
  Sarah T., 123
  William, 116
  William E., 116, 123
Wynn
  C. W., 112
  Charles, 131
  Richard, 9
Yancey
  Absalom, 3, 4

Ann, 3, 4
Charles, 3, 4, 58, 88
Henry, 43, 91, 109
Hezekiah, 58
Jane, 4
Kesiah, 3, 4, 58, 88
Lewis, 58
Martha, 4
Mary, 4
Richard, 58
Richard Jr., 58
Robert Sr., 58
Samuel, 58
Tryon, 37
Yarbrough
  William, 16
York
  Mary, 79
  Thomas, 79
  Thomas, Sr, 60, 77
  Thos. A, 60
  William C., 62
Young
  D. A., 114
  D. J., 7, 70, 86, 109, 110, 120, 128
  David J., 87, 113, 116, 120, 121, 133
  Demetrias E, 111
  Henry, 34
  J. H., 119
  James, 57, 113
  James H., 114, 116, 127, 134
  James, Dr, 23
  Jas., 63
  John, 105
  John W., 105, 107, 115, 130
  Julia, Mrs, 134
  Julian, 113, 133
  Mary, 105
  Nancy 34
  Richard, 134
  Saml, 30
  Samuel, 24
  Sarah, 24
  William, 105

Trudie **Davis-Long** has an interest in researching the Piedmont area of North Carolina and Virginia, an area where many of her paternal grandparent's families originated.

In addition to the Paw Prints work listed below, she has been the newsletter editor for the Frederick County, Maryland Genealogical Society for the past 12 years and is employed as an operating room nurse at a Rockville, Maryland hospital.

Trudie and long-time business partner Edie **Eader** are the owners of Paw Prints, Inc., P O Box 52, Monrovia, MD 21771 which publishes books based on records of Frederick County, Maryland. Their current works available in print are:

The Annotated Diary of James W. Lantz of Carroll County, MD 1857-1891 2002

The Jacob Engelbrecht Marriage Ledger of Frederick County, Maryland 1820-1890 1994

The Jacob Engelbrecht Death Ledger of Frederick County, Maryland 1820-1890 1995

The Jacob Engelbrecht Property and Almshouse Ledgers of Frederick County, Maryland 1996

Frederick County, Maryland Will Index 1744-1946 1997 compiled by Susanne **Flowers**.

www.ingramcontent.com/pod-product-compliance
Lightning Source LLC
Chambersburg PA
CBHW060527090426
42735CB00011B/2406